Adobe
Edge Animate

the missing manual®

The book that should have been in the box®

D0731375

Chris Grover

O'REILLY®

Beijing | Cambridge | Farnham | Köln | Sebastopol | Tokyo

Adobe Edge Animate: The Missing Manual

by Chris Grover

Copyright © 2013 Chris Grover. All rights reserved.
Printed in the United States of America.

Published by O'Reilly Media, Inc.,
1005 Gravenstein Highway North, Sebastopol, CA 95472.

O'Reilly books may be purchased for educational, business, or sales promotional use.
Online editions are also available for most titles (*http://my.safaribooksonline.com*).
For more information, contact our corporate/institutional sales department: (800)
998-9938 or *corporate@oreilly.com*.

October 2012:   First Edition.

Revision History for the 1st Edition:

    2012-10-26   First release

See *http://oreilly.com/catalog/errata.csp?isbn=9781449342258* for release details.

ISBN 13: 978-1-449-34225-8

[LSI]

Contents

Part One: **Working with the Stage**

The Missing Credits

ABOUT THE AUTHOR

 **Chris Grover** is a veteran of the San Francisco Bay Area advertising and design community, having worked for over 25 years in print, video, and electronic media. He has been using and writing about computers from the day he first fired up his Kaypro II. Chris is the owner of Bolinas Road Creative (*www.BolinasRoad.com*), an agency that helps small businesses promote their products and services. He's also the author of *Office 2011 for Macintosh: The Missing Manual*, *Premiere Elements 8: The Missing Manual*, *Google SketchUp: The Missing Manual*, *Flash CS6: The Missing Manual*, and *Word 2007: The Missing Manual*. Email: *chris@BolinasRoad.com*.

ABOUT THE CREATIVE TEAM

Nan Barber (editor) has been working on the Missing Manual series since its inception. She lives in Massachusetts with her husband and various Apple products. Email: *nanbarber@oreilly.com*.

Carla Spoon (proofreader) is a freelance writer and copy editor. An avid runner, she works and feeds her tech gadget addiction from her home office in the shadow of Mount Rainier. Email: *carla_spoon@comcast.net*.

Melanie Yarbrough (production editor) lives, works, and does pretty much everything else in Cambridge, MA. When not ushering books through production, she's baking and writing up whatever she can imagine. Email: *myarbrough@oreilly.com*.

Bob Pfahler (indexer) is a freelance indexer who indexed this book on behalf of Potomac Indexing, LLC, an international indexing partnership at *www.potomacindexing.com*. Besides the subject of computer software, he specializes in business, management, biography, and history. He can be reached at *bobpfahler@hotmail.com*.

Jacques Surveyer (technical reviewer) is a long-time Flash developer of the Air, Swift3D, and SwishMax variety who finds Adobe's move to HTML5 animation via Edge of keen interest. See more coverage at *www.theopensourcery.com/keepopen* or ask for more at *jbsurv@thephotofinishes.com*.

Darrell Heath (technical reviewer) is a freelance designer and web developer from Newfoundland and Labrador, Canada with a background in Information Technology and visual arts. He also authors weekly tutorial content for NAPP and in his spare time is offering design related tips through his blog at *www.heathrowe.com/blog*. Email: *darrell@heathrowe.com*.

ACKNOWLEDGEMENTS

Thanks to all the pros and friends on the Missing Manual team who worked to get this book into your hands. A special thanks again to Nan Barber whose skill, patience and planning has guided me through many books. Thanks also to Carla Spoon for catching typos and other embarrassing goofs on my part. I'm extremely grateful to Melanie Yarbrough, the production editor, for her work in putting all the parts together. Much appreciation also goes to Jacques Surveyer and Darrell Heath who provided their technical expertise while we explored this great new design/development tool. As always, thanks and love to Joyce, my wife, who makes work and play fun.

—Chris Grover

THE MISSING MANUAL SERIES

Missing Manuals are witty, superbly written guides to computer products that don't come with printed manuals (which is just about all of them). Each book features a handcrafted index and cross-references to specific pages (not just chapters). Recent and upcoming titles include:

Access 2010: The Missing Manual by Matthew MacDonald

Buying a Home: The Missing Manual by Nancy Conner

CSS: The Missing Manual, Second Edition by David Sawyer McFarland

Creating a Website: The Missing Manual, Third Edition by Matthew MacDonald

David Pogue's Digital Photography: The Missing Manual by David Pogue

Dreamweaver CS5.5: The Missing Manual by David Sawyer McFarland

Droid 2: The Missing Manual by Preston Gralla

Droid X2: The Missing Manual by Preston Gralla

Excel 2010: The Missing Manual by Matthew MacDonald

Facebook: The Missing Manual, Third Edition by E.A. Vander Veer

FileMaker Pro 12: The Missing Manual by Susan Prosser and Stuart Gripman

Flash CS6: The Missing Manual by Chris Grover

Galaxy S II: The Missing Manual by Preston Gralla

Galaxy Tab: The Missing Manual by Preston Gralla

Google+: The Missing Manual by Kevin Purdy

Google Apps: The Missing Manual by Nancy Conner

Google SketchUp: The Missing Manual by Chris Grover

HTML5: The Missing Manual by Matthew MacDonald

iMovie '11 & iDVD: The Missing Manual by David Pogue and Aaron Miller *iPad 2: The Missing Manual, Third Edition* by J.D. Biersdorfer

iPhone: The Missing Manual, Fifth Edition by David Pogue

iPhone App Development: The Missing Manual by Craig Hockenberry

iPhoto '11: The Missing Manual by David Pogue and Lesa Snider

iPod: The Missing Manual, Tenth Edition by J.D. Biersdorfer and David Pogue

JavaScript & jQuery: The Missing Manual, Second Edition by David Sawyer McFarland

Kindle Fire: The Missing Manual, Second Edition by Peter Meyers

Living Green: The Missing Manual by Nancy Conner

Mac OS X Lion: The Missing Manual by David Pogue

Mac OS X Snow Leopard: The Missing Manual by David Pogue

Microsoft Project 2010: The Missing Manual by Bonnie Biafore

Motorola Xoom: The Missing Manual by Preston Gralla

Netbooks: The Missing Manual by J.D. Biersdorfer

NOOK Tablet: The Missing Manual by Preston Gralla

Office 2010: The Missing Manual by Nancy Connor, Chris Grover, and Matthew MacDonald

Office 2011 for Macintosh: The Missing Manual by Chris Grover

Palm Pre: The Missing Manual by Ed Baig

Personal Investing: The Missing Manual by Bonnie Biafore

Photoshop CS5: The Missing Manual by Lesa Snider

Photoshop Elements 10: The Missing Manual by Barbara Brundage

PHP & MySQL: The Missing Manual, Second Edition by Brett McLaughlin

PowerPoint 2007: The Missing Manual by E.A. Vander Veer

Premiere Elements 8: The Missing Manual by Chris Grover

QuickBase: The Missing Manual by Nancy Conner

QuickBooks 2012: The Missing Manual by Bonnie Biafore

Quicken 2009: The Missing Manual by Bonnie Biafore

Switching to the Mac: The Missing Manual, Lion Edition by David Pogue

Wikipedia: The Missing Manual by John Broughton

Windows Vista: The Missing Manual by David Pogue

Windows 7: The Missing Manual by David Pogue

Word 2007: The Missing Manual by Chris Grover

Your Body: The Missing Manual by Matthew MacDonald

Your Brain: The Missing Manual by Matthew MacDonald

Your Money: The Missing Manual by J.D. Roth

For a full list of all Missing Manuals in print, go to *www.missingmanuals.com/library. html.*

Introduction

It may be hard to imagine, but once upon a time, pages on the World Wide Web didn't have pictures, let alone animations, videos, and interactive graphics. All these elements were added through trial, error, debate, and debunk. Changes came when brave souls (like you) forged ahead and made things work with the tools at hand. If a commercial product worked well and was widely adopted, it became the de facto standard. Adobe's PDF (portable document files) and Flash animation player are well-known examples. However, there's always been a problem with proprietary and patent-encumbered technologies on the Internet. They're like a toll road in the center of a major city. On the other hand, authorities and standards-writing groups have been known to create "standards" that few browser and web developers follow. Strictly structured XHTML pages fall into this category. The solution is to create standards for the Internet that are practical, usable, and don't stifle creativity. Of course, that's easier said than done.

With HTML5, the standards-writing crowd (also known as the W3C) is working hard to give the Internet community a roadmap that takes into account where we've been and where we're heading. There are a number of exciting new features in HTML5, but perhaps most visible are the new ways to present and animate graphics. If you're thinking, "That sounds a lot like Adobe Flash," you're right. One shiny new feature of HTML5 provides a non-proprietary, standard way to change graphics, color, size, shape, and position over time. The technique uses newly defined HTML tags, the power of JavaScript, and its jQuery companion library. These open-source technologies are available to everyone, whether they're designing web pages or building the next great web browser.

■ Why Use Adobe Edge Animate?

If you need a compelling reason to learn yet another animation technology, here are three good ones: iPhone, iPod, and iPad. In fact, if you're a Flash designer or developer, you're probably already dialed in to the famous debate between Apple and Adobe regarding Flash. As a web designer and developer, more important than the debate is the fact that Flash content on web pages can't be viewed by the most popular mobile devices on the planet. However, if you use HTML5 and JavaScript, you can capture that Apple audience and more.

So why should you use an Adobe product to create HTML5 web content? It's an understatement to say that most graphic artists view the world differently from computer programmers. If you're an artist, you may not be entirely comfortable describing each circle, color, and line in your artwork by typing out JavaScript code, even though it's theoretically possible. You're probably more inclined to use a tool that reminds you of Adobe Illustrator, Photoshop, or Flash. That's exactly where Animate fits in. Animate has a timeline like the ones in Flash and After Effects. The Elements and Properties panels will remind you of your favorite drawing and photo tools. If you use Animate to develop HTML5 graphics, then you can concentrate on creating and fine-tuning your artwork. Animate will generate the HTML5 and JavaScript/jQuery code that's needed for your web pages.

> **NOTE** Although "Adobe Edge Animate" is the program's formal name, in this book you'll often see "Animate" for short.

■ Where to Find Adobe Edge Animate

If you don't already have Adobe Edge Animate on your computer, you can get Version 1.0 from Adobe as part of a free Adobe Cloud membership. Go to *http://html.adobe.com/edge/animate/*. Click the Get Started button. You know the drill. Provide your name, email address and a password and you're signed up. If you want more details on how to install Animate on your computer, check out Appendix A.

■ About This Book

Despite the many improvements in software over the years, one feature has grown consistently worse: documentation. With the purchase of most software programs these days, you don't get a single page of printed instructions. To learn about the hundreds of features in a program you're expected to use online electronic help, but with a brand new product, like Adobe Edge Animate, the help files are minimal.

But even if you're comfortable reading a help screen in one window as you try to work in another, something is still missing. At times, the terse electronic help screens assume that you already understand the discussion at hand and hurriedly skip over important topics that require an in-depth presentation. In addition, you don't always get an objective evaluation of the program's features. (Engineers often add technically sophisticated features to a program because they *can*, not because you need them.) You shouldn't have to waste your time learning features that don't help you get your work done.

The purpose of this book, then, is to serve as the manual that should have been in the box. In this book's pages, you'll find step-by-step instructions for using every Animate feature, including those you may not even have quite understood, let alone mastered, such as moving the HTML5 and JavaScript code into your web pages or making changes to existing pages using Animate. In addition, you'll find clear evaluations of each feature that help you determine which ones are useful to you, as well as how and when to use them.

> **NOTE** This book periodically recommends *other* books, covering topics that are too specialized or tangential for a manual about Animate. Careful readers may notice that not every one of these titles is published by Missing Manual-parent O'Reilly Media. While we're happy to mention other Missing Manuals and books in the O'Reilly family, if there's a great book out there that doesn't happen to be published by O'Reilly, we'll still let you know about it.

Adobe Edge Animate: The Missing Manual is designed to accommodate readers at every technical level. The primary discussions are written for advanced-beginner or intermediate computer users. But if you're a first-timer, special sidebar articles called Up to Speed provide the introductory information you need to understand the topic at hand. If you're an advanced user, on the other hand, keep your eye out for similar shaded boxes called Coders' Clinic and Designer's Toolbox. They offer more technical tips, tricks, and shortcuts for the experienced computer fan.

Macintosh and Windows

Animate works almost precisely the same in its Macintosh and Windows versions. Every button in every dialog box is exactly the same; the software response to every command is identical. In this book, the illustrations have been given even-handed treatment, rotating between the two operating systems where Animate is at home (Windows 7 and Mac OS X).

One of the biggest differences between the Mac and Windows versions is the keystrokes, because the Ctrl key in Windows is the equivalent of the ⌘ key on the Mac.

Whenever this book refers to a key combination, you'll see the Windows keystroke listed first (with + symbols, as is customary in Windows documentation); the Macintosh keystroke follows in parentheses (with - symbols, in time-honored Mac fashion). In other words, you might read, "The keyboard shortcut for saving a file is Ctrl+S (⌘-S)."

About the Outline

Adobe Edge Animate: The Missing Manual is divided into three parts, each containing several chapters:

- **Part One: Working with the Stage** starts off with an introduction to the Animate workspace. You'll learn some more details about how Animate performs its magic by creating HTML, JavaScript, and CSS code. Then you'll roll up your sleeves and create graphics within Animate and import artwork from other programs. Along the way, you'll begin to work with Animate's Timeline and Properties panel to make things move. Chapter 3 is devoted to working with text and you'll see how easy it is to make text elements change size, shape, and color.

- **Part Two: Animation with Edge Animate** is all about animating the elements on the stage. You'll learn advanced techniques for working efficiently in Animate. Animation is time-consuming work, but you can save lots of time by reusing and recycling your previous work with symbols. You'll learn to manage and edit the timeline and the transitions you create. One chapter in this section is devoted to triggers and actions. You use these tools to automate your animation and give interactive control to your web pages. The last chapter is devoted to Animate symbols, a handy tool for grouping elements and reusing art and code. Symbols speed up the development process and add consistency to your compositions.

- **Part Three: Edge Animate with HTML5 and JavaScript** gets into the nitty-gritty details of working with code. This book doesn't attempt to be an advanced JavaScript programmer's manual. Instead, you'll learn how to selectively tweak bits of code to make some animation magic. Some of the most interesting projects are covered in this chapter, where all the skills learned in the previous chapters come in to play.

- **Part Four: Publishing Animate Compositions** helps you deliver your Animate masterpiece to an audience—that's done by publishing your composition. In this section, you learn how to develop responsive designs that look good whether they're viewed on a desktop computer, a smartphone, or a high-def TV. You'll also learn how to accommodate browsers that aren't up to date with HTML5 capabilities.

Appendix A explains how to install Animate on both Windows and Mac computers. You'll also find tips on where to look for discussions and additional Animate resources. Appendix B: Menu by Menu briefly describes each menu command and its function.

■ The Very Basics

You'll find very little jargon or nerd terminology in this book. You will, however, come across a few terms and concepts that you'll encounter frequently in your computing life:

To use this book (and indeed to use Adobe Edge Animate), you need to know a few basics. This book assumes that you're familiar with a few terms and concepts:

- **Clicking.** This book includes instructions that require you to use your computer's mouse or trackpad. To *click* means to point your cursor (the arrow pointer) at something on the screen and then—without moving the cursor at all—press and release the left button on the mouse (or laptop trackpad). To *right-click* means the same thing, but pressing the *right* mouse button instead. (Usually, clicking selects an onscreen element or presses an onscreen button, whereas right-clicking typically reveals a *shortcut menu*, which lists some common tasks specific to whatever you're right-clicking.) To *double-click*, of course, means to click twice in rapid succession, again without moving the pointer at all. And to *drag* means to move the cursor while holding down the (left) mouse button the entire time. To *right-drag* means to do the same thing but holding down the right mouse button.

  When you're told to *Shift-click* something, you click while pressing the Shift key. Related procedures, like *Ctrl-clicking*, work the same way—just click while pressing the corresponding key.

- **Menus.** The *menus* are the words at the top of your screen: File, Edit, and so on. Click one to make a list of commands appear, as though they're written on a window shade you've just pulled down. Some people click to open a menu and then release the mouse button; after reading the menu command choices, they click the command they want. Other people like to press the mouse button continuously as they click the menu title and drag down the list to the desired command; only then do they release the mouse button. Both methods work, so use whichever one you prefer.

- **Keyboard shortcuts.** Nothing is faster than keeping your fingers on your keyboard to enter data, choose names, trigger commands, and so on—without losing time by grabbing the mouse, carefully positioning it, and then choosing a command or list entry. That's why many people prefer to trigger commands by pressing combinations of keys on the keyboard. For example, in most word processors, you can press Ctrl+B to produce a boldface word. In this book, when you read an instruction like "Press Ctrl+L to insert a label," start by pressing the Ctrl key; while it's down, type the letter L; and then release both keys.

About→These→Arrows

Throughout this book, and throughout the Missing Manual series, you'll find sentences like this one: "Open the System Folder→Preferences→Remote Access folder." That's shorthand for a much longer instruction that directs you to open three nested folders in sequence, like this: "On your hard drive, you'll find a folder called System Folder. Open that. Inside the System Folder window is a folder called Preferences; double-click it to open it. Inside that folder is yet another one called Remote Access. Double-click to open it, too." Similarly, this kind of arrow shorthand helps to simplify the business of choosing commands in menus, as shown in Figure I-1.

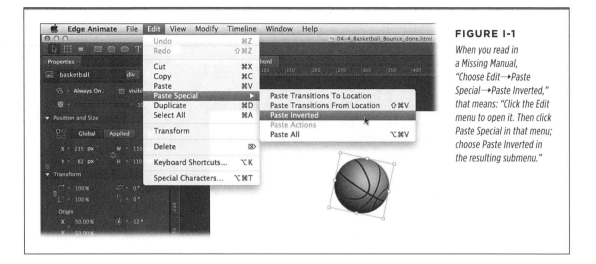

FIGURE I-1

When you read in a Missing Manual, "Choose Edit→Paste Special→Paste Inverted," that means: "Click the Edit menu to open it. Then click Paste Special in that menu; choose Paste Inverted in the resulting submenu."

■ About the Online Resources

As the owner of a Missing Manual, you've got more than just a book to read. Online, you'll find example files so you can get some hands-on experience, as well as tips, articles, and maybe even a video or two. You can also communicate with the Missing Manual team and tell us what you love (or hate) about the book. Head over to *www.missingmanuals.com*, or go directly to one of the following sections.

Missing CD

This book doesn't have a CD pasted inside the back cover, but you're not missing out on anything. Go to *www.missingmanuals.com/cds/animatemm* to download all the examples and exercises that are covered in this book. You can download all the files in one big ZIP file or you can download the files chapter by chapter. Most examples are made up of several files, which might include a web page (.html), images (.jpg), JavaScript code (.js), and style sheets (.css), so it's important to keep the files and their folders together or the examples may not work. Example and exercise folders and files are numbered, so when you see *03_2-MyExample*, you'll know that this example is from Chapter 3 and it's the second folder for the chapter.

For many of the exercises, there are completed examples that you can use to check your own work. A completed example includes the word *done* in the filename as in *03-3_MyExample_done*.

Finally, so you don't wear down your fingers typing long web addresses, the Missing CD page also offers a list of clickable links to the websites mentioned in this book.

Registration

If you register this book at oreilly.com, you'll be eligible for special offers—like discounts on future editions of *Adobe Edge Animate: The Missing Manual*. Registering takes only a few clicks. To get started, type *http://oreilly.com/register* into your browser to hop directly to the Registration page.

Feedback

Got questions? Need more information? Fancy yourself a book reviewer? On our Feedback page, you can get expert answers to questions that come to you while reading, share your thoughts on this Missing Manual, and find groups for folks who share your interest in web design and animation. To have your say, go to *www.missingmanuals.com/feedback*.

Errata

In an effort to keep this book as up-to-date and accurate as possible, each time we print more copies, we'll make any confirmed corrections you've suggested. We also note such changes on the book's website, so you can mark important corrections into your own copy of the book, if you like. Go to *http://tinyurl.com/animate-mm* to report an error and view existing corrections.

■ Safari® Books Online

 Safari® Books Online is an on-demand digital library that lets you easily search over 7,500 technology and creative reference books and videos to find the answers you need quickly.

With a subscription, you can read any page and watch any video from our library online. Read books on your cellphone and mobile devices. Access new titles before they're available for print, and get exclusive access to manuscripts in development and post feedback for the authors. Copy and paste code samples, organize your favorites, download chapters, bookmark key sections, create notes, print out pages, and benefit from tons of other time-saving features.

O'Reilly Media has uploaded this book to the Safari Books Online service. To have full digital access to this book and others on similar topics from O'Reilly and other publishers, sign up for free at *http://my.safaribooksonline.com*.

Working with the Stage

PART

1

Introducing Adobe Edge Animate

Travelers on the World Wide Web expect strong graphics. They appreciate animation that contributes to the subject as long as it doesn't waste their time. Done well, animation draws attention to important details, shows how things work, and helps site navigation. But, graphics certainly weren't first and foremost when the Web was created. The language used to display web pages is called HTML—short for *HyperText Markup Language*. Like any language, HTML has evolved and continues to adapt to current needs and new ideas. The latest step in that evolution is HTML5, which combined with other technologies like CSS3, JavaScript, and jQuery, presents the beautiful interactive pages you visit today.

Instead of creating graphics and visual effects manually by writing code, artists can use Adobe Edge Animate—a tool that's a much better fit for designers. This chapter starts off by explaining how Animate works to write HTML code that a web browser can read. Then it offers a quick introduction to the main parts of the Animate workspace. Finally, you'll take Animate for a test drive, where you'll make an image move and create text that fades in and out. Your first hands-on experience will be quick and easy. Consider this first adventure an overview—the following chapters will reveal the details.

Creating and Saving Edge Animate Projects

Animate's role in life is to help you make web pages that come alive with motion. You design the graphics using familiar visual tools, while Animate writes the underlying code. It's as if you hired an HTML/CSS/JavaScript/jQuery coder for your design team. One good way to understand what goes on behind the scenes is to create and save an empty Animate project. Fire up Edge Animate as you would any other application on your computer. That means the process is slightly different for Windows and Mac computers. If you plan on using Animate a lot (and why wouldn't you?) you can use any of the familiar tricks to create handy shortcuts. In Windows, you can pin an Animate shortcut to your Start menu or the taskbar. On a Mac, you can add Animate to the Dock.

When you first start Animate, you're greeted by a splash screen. On the right side of the screen, you see links to lessons and other Adobe resources. On the left are links to create a new file or open previously created files. Click Create New and then, once Animate is running, you reach a workspace with a number of panels and more links to Adobe lessons. Don't worry about those details now; you'll explore them later in this chapter. Create a new folder on your computer desktop and call it *Edge Barebones*. Next, do the project creation two-step. Go to File→New and then File→Save As. Find the Edge Barebones folder on your desktop and save your project with any name you want. Now, examine the contents of the folder. You'll find five files and a folder like the ones in Figure 1-1. If you've spent time developing web pages, you'll see some of the usual suspects and maybe a newcomer or two:

- The **.an** file is used by Animate to keep track of your project.

- The **.html** file describes a web page using HTML code, like any of the gazillion web pages on the Internet.

- The **.js** files hold JavaScript code that's specific to your project. Right now your project is barebones, but the code defines the empty animation stage and performs other tasks that are necessary for all Edge Animate projects.

Open the folder that's named *edge_includes,* and you'll find more JavaScript files. These are libraries of JavaScript code. One is specific to Animate; the others are standard JavaScript libraries. These libraries are referenced by the code in the HTML page that Animate created. They serve as the engine behind your Animate project. In short, they make things move.

Unlike a word processor or a spreadsheet, which create single files, Animate creates several files, and it needs those files to build the project and to display your masterfully designed page in a browser. If you delete or move one of these files, chances are you'll confuse Animate and anyone who views the web page. So one thing to learn from this bare-bones exercise is proper folder and file management:

- Create separate folders for each project you tackle, including the exercises in this book. (You may want to put them all in a main Animate project folder.)

- Don't delete, move, or rename the files and folders that Animate creates until you fully understand their relationships.

NOTE Actually, all your projects could share the files in the *edge_includes* folder. For now, it's easiest to let Animate create new files for each project. They don't take up that much storage space on your computer.

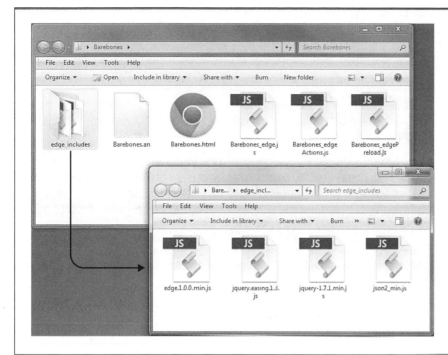

FIGURE 1-1

Animate automatically creates several files and folders as you work. It's important not to move, delete, or rename these files, or your animation won't work as expected. You add your work to a website by copying these files to the web server.

A Tour of the Animate Workspace

Once you've gone past the splash screen by creating a new file or opening an old one, you see a workspace with several panels and a small toolbar, as shown in Figure 1-2. The name for each panel appears on a tab at the top. The Elements, Properties, and Timeline panels and the Tools toolbar all hold tools and widgets you use to create your animation masterpieces. The largest panel is the stage, where you build your animation. Its tab displays the name of your project.

- The **stage** is where you display and animate the graphics and text for your web page audience. When you save your project, Animate records the text and graphics and saves the description as a web page in HTML code. Open the page in a browser, and it plays back just as it appeared on the Animate stage. The stage has defined boundaries, and it's possible to hide or position elements so that they are offstage.

- **Elements** are objects that you add to the stage, and as a result they appear on your finished web page. Elements may be artwork, photographs, or text.

- Elements have **properties** that affect their position and appearance on the stage. You manage those properties using the Properties panel.

- The **Timeline** keeps track of elements and their properties over the course of time. When an element's properties change, that may change its position on the stage and its appearance.

- The **Library** keeps track of images that you import into your project. It provides easy access to the symbols that you create in Animate.

- **Tools** appear at the top of the main workspace. You use these to create, select, and modify elements on the stage. It's a small toolbox, but you may be surprised at how much it can do.

- The **Lessons** panel at right provides links to Adobe's introductory lessons, which can be helpful when you're starting out. The right panel gives you step-by-step instructions, with the results appearing in a sample file on the stage. After you've checked out the lessons, click the X on the Lessons tab to hide it and recover some valuable workspace.

TIP You may think of these workspace boxes as panels or palettes, but Adobe lists them all under the Window menu, where you can show or hide each with a mouse click.

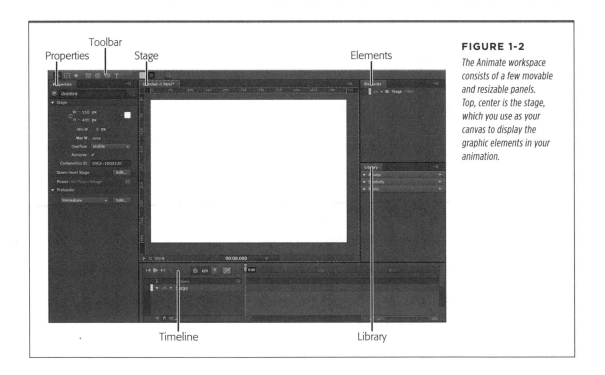

FIGURE 1-2

The Animate workspace consists of a few movable and resizable panels. Top, center is the stage, which you use as your canvas to display the graphic elements in your animation.

Properties   Toolbar   Stage   Elements

Timeline   Library

The Animate workspace takes its cues from other Adobe products. If you've used recent versions of Dreamweaver, Photoshop, or Flash, you'll feel right at home. If this is your first foray into Adobe territory, the techniques you learn here can be applied when you explore other applications.

Initially, all the panels are pieced together like a puzzle, but you aren't stuck with that arrangement. You can resize the panels within the workspace, or you can drag panels out so that they float independently. Want to make the timeline bigger? To resize it while it's grouped snugly with the others, drag one of its edges. As it changes size, the surrounding panels change to accommodate the new arrangement. Want to move the Properties panel to a second monitor? Just drag its tab anywhere you want; the panel follows. If you have trouble freeing a window, click the small menu button in its upper-right corner (Figure 1-3) and choose Undock Panel. It will pop out from the main Animate workspace.

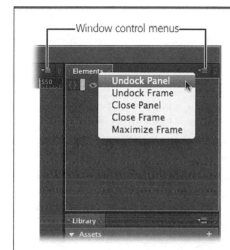

—Window control menus—

FIGURE 1-3

Use the menu in the upper-left corner of the individual panels to open, close, dock, and undock the panels. You can group several panels by dragging one tab over the edge of another panel. Panels that are grouped in this way are called frames.

Saving a Custom Workspace

Two scenarios may arise when you start dragging panels all over the place: Either you love the new layout or you hate it. Suppose you find the perfect layout for your work style and equipment. Perhaps you have a dual-monitor system and you like to have the stage and timeline fill one screen while Properties, Elements, and Library panels camp out on the other. You can save the workspace layout using the Windows→Workspace. Initially, the menu is set to Default, as shown in Figure 1-4. Choose New Workspace, and a dialog box appears, where you can provide a custom name, such as "Dual Screen," for your custom workspace. Click OK, and now your newly named workspace joins the workspace menu. Just choose it whenever you want to use your handy Dual Screen workspace.

On the other hand, perhaps through dragging, tugging, and hiding panels you've arrived at a completely unworkable situation. You just want everything back the way it was when you started. Choose Default or any of the other workspace options, and all those panels jump back in place. Use the Reset option to return the currently selected workspace to its last saved arrangement.

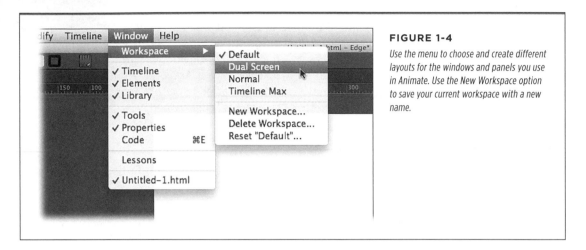

FIGURE 1-4

Use the menu to choose and create different layouts for the windows and panels you use in Animate. Use the New Workspace option to save your current workspace with a new name.

NOTE To help you keep your bearings, most of the time this book uses the Default workspace.

Building Your First Animation

It's a long-standing coder's tradition to program a "hello world" test when first tackling a new language. In this case, Animate is going to write the code that displays your web page and animation, but why break with tradition? To dip your toe in the animation waters, you'll develop a hello-world page Animate-style. The blue marble of the earth will rise onto the stage, and the words "Hello World" will fade in and then fade out. You can use your own earth picture, or you can use *01-1_Hello_World* from *www.missingmanuals.com/cds/animatemm*. The folder contains one image, *planet_earth.png*, which is used for this exercise.

If you want to see the final working example before you build it yourself, grab *01-2_Hello_World_done* from the Missing CD. Download and unzip it to find a folder that holds several files. You can view the completed project by opening *01-2_Hello_World_done.html* in any browser that's HTML5 capable. If you're not sure whether your browser can handle HTML5, see the box on page 14.

NOTE You can find all the examples for this book at *www.missingmanuals.com/cds/animatemm*. Animate projects produce several different files and folders, such as HTML, JavaScript, and graphics, so the files for each exercise are in a folder. Individual examples are numbered. In the case of *01-1_Hello_World*, the *01* at the beginning stands for Chapter 1 and *-1* indicates that it's the first exercise in the chapter. Completed examples for comparison are often included and have the word *done* in the filename, as in *01-2_Hello_World_done*.

1. Start Animate and go to File→New to create a new document.

   When you create a new document, you start off with an empty stage. You see "Stage" as the only element listed in the Elements and Properties windows. As you see in the Properties panel, the stage has dimension, color, and other properties. You'll learn more about each of these properties later.

2. Create a folder for your project and then choose File→Save As to save your file with a name like *Hello_World* or *First_Try*.

   You can create a folder outside of Animate using Windows Explorer or Finder, or you can create a new folder as part of a File→Save As command. It's a good practice to save your Animate project immediately with a helpful name. That way you won't end up with a bunch of "untitled" projects that you don't remember. Also, it makes it easy to save your work early and often with a quick Ctrl+S or ⌘-S. As explained on page 2, it's best to save each Animate project in its own folder because Animate creates several files and an *edge_includes* folder when you first save a project.

TIP A quick look at the Animate window tells whether your most recent work has been saved. If your work is unsaved, Animate shows an asterisk next to the filename at the top of the window.

3. In the Properties window, click the white Background Color swatch.

   A panel appears where you can choose a color (Figure 1-5). If you prefer a strictly visual approach, click the *spectrum* bar at the left for a basic hue and then click inside the square to fine-tune your selection. In some cases, you may have a specific color specification in RGB (red-green-blue) format or as a hexadecimal number. For more details on color management, see the box on page 22.

4. When the color picker appears, choose a dark blue color to represent deep space.

   If in doubt, try R=30 G=45 B=90 A=100 for this project. Animate uses Adobe's standard method for choosing numbers. When you see a highlighted number, that means you can either click and then type in a number, or you can click and drag to "scrub" in a number. Drag right to increase the number, left to decrease.

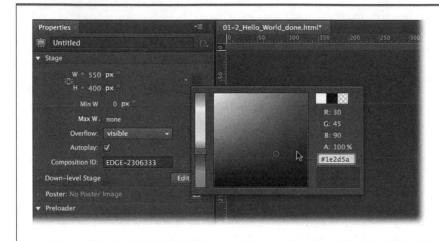

FIGURE 1-5

Animate uses the RGB (red-green-blue) color space used by most computer monitors and TV sets. The A stands for Alpha channel and controls opacity/transparency. The color picker lets you specify colors by pointing and clicking or typing in numbers.

5. Still in the Stage properties panel, change the Overflow to hidden.

   The Overflow property controls the visibility of items when they are viewed in a web browser. On a web page, the stage may represent just a portion of the entire web page. You can control the visibility of elements outside of the stage's rectangle. Change this property to hidden when you don't want to see elements that are offstage.

6. Choose File→Import. Using the Import window that appears, find and select *planet_earth.png*. Click Open to import the image into your project.

   The *planet_earth.png* image was in the *01-1_Hello_World* from the Missing CD (*www.missingmanuals.com/cds/edgepv7mm*). After you import a file to your Animate project, it is listed in the Elements window and is displayed on the stage. It's automatically selected, so you see the properties for the newly imported element in the Properties window. The "planet_earth" has visibility properties at the top of the panel. Right below are Position and Size properties. Below those, you see the Transform properties that let you rotate, skew, and scale elements. Below that, the source file is listed—a handy point to keep in mind when you're trying to remember, "What the heck was the name of that file anyway?"

> **NOTE** There's another bit of behind-the-scenes Animate magic going on here, too. When you import an image, Animate automatically creates an *images* folder in your project. It makes a copy of the image you select and puts the copy in the images folder. You'll also find your imported image listed under Assets in the Library panel.

7. In the Properties panel, click the ID box at the very top and change planet_earth to *World*.

As Animate imports graphics, it names them using the file name. In some cases, that may be fine, but often you'll want to rename the element inside of Animate. Keep in mind this doesn't change the filename of your graphic. The ID *World* is used when you're working in Animate.

IDs serve an important function in HTML code, as you'll learn later in this book. Notice that in the Elements panel your World appears with its new name. Because it's on the stage, World also appears in the timeline.

TIP Names of non-animated elements may or may not appear in the timeline. You can show and hide them using the "Only show animated elements" button below the timeline (see Figure 1-6).

---

8. In the timeline, make sure the playhead is at 0:00.

If you haven't made any timeline changes since you created this project, the playhead is at 0:00, marking the first moment or frame of the animation, as shown in Figure 1-6. If you need to move the playhead, drag the gold-colored, bottom part of the playhead. The top part is called the *pin*. It should follow automatically. You'll learn more about the two-part playhead in the following steps.

9. Drag the World past the bottom of the stage.

As mentioned in step 5, you can control whether offstage items are displayed on the web page. With Overflow set to hidden, when you're in the Animate workspace, offstage elements appear a little darker than usual. When the final project is viewed in a browser, these elements will be hidden.

10. In the timeline, make sure that the Auto-Keyframe Mode button is pressed.

When the Auto-Keyframe Mode button (Figure 1-6) is pressed, keyframes are automatically created in the timeline as you make changes to element properties. Keyframe markers look like diamonds. You'll learn all about keyframes and other timeline features in Chapter 4.

NOTE In the timeline, buttons have a pushed-in appearance when they're turned on. They may also sport a bit of color. For example, the Auto-Keyframe Mode button, which looks like a stopwatch, has a bright red face when it's on.

---

11. In the timeline, make sure that the Auto-Transition Mode button is pressed.

When this button is pressed, Animate creates smooth transitions instead of abrupt changes. In this case, the World graphic will smoothly move from one position to another.

12. Drag playhead to 0:01 on the timeline.

In the timeline, 0:01 marks 1 second into the animation. A red line extends downward from the playhead, providing a marker for all the element and property layers.

13. With the World still selected, in the Properties panel, go to Position and Size and click the diamond shaped buttons next to X and Y.

Two diamond-shaped keyframes appear in the timeline marking the position for the Left and Top edge of the World graphic. The X and Y properties set the position of elements on the stage. (Position properties are covered in detail on page 20.) By clicking the diamond next to Location in the Properties panel, you manually recorded the World's location on the stage. As a result, the World stays in the same X/Y position for the first second of the animation.

NOTE Animate automatically assigns a reference color to each element in your project. The color appears in the timeline next to the name, and it's also used to display transitions—changes in property values. You see the same color next to the names in the Elements window. When you're dealing with dozens or hundreds of elements, the color-coding comes in handy.

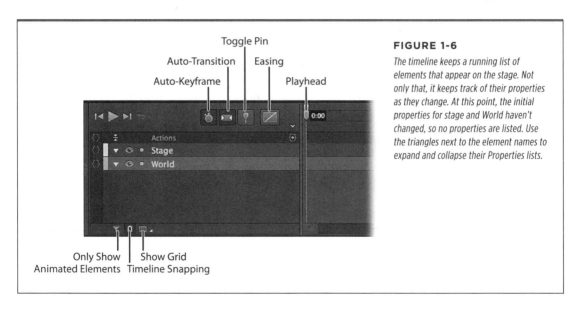

FIGURE 1-6

The timeline keeps a running list of elements that appear on the stage. Not only that, it keeps track of their properties as they change. At this point, the initial properties for stage and World haven't changed, so no properties are listed. Use the triangles next to the element names to expand and collapse their Properties lists.

14. Click the Toggle Pin button, then drag the bottom, gold part of the playhead to 0:03.

To animate an element, you change its properties over a specific period of time. The playhead and the pin let you mark two points in time, as shown in Figure 1-7.

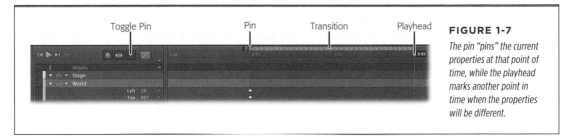

Toggle Pin   Pin   Transition   Playhead

FIGURE 1-7

The pin "pins" the current properties at that point of time, while the playhead marks another point in time when the properties will be different.

15. Drag the World graphic so that Earth is visible on the stage.

    You can center the image on the stage, or you can choose some other eye-pleasing layout.

16. Click the Toggle Pin button, then press the Home key and then press the space bar.

    When you press Home, the playhead returns to 0:00. Pressing the space bar plays your animation so you can preview the action on the stage.

17. Move the playhead back to 0:00, and then in the toolbar, click the letter T.

    The text tool is selected, and the cursor changes to a cross.

18. Click on the stage and type *Hello World*. When you're done, close the text window by pressing ESC or clicking the X button in the upper-right corner.

    The words "Hello World" appear on the stage, but they're probably not positioned or formatted as you want.

19. In the Properties window, set the ID for the text box to HelloWorld.

    Naming your text makes it easier to identify in the timeline and the Elements panel. Animate doesn't permit space in names, so you need to use HelloWorld or Hello_World.

20. Using the Properties panel, format the text.

    Change the text color to white or a very light blue. Choose Arial Black or another bold font. Adjust the size so it nearly fills the screen (72 px works well with Arial Black). Animate notes each change to the text in the timeline, adding property layers and creating keyframes.

21. Position the text.

    If you're not sure about the placement, try it centered horizontally and about a third of the way down the stage.

22. With the playhead still at 0:00, set the opacity to 0.

    The Opacity slider is at the top of the Properties panel. This means the text will not be visible at the beginning of the animation. Only the selection box shows and that will disappear as soon as you click something else. Don't worry, though—you can select any element, whether it's visible or not, by clicking its name in the Elements panel.

23. Make sure Toggle Pin is turned off.

    When Toggle Pin is off, the button doesn't appear pushed in and the pin moves with the playhead.

24. Drag the playhead to 0:02. With the text selected, click the diamond next to Opacity in the Properties panel.

    As you drag the playhead, you see the *World* move on the stage. Filmmakers and animators refer to dragging the playhead as *scrubbing*, a quick and easy way to review a segment of your animation. Clicking the Opacity diamond creates a keyframe at the 2-second mark where the text is still invisible.

25. Turn Toggle Pin back on, then drag the playhead to the 0:03 mark.

    With the pin at 0:02 and the playhead at 0:03, you're ready to create another transition.

26. With the HelloWorld text box selected, set its opacity to 100.

    Animate creates a transition so that the text gradually changes from 0 to 100 percent opacity between 0:02 and 0:03 in your animation.

27. Drag the pin to the 0:03 mark, then drag the playhead to 0:04. Set the opacity back to 0.

    The text disappears again.

28. Press Ctrl+S (⌘-S) to save your work.

    As explained earlier, Animate saves your animation as a collection of HTML and JavaScript files. The main HTML file uses the name you provided in step 2, when you first saved your project. So, for example, you may see *Hello_World.html* in the project folder. When you imported the *planet_earth.png* image, Animate created an images folder and placed a copy of the graphic in the folder.

Your simple animation is complete. You can preview it in Animate by pressing Home and then the space bar. The earth rises into view, and your message fades in and then fades out (Figure 1-8). The entire animation takes 4 seconds.

FIGURE 1-8

You can watch your entire animation inside of Animate by pressing Home and then the space bar. You can preview the animation in your web browser by choosing File→Preview In Browser.

Viewing Your Animation in a Browser

Your audience won't be viewing your animation in Animate; they'll be watching it in the familiar comfort of their favorite web browser. That means you need to review your work in a browser—preferably more than one browser. For a quick look, choose File→Preview In Browser. Animate starts your browser, if it isn't already running, and opens the HTML file that was created when you saved your project. That single HTML file describes the web page for your audience. All they have to do is load the page in a browser. The HTML code is actually the hub for all the other files the animation needs. It references the *planet_earth.png* image, which is stored as a separate file in the images folder. It also references the multiple JavaScript files needed to make everything run.

In animation, timing is everything. You may not be entirely pleased with the pace or other aspects of your Hello World experiment. In the coming chapters, you'll learn all about fine-tuning elements on the page so they look just right.

Here's a quick list of some important points to remember from this chapter:

- Animate creates multiple files and folders, so it's best to keep each project in a folder all its own.

- You can create and save a custom workspace that suits your work habits and your equipment.

- When you import a photo or graphic file, Animate creates a copy and stores that in the Images folder.

- Select an element on the stage or in the Elements panel and you see its properties listed in the Properties panel.

- To change the location or appearance of an element, select it and then change its properties. For example, change the location properties to move an element. Change the color or opacity properties to change its appearance.

- In the timeline, keyframes record an element's properties at a given point in time.

- Animation occurs when properties change over time. These changes are marked by keyframes in the timeline.

- Transitions can be smooth (gradually changing over time) or abrupt.

- Handy keyboard shortcuts to remember: Home moves the playhead to the beginning of the timeline. Space plays the animation in Animate. Ctrl+Enter (⌘-Return) plays the animation in your web browser.

UP TO SPEED

HTML5 Browsers on the Leading Edge

The industry transition to full HTML5 compatibility isn't an overnight event. The features that make up the complete HTML5 specification are being implemented gradually over time in different browsers. If you want to test your browser's compatibility, head over to *http://html5test.com*. Free to use, this website provides a list of the HTML5 features your browser supports. Click the "other browsers" tab to see how your browser ranks with the competition.

If you're developing pages with Animate and expect a wide and diverse audience, you may want to test your work using several different browsers. The last couple of versions of Chrome, Firefox, Internet Explorer, and Safari would be a good start. You'll be pleased to know that most browsers in mobile devices are pretty HTML5 savvy.

There are some great resources for developers to learn more about browser capabilities. For example, *http://caniuse.com* displays a list of HTML5, CSS, and JavaScript elements. Click one of the elements listed, and you see a chart that explains which browsers and versions support the element. Another site, *http://html5please.us*, provides similar services.

Creating and Animating Art

As the name implies, Animate is an animation management tool. Using Edge Animate, you determine what elements show on the stage, their position, and their appearance. You can create text and simple visual elements within Animate, but it's likely that you'll create more complicated artwork in some other program like Illustrator, Photoshop, or Fireworks.

This chapter examines what types of graphics you can and can't create within Animate. It starts off by defining the stage and the ways you can modify it. You'll learn about all the properties of the rectangle and rounded rectangle. With creativity, you can also create some distinctly non-rectangular shapes. Along the way, you'll learn how to quickly align and arrange objects on the stage and test-drive the transform and clipping tools. But you're not stuck in Animate: You'll also learn how to import artwork from your other favorite applications, such as Illustrator or Fireworks (and you'll get some tips about the best free graphics programs you can find on the Web).

Setting the Stage

As the Bard said a few hundred years ago, "All the world's a stage." That's certainly true in Edge Animate. As explained in Chapter 1, when you place an element on the stage, it's visible to your audience. There are a couple of ways to hide or remove elements from the stage. If you have the stage Overflow properties set to hidden, then you can exit stage right, left, top, or bottom by moving the element off stage. At least, it's not visible when viewed in a browser. The Hello World exercise also demonstrated how to perform disappearing acts by using the Opacity property.

The stage that you work with in Edge Animate represents a portion of a web page when it's viewed in a browser. The stage has a limited number of properties. The most obvious are its dimensions and background color, but you'll want to understand them all. Here's the rundown starting from the top of the Properties panel:

- The **ID**, as you might guess, is the name of your animation. When you save a project, Animate creates a web page, also known as an HTML document. Most browsers show the ID of the web page in a tab or the window's title bar.

- Initially, stage **dimensions** are shown as W (width) and H (height) properties in pixels. No big surprises here. You can type in or scrub in the width and height of the stage. The stage doesn't have to appear in the upper-left corner of a web page; on page 168, you'll learn how to reposition it. For example, if your Animate composition is a banner ad, you might create a tall, narrow stage and then position it on the left side of the page.

  Use the link next to the W and H properties to lock and unlock your stage's aspect ratio. When Link Width and Height is unbroken, changing one dimension automatically changes the other so that the stage stays proportionate; when the link is broken, you can change W and H independently.

  You can change the measurement from pixels (px) to a percentage (%). For example, if you set the stage width to 80%, the stage will be 80 percent the size of the web browser window that it's viewed in. This feature is great if you're developing a page for computers, tablets, and phones. What's more, if the browser window is resized, the stage automatically adjusts to the new size. For more details on designing pages for multiple screen sizes, see the box on page 23. Chapter 10 covers publishing issues and includes more details about designing pages that respond to the size of devices and web browsers.

- The **background color** is set using a color picker. In the Properties panel, click the color swatch and a color picker appears, as shown in Figure 2-1. Click the bar (also called the *spectrum*) on the left to choose a hue, and then click in the larger square to fine-tune the shade. The circle is positioned over the selected color, and the swatch in the lower-right corner displays it. The three swatches at top right make it easy to quickly choose a white, black, or transparent background. If you work with a team, you may be given a color spec in RGB or hexadecimal formats. On the other hand, if you're calling the shots, you may want to specify a color for other designers. For the details on specifying a color by numbers, see the box on page 22.

- Use **Min W** and **Max W** to set the minimum and maximum width for the stage. Web pages aren't a fixed size. Your page may be viewed on a smartphone or a big screen TV. On top of that, your audience may resize the browser window. You can gain some control over how your project looks by setting a minimum and maximum width. You can use pixels to set an absolute value or you can use a percentage for responsive designs. Initially, Max W is set to none. To turn it on, click the label and deselect none. At that point, the value appears in the panel and you can make adjustments.

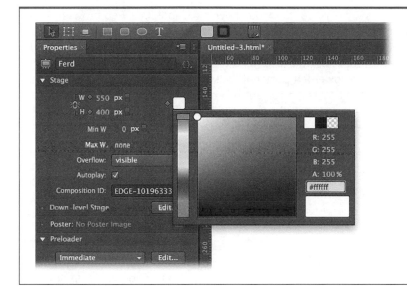

FIGURE 2-1

Animate presents the same color picker whether you are choosing the color for the stage, text, or a drawn object. The selected color shows in the lower-right corner. You can dial in your color by eye or type in a color spec.

- The **Overflow** menu controls the way elements appear when they're offstage. Often, you'll want to set this menu to *hidden,* which makes elements outside the stage's rectangle invisible. The hidden option works well when you want to have elements enter and exit the stage. If you set the menu to *visible,* elements that move beyond the boundary of the stage remain visible as long as there's room on the web page. The *scroll* option places scroll bars at the right and bottom of the stage, making it possible to view elements that move outside the specified dimensions of the stage. The *auto* option automatically adds scroll bars if content exists beyond the confines of the stage.

- Use the **Autoplay** checkbox to tell your animation to automatically run when its web page is loaded in a browser. If the box is turned off, you must use a JavaScript trigger to run the animation.

- The **Composition ID** is used to identify this particular stage and its accompanying timeline. This becomes important when you have more than one Animate composition on a single web page. You'll learn more about this in the JavaScript chapters.

- The **Down-level Stage** and **Poster** properties create alternative elements for web browsers that aren't HTML5 savvy.

- The **Preloader** is responsible for loading all the resources needed to display your composition on a web page. Those resources include JavaScript libraries and graphics. You'll learn more about these controls in Chapter 10.

■ Viewing the Stage

You can change your view of the Stage in Animate. Initially, you see it Actual Size—that is 100%. This gives you a good idea how it will look in a web browser. When you're doing intricate work you may want to zoom in for more precision. Press Ctrl+= (⌘-=) and everything gets bigger. If you're working with a large stage there may be times when you want to zoom out to get the entire picture. The command for that is Ctrl+_ (⌘-_). In the lower-left corner of the stage, there's a magnifying glass icon and a number that indicates the current zoom level as a percentage. You can use it to adjust the view, too. Just click type in a number or click and drag to scrub in a new value. When you want to quickly jump back to actual size, press Ctrl+1 (⌘-1).

> **TIP**   If you use other Adobe tools, the shortcut keys for zooming in and out are probably familiar. If you're knew to the Adobe realm, you may wonder, why the odd commands? Take a look at your keyboard and you notice that the equal (=) character shares space with the plus (+) character. The underscore (__) shares space with minus (-). It's easier to remember these commands if you think plus and minus. Just don't hold down the Shift key when you use them.

You can scroll your view of the stage, just like you scroll around a browser window to change the view, using your mouse or touch pad. After you move up or down, left or right, there's a quick way to center the stage in the window. Click the button the button in the lower-left corner of the window that looks like a gun sight.

■ Creating Art in Animate

In its current incarnation, Edge Animate's drawing tools are limited—no pen tool, no gradients. Why is its art so primitive compared with other Adobe products such as Flash or Illustrator? Part of the reason is that Edge Animate is new. It's likely that Adobe implemented the graphics features that were easiest first and that Animate will become more full featured over time. Keep in mind that every time you create a graphic object in Animate, it's busy behind the scenes writing code in JavaScript to describe that object. If you're a conspiracy theorist, you might think Adobe wants you to spring for Illustrator or one of the other artist's tools it sells in its Creative Suite. In fact, if you want to create vector graphics with complex paths, you need to use a tool like the pay-to-play Illustrator (*www.adobe.com*) or the open source Inkscape (*www.inkscape.org*).

The next section describes in detail the properties of the rectangle. However, many of these properties are used by other objects, such as blocks of text and artwork that you import into Animate. So when you're learning all about rotating, skewing, and scaling rectangles, keep in mind that you can rotate, skew, and scale text and photos, too.

> **TIP** If you're on a budget, you may want to use one of the free, open-source applications that create art. Inkscape (*www.inkscape.org*) is a vector-based drawing program (similar to Illustrator), and GIMP (*www.gimp.org*) is a raster-based photo editing application (similar to Photoshop). For an online photo editor, consider Pixlr (*www.pixlr.com*).

Rectangles: Building a Basic Box

Using the Rectangle tool (M), you can add blocks of color to the stage. These blocks are great if you want to differentiate portions of the web page. For example, perhaps you want to make a sidebar. Add a rectangle, and then you can place text or graphics over the rectangle, setting it off from the rest of the page. Chances are you know the basic drill for creating a rectangle. Click the Rectangle tool on the Tools palette, and then click and drag on the stage to mark its shape. To create a square, hold the Shift key while you drag. The new element appears on the stage, and it's automatically selected, so you see eight white squares around the border that represent handles (Figure 2-2). You can continue to change the size and shape of the rectangle after it's drawn by dragging the handles.

Here are the basic properties that describe your rectangles:

- **ID.** As soon as you draw a rectangle on the stage, it's listed in the Elements panel. When the rectangle is selected, its properties appear in the Properties panel. As with all your Animate elements, you probably want to give your rectangle a meaningful ID, such as LeftSidebar or Header. Otherwise, you'll be searching through Rectangle1, Rectangle2, and Rectangle3 trying to find the one you want. To rename your rectangle, select it and change the ID at the top of the Properties panel. As an alternative, you can double-click the name in the Elements panel.

- **Display.** Some elements are always on stage while others may come and go. The Display menu gives you a way to easily hide an element until it is needed. Your three choices include: Always On, On, and Off.

- **Overflow.** The overflow control for your rectangle works like the one for your stage, except it explicitly applies to the rectangle.

- **Opacity.** Use the slider near the top of the Properties panel when want to control the Opacity of the entire rectangle. When you want to adjust the opacity of the border or background independently, click their color swatches (explained under Color) and change the A (alpha property).

- **Tag.** Check out Rectangle in the Elements panel and see <div> after the name. Your rectangle is automatically assigned an HTML <div> tag. Animate uses these tags to identify, position, and transform elements. With other Elements, Edge Animate lets you choose different tags. For example, when you add a photo to your animation, there are good reasons to use a <img> tag instead of <div>. Chapter 7 covers HTML code in detail.

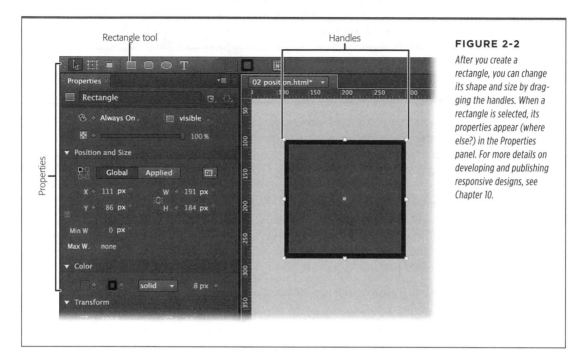

FIGURE 2-2

After you create a rectangle, you can change its shape and size by dragging the handles. When a rectangle is selected, its properties appear (where else?) in the Properties panel. For more details on developing and publishing responsive designs, see Chapter 10.

- **Position.** Underneath the name in the Properties panel, you see the Position and Size properties. The upper-left corner of the stage is referenced as X=0, Y=0. Moving from left to right increases the X value. Moving from top to bottom increases the Y value. Initially, your rectangle's position is referenced by the upper-left corner. You can change that reference point, using the "Relative to" tool. It looks like a box with a square at each corner. Suppose you need to place a copyright notice in the lower-right corner of the the stage. Naturally, you want to use the lower-right corner as the reference point. Position the copyright notice where you want it. Set the stage W and H to percentages for a responsive design. Then, in the "Relative to" box (Figure 2-3), click the square in the lower-right corner.

- **Global/Applied.** These two large buttons play an important role in positioning elements. They work like a toggle, you can only select one at a time. Initially the Global button is selected. That means that the position and other settings are relative to the Stage. When you're starting out with simple composition, this is the best setting. Later in this book, you'll learn how to group elements in symbols and DIV tags. These elements act as containers for other elements. Choose Applied and the Position and Size settings are relative to the underlying values of these containers.

- **Size.** Next to the Location properties are the Size properties: W (width) and H (height). These change automatically when you drag a rectangle's handles. You can also type in or scrub in a specific number. Initially for rectangles, the size properties use pixels as the unit of measure. However, you can change from pixels to percentage. So a rectangle with a width of 20% would be 20 percent of the width of the stage. Use the link next to the W and H properties to lock and unlock the aspect ratio for your rectangle. When the Link Width and Height is unbroken, changing one dimension automatically changes the other so that the rectangle stays proportionate. When the link is broken, you can change W and H independently. The box on page 23 offers some strategies for creating animations that resize gracefully with changes in the browser window. This bit of magic, sometimes called "responsive" or "fluid" design is accomplished by using percentage sizes, minimum and maximum widths, the corner reference box, and other tools that help your animation adapt to the size of the browser window.

- **Color.** Rectangles have two basic parts: border color and background color. Border color marks the outer edge of the rectangle, while background color is the color inside the box. (Other programs sometimes call these properties *stroke* and *fill*.) You can assign separate colors to the border and background, or you can make them transparent by setting the Alpha channel to zero. There are two additional properties for the stroke. You can set the size in pixels (px) and you can choose among a solid stroke, a dashed stroke, a dotted stroke, or none   no stroke at all. The toolbar at the top of the workspace gives you another way to quickly change the background and border color of a selected element. It works just like the color picker in the properties panel.

TIP   At the time of this writing, Animate didn't offer any way to create color gradients. That's where one color blends into another color. These effects are standard tools for graphic artists. If you want to use gradients, you'll need to create your art in Photoshop, Illustrator, or Fireworks and then import it into Animate. If you want to create a gradient that blends to transparency, letting the background show through, use the PNG32 graphic format.

Selecting and Copying Elements

When it comes to selecting, cutting, and pasting objects, Animate works like most other computer programs. You use the same techniques for objects you create in Animate, like rectangles and text, or artwork that you import (as explained on page 38). You use the Arrow in the Tools palette to do the heavy lifting. Click once on an element to select it. Shift-click on another element to add it to the selection. Animate has a handy command (Ctrl+A or ⌘-A) to select everything on the stage. You can easily deselect objects by clicking on an empty spot around the edge of the stage.

Animate also provides the usual suspects when it comes to Cut (Ctrl+X or ⌘-X), Copy (Ctrl+C or ⌘-C), and Paste (Ctrl+V or ⌘-V). The Duplicate command (Ctrl-D or ⌘-D) combines copy and paste into one function. When you're in need of several carefully rounded and shaded rectangles, it's much easier to create one and then clone it with Duplicate. (If you prefer menus to shortcut keys, you'll find all these commands on the Edit menu.)

When you duplicate an element that's on the stage, you also duplicate any transitions that may have been created for that element. If you don't want the transitions, use Copy (Ctrl+C or ⌘-C) and Paste (Ctrl+V or ⌘-V). You'll find details for editing transitions on page 87.

GEEK SPEAK

Understanding Color Specs and the Color Picker

If you're new to digital art, the various ways to specify color may seem confusing. As an artist, you know that color doesn't exist in a vacuum. The colors you get when you mix pigments aren't the same as the colors you get when you mix different colored lights, which is how a computer monitor works. Artists working in oil paint or pastel use the red-yellow-blue color model, while commercial printers use the cyan-magenta-yellow-black model. In the world of computer graphics, the color model you use is red-green-blue, or RGB.

The Animate color picker (Figure 2-1) has three different ways to reference a color using the RGB color model. You can pick a color visually using the spectrum bar and the square next to it. As you do so, different numbers appear on the right. The R, G, and B numbers represent the quantity of red, green, or blue added to the mix. The numbers range from 0 (0 percent) to 255 (100 percent). Why the odd numbers? Computers like powers of two and 256 (2^8) falls in that category. Computers also start their counting at zero. As a result, RGB colors use a scale from 0 to 255 to mix colors. The advantage to you, the human artist, is that you have more precision in identifying colors than if you used 0 percent to 100 percent.

So what about that A? The A stands for Alpha channel, which controls the overall opacity for the final mixed color. When A is zero, the color is completely transparent. You can use the Alpha channel whether you specify a color using the visual tools or one of the number systems.

In the coder's world, there's another common way to specify a color, and that's done with hexadecimal numbers. Hexadecimal numbers are base 16 instead of the base 10 numbers people usually use. (How's that for a flashback to math class?) Hexadecimal numbers translate more easily into binary numbers than our familiar decimal system. The hexadecimal number system uses 16 symbols (2^4) to represent numbers instead of the usual 0-9. When the common numeric symbols run out, hexadecimal uses letters. So the complete set of number values looks like this: 0, 1, 2, 3, 4, 5, 6, 7, 8, 9, A, B, C, D, E, F.

To specify an RGB color with hexadecimal numbers, you use six places. The first two numbers represent the amount of red in the mix, the second two numbers represent green, and the final two numbers represent blue. So a color specification might look like this: 0152A0. Or this: 33CCFF. At first, it seems odd to see letters in numbers, but after a while you get the hang of it. So the hexadecimal FF0000 is a bright, pure red, while 0000FF is a bright blue.

In Animate, hexadecimal numbers are differentiated from base 10 numbers by placing a pound sign (#) in front. That's the way the color picker shows the hexadecimal number for your color selection, as you can see in Figure 2-1.

TIP Even though you can quickly create new elements using the copy-and-paste technique, you may still want to give each new element a unique, useful name. All you'll get from Animate are less-than-helpful names like RectangleCopy and RectangleCopy2.

DESIGNER'S TOOLBOX

Gracefully Resizing Elements for Browsers

Web design is not a good job for control freaks: More often than not, the audience controls the view. Visitors to your web pages can resize the browser window on a whim. You don't know whether your masterpiece will be displayed in all its glory across a 30-inch monitor or scrunched down to a small portion of a 13-inch laptop screen. Your audience can change key visual elements, such as the font size. Then, there's the device question: computer, tablet, smartphone...or the LCD display in a car's dashboard? Who knows? So the designer's challenge is to create pages that work under all crazy circumstances. The bad news: You'll never be able to anticipate every circumstance or get complete control. The good news: Animate helps you create pages that adapt to their environment.

Fixed-Size Design. First of all, you can always create animations that have a fixed size. Just use the pixel (px) unit for setting the size of the stage and all the elements displayed on the stage. With these settings, the stage and its elements will displayed in a browser at a fixed size. Then, for example, if the browser window isn't as big as the stage, the audience sees only a portion of the stage. They'll have to resize or scroll to see the rest. Alternately, if they're viewing the page on an enormous monitor, it may seem too small. They may need to adjust some of their browser settings to zoom in on the page. That said, if you're just learning Animate, you may want to used fixed width at the start. It's less confusing while you're working on your fundamental skills.

Fluid Design. A more fluid alternative is to use percentages instead of fixed pixel sizes. Want the stage to be as wide as the browser window? Set the X property to 100%. Even if your visitor resizes the window, the stage width adapts to the available space. Often, you'll want the elements on the stage to scale with the browser window, too. Suppose you have a sidebar that looks good at a quarter of the display width. Set that element to 25%. Now, both the stage and the sidebar change as the width of the browser window changes. When you use fluid design, you'll need to make decisions about each element, determining the best method for changing to accommodate the browser window. You may come up one solution for a text box and a different solution for graphics or photos.

Your tools for fluid design are in the Position and Size subpanel, shown in Figure 2-3. The Relative Position Point box lets you designate one of four corners as a position reference point for the X and Y properties. The Global and Applied toggle buttons let you choose whether the settings are relative to the Stage or to the parent <div> or symbol that contains the element. Click the button in the lower-left corner of the Position and Size subpanel to see more options. Then you'll see the Min W and Max W settings, which let you establish limits for stretch and squashing elements. And of course, choosing percentages for Position and Size is the key to a fluid design. You can use percentages for width (W) and height (H). You can also use percentages for position on the stage X and Y.

As you can see, there are a lot of settings to consider. To get a handle on how they all work in combination takes patience and practice. The solution for any particular project usually requires some experimentation. To help you get started, Animate offers some presets for common situations. In the upper-right corner of the Position and Size subpanel, there's a menu offering different solutions. Select an element, then choose an option like Scale Position or Scale Size. You'll find more tips throughout this book to help you create animations that respond to different browser situations. Chapter 10 is devoted to publishing and includes more details and tips on responsive page designs.

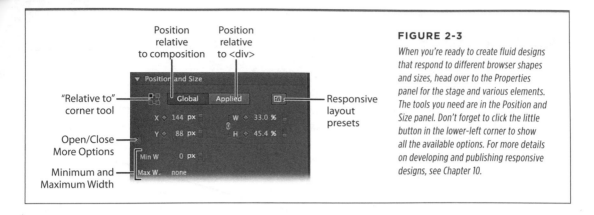

Position
relative
to composition

Position
relative
to <div>

"Relative to"
corner tool

Open/Close
More Options

Minimum and
Maximum Width

Responsive
layout
presets

FIGURE 2-3

*When you're ready to create fluid designs
that respond to different browser shapes
and sizes, head over to the Properties
panel for the stage and various elements.
The tools you need are in the Position and
Size panel. Don't forget to click the little
button in the lower-left corner to show
all the available options. For more details
on developing and publishing responsive
designs, see Chapter 10.*

Transforming Your Rectangle

The Transform properties, along with the Transform Tool (Q), are there to help
you fold, spindle, and mutilate your rectangles. Well, actually the transforms are
called Rotate, Skew, and Scale. The other property in the Transform group is called
Transform Origin. You can think of the origin as an anchor point for your rectangle.
It appears as a target symbol when the rectangle is selected. Initially, the origin
is at the midpoint. So if you rotate the rectangle, it spins around the midpoint. If
you move the transform origin to the bottom-right corner by setting X=100% and
Y=100%, your rectangle will rotate around that bottom-right corner point. Using the
X and Y Transform Origin properties, you can move the origin to any point in your
rectangle. As you make adjustments, the target symbol moves over the surface of
the rectangle. If you don't mind eyeballing it, choose the Transform Tool (Q) and
then you can drag the transform origin to a new point as shown in Figure 2-4.

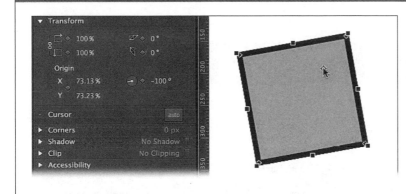

FIGURE 2-4

The transform origin point is the center of the universe when it comes to rotating, skewing, or scaling elements on the stage. You can reposition the transform origin using the Origin X and Y properties shown here in the Transform panel.

- **Rotate.** The Rotate properties are straightforward. When you create an element, like a rectangle, the Rotate property starts out at 0 degrees. You can manually rotate an object with the Transform tool (as shown in Figure 2-5, top) or you can use the Properties panel. If you want to spin your rectangle, change the Rotate property. If you want the spinning motion to take place over time, you need to create two keyframes in the timeline at different points in time with different Rotate properties. (For more details on the timeline and keyframes, see page 73.) If your first rotation keyframe is set to 0 and your second is set to 360, the rectangle spins in a complete circle. Set that second keyframe to 720, and it spins twice.

- **Skew.** The Skew properties turn your rectangle into a parallelogram by sliding two opposing sides in different directions (Figure 2-5, bottom). The top Skew property slides the top and bottom sides, and the bottom Skew property slides the left and right sides. You can apply both types of skew to a single object. The best way to get the hang of the Skew properties is to jump in and start playing with it.

- **Scale.** When you scale a rectangle, you change its size—making it smaller or larger. The Scale properties represent a percentage of the original object in the horizontal and vertical direction. As with the Size properties (page 21), the link to the left of the numbers lets you choose whether or not the scaling is proportionate.

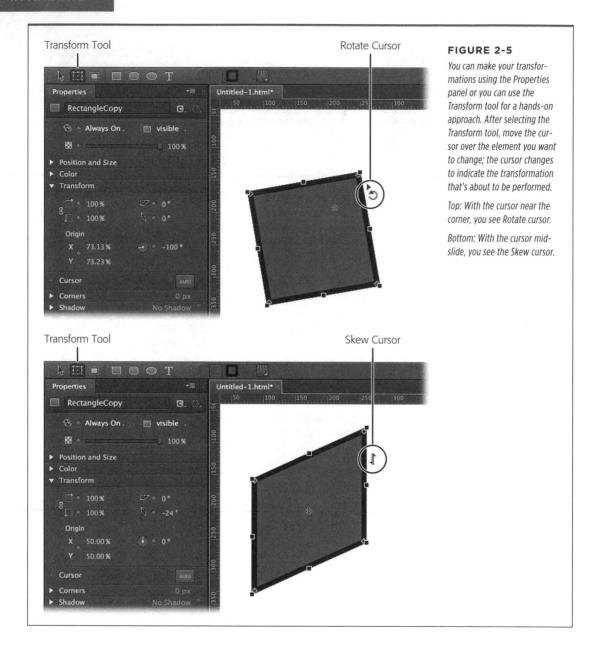

Transform Tool

Rotate Cursor

Transform Tool

Skew Cursor

FIGURE 2-5

You can make your transformations using the Properties panel or you can use the Transform tool for a hands-on approach. After selecting the Transform tool, move the cursor over the element you want to change; the cursor changes to indicate the transformation that's about to be performed.

Top: With the cursor near the corner, you see Rotate cursor.

Bottom: With the cursor mid-slide, you see the Skew cursor.

Aligning, Distributing, and Arranging Elements

The maxim that "everything has its place" is certainly true when it comes to anima-tion. With more than one element on the stage, their relationship to each other is critical. Designers often have a specific grid in mind when they're creating printed pages or web pages. It's best when boxes of text or graphics are aligned with this invisible grid. When several elements are aligned, it usually looks best when there's an equal distance between them. You can spend a lot of time eyeballing the stage to try to get everything just right, but fortunately, you don't have to.

To experiment with Animate's Arrange, Align, and Distribute tools, you may want to create three or four simple objects from the Rectangle and Rounded Rectangle tools like the ones shown in Figure 2-6. As you drag elements around the stage, you'll notice magenta-colored lines sprouting from the edges and midpoints. These are Smart Guides, and they can help you to quickly align one or more objects while you're mid-move. In many cases, that may be all the help you need.

> **TIP** If you find the Smart Guides distracting, you can toggle them on and off as needed with Ctrl+U or ⌘-U.

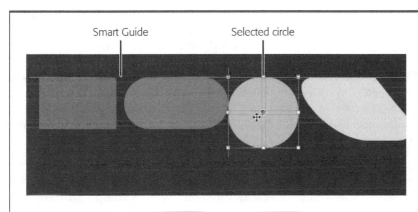

Smart Guide   Selected circle

FIGURE 2-6

Smart Guides are smart enough to hide when you don't need them. However, they show up when there's a job to do. Here the Smart Guide appears to help align the top edge of these four shapes. You can use guides to align any edge or the midpoint of an element.

For more formal alignment needs, turn to the Modify→Align menu. For align to work, you need to select at least two elements. You can select the elements on the stage or you can use the Elements panel. To use these commands, select all the elements that you want to align and then choose one of the options:

- Modify→Align→Left
- Modify→Align→Horizontal Center
- Modify→Align→Right

- Modify→Align→Top
- Modify→Align→Vertical Center
- Modify→Align→Bottom

You use the Modify→Distribute commands to put equal distance between three or more elements on the stage. You can choose which part of your elements the distribute command uses for the process and whether the action takes place along the horizontal or vertical axis. The specific commands are:

- Modify→Distribute→Left
- Modify→Distribute→Horizontal Center
- Modify→Distribute→Right
- Modify→Distribute→Top
- Modify→Distribute→Vertical Center
- Modify→Distribute→Bottom

Rulers and Manual Guides

The stage includes that help you place elements with precision. You can show and hide the rulers using the View menu (View→Rulers) or with the shortcut key: Ctrl+R (⌘-R). The rulers extend beyond the edges of the stage, but there are markers that indicate the stage's current size. For help with alignment chores, create guides by clicking on either the horizontal or vertical ruler and dragging toward the stage. Your guide follows and stays in place when you release the mouse button. If that's not the perfect spot, you can drag your guide to a new location. When you no longer want a guide, you can remove it by dragging it back to the ruler. To avoid inadvertently selecting and moving a guide, use the View→Lock Guides command. This locks them in place until you use View→Unlock Guides to free them again.

For quick help with alignment work, turn on Snap to Guides (View→Snap to Guides). You can drag multiple guides onto the stage for various alignment duties and you can show and hide all the guides at once using the View→Guides command (Ctrl+; or ⌘-;).

Arranging Elements: Z-Order

In addition to horizontal and vertical position, there's another way you can arrange objects on your stage. As you create elements, you may notice that new elements appear to be in front of the older elements, and if you drag a new element to the same X/Y position on the stage, it hides an older one. If you're familiar with Photoshop, you might think of this positioning as "layers." In geek-speak, it's often referred to as the Z-layer or the Z-order, because this third dimension is known as the Z axis. You can examine the Z-order of the elements on the stage by simply looking at the Elements panel. Elements at the top of the list are closer to the front. If you want to change the order, just drag an element to a new position in the panel. Animate also gives you menu commands and shortcut keys to rearrange elements:

- Modify→Arrange→Bring to Front (Ctrl+Shift+] or Shift-⌘-])

- Modify→Arrange→Bring Forward (Ctrl+] or ⌘-])

- Modify→Arrange→Send Backward (Ctrl+[or ⌘-[)

- Modify→Arrange→Send to Back (Ctrl+Shift+[or Shift-⌘-[)

■ A Rectangular Animation

Roll up your sleeves. Enough theory, it's time for some animation. In this exercise, you create four rectangles. You give them names, apply color, and skew them. Then you position them on the stage and make them move, change shape, and then appear to dissolve. It's the sort of effect that might be part of a banner ad or the introduction to a more complex animation. You don't need any Missing CD files to tackle this exercise. However, if you want to see the finished project, check out *02-1_Color_Bars_done.zip*.

This exercise is divided into two parts. In the first set of steps, you create and position the color bars:

1. Open and save a new Animate project with the name *Color_Bars*.

   Don't forget to create a new folder for your project.

2. Set the stage color to white and the dimensions to W=550px and H=400px.

   Animate remembers the last stage settings you used. So if you followed previous exercises or experimented on your own, you may need to make these changes.

3. In the timeline (Figure 2-7), make sure that the Auto Keyframe Mode and Auto Transition Mode buttons are pressed.

   If you move your cursor over the buttons, tooltips show their names. For example, at the top of the timeline you see: Auto-Keyframe Mode, Auto-Transition Mode, Toggle Pin, and Easing.

4. Draw a rectangle and in the Properties→ID, type *Red*.

   The ID box appears at the top of the Properties panel when the rectangle is selected.

5. In Properties, click the background color and set it to pure red, and set the border to *none*.

   When you're done, the hex color number should be #ff0000.

6. Set the rectangle's size to W=550px and H=100px.

The quickest way to accomplish this is to type the dimensions in the Properties panel, but if you're a mouse master, you can drag the rectangle's handles. You may need to click the "link" button next to W and H to change the width and height independently.

7. Set the Skew (x) to 50 deg (degrees).

The horizontal skew is the top setting. A positive number slides the top edge to the left and the bottom edge to the right.

8. Position your red, skewed rectangle in the top-left corner of the stage so that only its point tip is visible. The Location properties should be X=-550px, Y=0px.

Ideally, just a red triangle shows in the top-left corner of the stage.

9. With the Red rectangle selected, press Ctrl+D (⌘-D). Change the ID of RedCopy to Green. Then, change the color to match.

The hex value for solid green is #00ff00. You can change the background color of a selected element in the Properties→Color subpanel or you can use the color swatches in the toolbar above the stage.

TIP   The Duplicate command Edit→Duplicate is identical to the two step process of choosing Copy (Ctrl+C or ⌘-C) and then Paste (Ctrl+V or ⌘-V). In either case, you have a new copy of the element with the word "Copy" tacked onto the end of the name.

---

10. Line up the top of the green rectangle with the bottom of the red rectangle (Y=100px). Then, hold the Shift key down and slide Green to the right until only the tip shows (X=430px).

Holding the Shift key down while you move an element helps to lock it to the horizontal or vertical axis as you drag it. You can still drag it off axis, but it's a little "sticky."

11. Create two more skewed rectangles, naming and coloring them Blue and Yellow. Position the rectangles on alternating sides of the stage.

The blue color is #0000ff, and yellow color is #ffff00. When you're done positioning the rectangles, the stage should look like Figure 2-7.

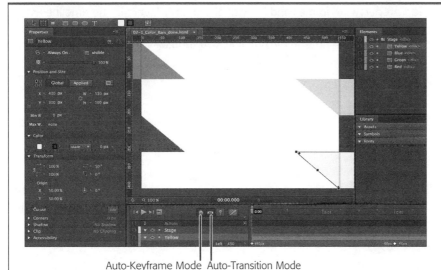

Auto-Keyframe Mode   Auto-Transition Mode

Animating by Adding Property Keyframes

Now that you've successfully created and positioned the color bars, it's time to make them move. Chapter 1 showed how the position of elements on the stage is controlled by property keyframes in the timeline. When the Auto-Keyframe Mode button is pressed, as shown in Figure 2-7, new property keyframes are created whenever you set or change a property. You can also create property keyframes manually by clicking the diamond-shaped buttons in the Properties panel. You want to lock in the Position, Size, and Opacity properties at the beginning of your animation by creating property keyframes. Then you'll move down the timeline and create different property keyframes. The result will be animation magic.

1. Make sure the timeline's playhead is at 0:00. Select the parallelogram named Red; then in the Properties panel, click the diamond-shaped buttons next to X, Y, W, H, and Opacity.

The X and Y properties are in the Position and Size subpanel. They control the position. The W and H buttons create keyframes for width and height. The Opacity slider is near the top of the Properties panel. The diamond buttons add property keyframes and individual property layers in the timeline as you can see in Figure 2-8. Property keyframes anchor a specific property value at a specific point in time. In the timeline, you should see property keyframes and property layers for:

- Left
- Top
- Width
- Height
- Opacity

If you don't see all those keyframes and property timelines under Red, you should create them manually by clicking the diamond button next to the missing property.

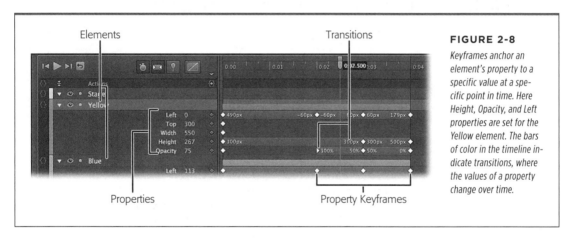

FIGURE 2-8

Keyframes anchor an element's property to a specific value at a specific point in time. Here Height, Opacity, and Left properties are set for the Yellow element. The bars of color in the timeline indicate transitions, where the values of a property change over time.

TIP You can expand and collapse the lanes (property rows) for each element by clicking the triangle button next to the element name. A button at the top-left of the word Actions, collapses or expands all lanes.

---

2. Repeat step 1 for the Green, Blue, and Yellow color bars to create the property keyframes and property layers for each.

   To speed things up, you can select all three bars first and then click the keyframe buttons.

3. Make sure the Auto-Keyframe Mode and Auto-Transition Mode are on (pressed in) and the other buttons are not.

   When Auto-Keyframe is on, Animate automatically creates property keyframes as you change elements on the stage (Figure 2-8). It's a two-step process. Move the playhead to a point in time and then change your element's properties. You can make changes in the Properties panel or you can make changes on the stage with the Selection and Transform tools.

4. In the timeline, drag the playhead to the 0:02 position.

   For this step, the pin should be toggled off (not pressed in).

5. Drag each of the rectangles across the stage until the tail end of the skewed rectangle is visible.

   At this point, most of the stage is covered by the color bars, with white triangles of the stage showing through at the edges. Remember to press the Shift key as you drag if you want to steady the bars' vertical position.

6. With all the rectangles selected, in Properties click the Add Key Keyframe for Opacity button. Drag the playhead back and forth to preview the animation.

   The opacity for each color bar is set to 100 percent at the 2 second point. Scrubbing the playhead gives you a quick look at the action.

7. Drag the playhead to the 0:03 marker.

   This position represents the point 3 seconds into your animation.

8. Select each rectangle and then change the height (H property) to 300 px and the opacity to 50 percent.

   This has the effect of making the rectangles grow, slicing vertically into one another, and at the same time start to blur. See Figure 2-9. Keep in mind, you may need to delink the W and H properties to change them independently.

9. Drag the playhead to the 0:04 marker. Then change each rectangle's height to 500 px and the opacity to 0 percent.

   The effect is that the rectangles keep growing and blur out of view.

Reviewing and Troubleshooting Your Animation

When you're finished with the exercise, it should look like *02-1_Color_Bars_done*. To watch your animation, press Home and then the space bar or use the controls on the timeline.

If the animation doesn't play as expected, the most likely culprit is a missing or misplaced property keyframe. Move the playhead to 0:00 on the timeline and check to make sure each color bar has the correct property values for:

- Left
- Top
- Width
- Height
- Opacity

It's a common mistake to assume that a property value is set at the start of an animation when it isn't. If there are still gremlins in the machine, compare the values at the 0:02, 0:03, and 0:04 positions with those in the Missing CD example file.

If you're in the mood to experiment, try staggering the bars' movement over time or changing the size, color, or skew properties in different ways. Add a background image or text to make the animation more interesting and the transparency revealing.

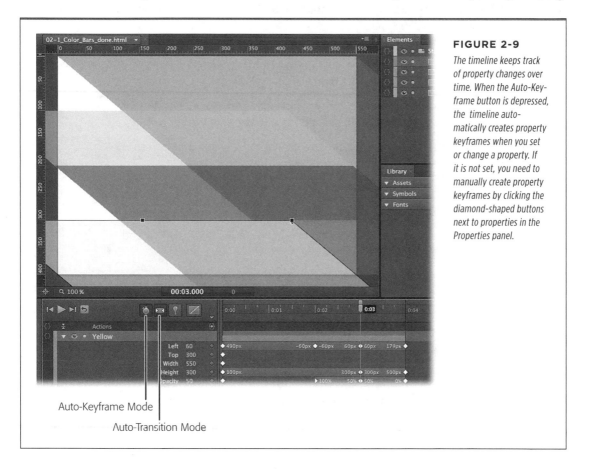

Auto-Keyframe Mode

Auto-Transition Mode

FIGURE 2-9

The timeline keeps track of property changes over time. When the Auto-Key-frame button is depressed, the timeline automatically creates property keyframes when you set or change a property. If it is not set, you need to manually create property keyframes by clicking the diamond-shaped buttons next to properties in the Properties panel.

Rounded Rectangles: More than Meets the Eye

OK, Animate pulls a fast one when it comes to the Rectangle, Rounded Rectangle, and Ellipse tools. The dirty little secret is that you can create all these shapes using the Rectangle tool and tweaking the properties. The reasons for this quirk have to do with the fact that JavaScript code is defining these shapes. You can check this by creating a shape with each tool and examining their properties. You can turn a rectangle into a rounded rectangle simply by adjusting the Corners→Radius properties, as shown in Figure 2-10. Likewise, you can square off a rounded rectangle using the same tools. So here's a look at how they work.

In a new Animate project, create a rectangle and leave it selected. Choose the Transform Tool (Q), then with the mouse, hover over the Corners keyframe diamond in the rounded rectangle properties, and the tooltip explains that it will "Add Keyframe for Top-left Radius, Top-right Radius..." and so on. (The actual tooltip message changes depending on the settings.) The three buttons at the top of the panel are labeled 1, 4, and 8. Below, you see a square made up of buttons where you can individually select the four corners of a rectangle. There's a number next to the corner buttons that's initially set to 0. A corner radius of zero means your rectangle has nice, sharp-edged corners. Click on the number and drag to the right to round off the corners. The number box accepts only positive numbers, so you can't drag left. Notice that as you drag, the black diamonds at the corners of your rectangle move to the center. These diamonds are control points for the corner radii. You can manually drag the diamonds on any rectangle to create and adjust rounded corners.

Reset your rectangle so that it's square, and then click the upper-right corner in the Properties panel. Change the radius setting and this time, you notice that the upper-right corner remains square while the others take on the rounded style. When a corner button is pressed in, that deselects the corner from the rounded settings.

Reset the rectangle once more and click the upper-right corner so it pops back out. Then click the 4 button at the top of the corner properties. Four new number boxes appear next to each corner. Now you can set each corner independently with different radius values. This gives you the ability to create irregular shapes even though, technically, they still have four corners. Combine this with the skewing and scaling properties, and you can create some really interesting amoeba effects. Click the 8 button, and each corner has two control numbers. This gives you the ability to move the control point off center, making a corner that is flatter on one side compared to the other. Notice that when you adjust the settings, the black diamond control point moves, too. You can always adjust your corners using either the number boxes or the control points in the rectangle.

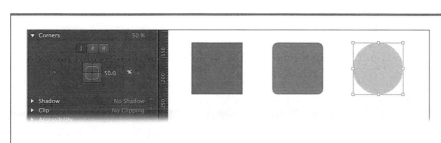

FIGURE 2-10

You turn a plain old rectangle into a rounded rectangle or an ellipse by adjusting the Corners properties. These shapes are identical except for their color and the Corners→Radius properties.

A Circle Is a Very Rounded Rectangle

You can experiment with the Corners→Radius properties by turning Rectangles into ovals and circles. For example, here are the steps to turn a square into a circle:

1. Click the Rectangle tool and, while holding the Shift key, drag out a box.

   Holding the Shift key down constrains the rectangle so that all sides are equal.

2. In the Corners properties, click the 1 button.

   With this setting, all the corners share the same corner radius value.

3. Click and drag the border radius number box until the square turns into a circle, as shown in Figure 2-11.

   It's possible to drag the number so that the corner radii pass one another at the center, but that's not necessary to create a circle.

> **TIP** You can turn your square into a circle using the Properties->Corners subpanel. Click the 1 button. Then, on the right side, click to change px to %. Then set the value to 50%.

FIGURE 2-11

The Corners→Radius tools give you a way to change any of the shapes you create using the Rectangle, Rounded Rectangle, or Ellipse tools. Here a square was rounded into a circle.

You can change and adjust your circle properties just as you would any other object that you create in Animate. By skewing your object, you can create ellipses. By scaling it, you can create ovals. And, of course, you can create anything in between a square and an ellipse with the right settings.

■ Adding Drop Shadows to Graphics

Drop shadows not only look cool, they give you a way to visually separate different elements. Apply a drop shadow to a graphic, and you make it look like it's floating above the stage. Add a shadow to the interior of an element, and you give it a more three-dimensional appearance. Shadows are often used with buttons to create a different appearance for over, clicked, and selected states. Animate gives you an easy way to create drop shadows and modify them to your needs and taste.

For a subtle shadow that sets an element off from the background, try the following steps:

1. Draw three elements on the stage.

2. Select one and then in the Properties panel, scroll down to the Drop Shadow controls shown in Figure 2-12. Click the button in the top-right corner to turn Drop Shadow on.

3. Click the color swatch and choose Black.

4. Click the horizontal offset and type *4*.

5. Click the vertical offset and type *4*.

6. Click the Blur radius and type *14*.

7. Click Spread and type *2*.

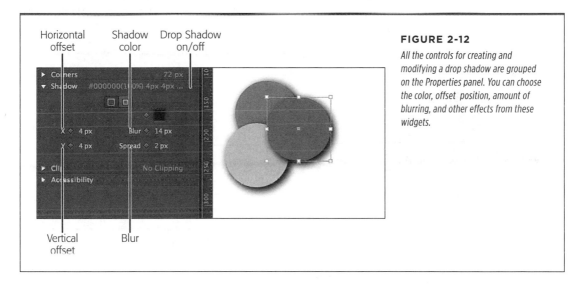

FIGURE 2-12

All the controls for creating and modifying a drop shadow are grouped on the Properties panel. You can choose the color, offset position, amount of blurring, and other effects from these widgets.

If you want one of the elements to look three dimensional, you can use the same settings but click the Inset button. Instead of appearing outside of the element, the shadow is created *inside* the element. As the name implies, the Spread property controls the size of the shadow making it spread in all directions. As with any other property, you can make the drop shadow change over time. With a little creativity, you can create the impression of the sun changing position in the sky, with shadows moving and changing shape. Shadows are an important tool for text, too: Text is more readable over a busy background when separated by a shadow. For tips on using shadows with text, see page 63.

TIP You can turn a shadow on and off with the click of a single button in the upper-right corner of the Shadow subpanel. There's no need to go back and tweak each shadow setting.

■ Clipping the Bits That Need Trimming

Adding art to your stage isn't an all or nothing affair. Animate gives you a tool to trim the edges of just about anything. The good news is, using the Clip tool couldn't be simpler. As with the Shadow properties, there's a single button in the upper-right corner of the subpanel that toggles the effect on or off. As you can see in Figure 2-13, there are four number settings representing the four edges of the selected element: top, bottom, left, and right. In most cases, it's easiest to click and drag over the number so you can watch how much Animate trims off the element. If you're more of a numbers person, you can click and type in a number. Once you've clipped an element you can move it around the stage—the trimmed bits remain hidden. What's more, you can animate the clipping properties like any Animate properties, so you can use this technique in animated transitions (as you'll see in Chapter 4). Clipping works with just about any element that appears on the stage, so you can also clip imported elements like photos or text boxes (Chapter 3) or symbols (Chapter 6). Clipping gives you yet another way to hide and reveal all or part of elements on the stage.

FIGURE 2-13

Here, the Clip tool has trimmed off the right and bottom edges of a rounded rectangle. Animate's native drawing tools are somewhat limited, but creative use of the Clip tool gives you an opportunity to make distinctly non-rectangular shapes.

■ Importing Art

It's easy enough to create basic shapes and text in Animate, but when it comes to complex artwork, you'll probably turn to your favorite art creation tools. For elaborate drawings and line art, that may be Adobe Illustrator. For photographs, you may use Photoshop, Lightroom, or iPhoto. Adobe Fireworks may be the ideal companion tool for Animate because both tools were designed to create Web content. No matter how you create JPEGs, GIFs, PNGs, or SVGs, you can import them into Animate and then animate them by changing their position on the stage and their appearance. There are two methods for storing and displaying images: bitmaps (technically called raster graphics) and vector graphics. For the details see the box on page 42. For tips on how to use specific file formats in Animate, read on.

- **Use JPGs for photos.** The JPG format is great for images that include lots of color and detail. JPG files, also known as JPEGs, are the familiar raster file format used on the web and in many cameras. (For details on the difference between raster and vector file formats, see the box on page 42.) The format was developed by the Joint Photographic Experts Group, hence the acronym. JPEGs use what is known as a lossy compression technique to create smaller file sizes. Image editors that work with JPEGs usually let you choose the degree of compression. If your image will only be viewed on a screen, you can crank up the compression. If it's headed to a photo printer and you want it poster size, you're going to need all those pixels. Adobe recommends using JPGs over PNGs because "90% of the time you'll get a smaller file with JPEG, which will reduce loading time of your compositions."

- **Use GIF files for preloader animated graphics.** Originally developed by CompuServe, one of the early online services. The acronym comes from Graphic Interchange Format. GIFs' popularity seems to be fading compared to JPEGs and PNGs, but you'll still find them on many websites. GIFs are raster graphics stored with a lossless compression technique, but use a limited color palette. The result is that an image with big swaths of solid colors, like a company logo or a bar graph, might result in a very small file. On the other hand, a photographic image won't compress as well and may not look as good in GIF as, say, in JEPG because of the limited number of colors. GIFs provide a couple of neat tricks. You can create animated GIFs using simple frame-by-frame animation. Programs like Adobe Fireworks and Flash make the process fairly easy. GIFs also let you designate parts of the image as transparent. That's great if you're placing an irregular shape, like an animated character, over an already developed background, like a room's interior.

- **Use PNG files when you need transparency.** PNG files were developed at a time when there were patent issues regarding GIF. Pronounced "ping," this abbreviation stands for Portable Network Graphics. The PNG format was designed to be used on the Web (as opposed to print graphics) and to improve upon features already popular in GIFs. PNGs use a lossless compression technique, provide a bigger color palette, can display animated sequences and can include transparency within the image. PNGs are well supported among modern web browsers, but there are probably still some older browsers out there that don't handle the format. The PNG format works well with Animate, in part because both were developed with the Web in mind.

- **Use SVG files _cautiously_ for graphics that need to be scaled.** SVG files are vector-based. The name stands for Scalable Vector Graphics. That means rather than recording a pixel-by-pixel map of an image, SVG files contain formulas that describe the lines, curves, shapes, and other details of an image. Animate "flattens" imported SVG graphics. That means if you resize an SVG image when you're working in Animate, it's likely to start looking pixelated—that jagged stair-step appearance that graphics get when they're enlarged. When this modified image is viewed in a browser, the pixelation shows. It's interesting to note that if you don't change the image within Animate, it resizes gracefully in a browser window, when it gets larger and smaller. When you create SVG files in a application like Adobe Illustrator, it's best to export to the SVG 1.1 format. Modern web browsers support SVG, but there are some inconsistencies. For this reason, Adobe suggests that, for now, it is safer to use PNG in most cases.

There's one difference in the way Edge handles artwork that you create using the built-in tools like the Rectangle tool, and art that's imported. Art created with the built-in tools is created on the fly with JavaScript code, while imported art is stored in its native format (JPG, SVG, PNG, or GIF) in the images folder. Those images are referenced by the HTML and JavaScript code. If the files themselves are renamed, moved, or missing, your audience is going to miss part of the show. If you want to update images that were created outside of Animate, just make the changes and save the file with the same name.

TIP It's a good idea to export images from your graphics program at the largest size they'll be used in your animation. That way you'll avoid the pixelation that occurs when bitmaps are scaled up. On the other hand, there's no need to make images bigger than they'll be displayed—all that does is slow down your composition's loading time. In the Sliding Show example, the stage is set to 600 × 400 pixels and each photo fills the stage. So, all the photos were saved at that same resolution. Reducing image size doesn't create the same ugly side effects. So you can take those 600 × 400 pixel images and use Animate to scale them down to 150 × 100 thumbnails of the photos and they'll look just fine.

Regardless of the file format, the process for importing artwork is the same. Go to File→Import and then find the file you want to bring into your project. The Missing CD folder *02-2_Sliding_Show* has three photos in JPEG format. You can practice by creating a new project complete with a new folder named *02-2_Sliding_Show* and import each of the photos. After you choose File→Import, a standard file/folder window opens for your PC or Mac. If you want to import all three files at once, just Shift-click to select them. As usual, Animate imports the files and, as a handy time-saver, names them based on the filenames. In this case, you'll find squirrel, farmhouse, and bike in your Elements panel. Each image is also automatically placed at the 0,0 position on the stage. You'll only see one of the images though, because they're covering one another. Remember that Z-order stuff on page 28?

TIP If you're a fan of drag-and-drop computing, it's worth noting you can drag the photos from a Windows Explorer or Finder folder and drop them right on the stage in your animation. Animate even has the courtesy to display the X/Y coordinates to help you position the imported graphics.

Showing and Hiding Elements

Sometimes you may have so many elements on the stage that you can't find or identify the one you want. The Elements panel can help you isolate and identify elements on the stage by showing and hiding them. To the left of each filename is an eyeball toggle button (Figure 2-14). When the eye is displayed, the object is visible on the stage. Click the eye and it turns into a circle; the element is hidden from view in Animate.

You can identify each of the imported photos by temporarily hiding the others. The show/hide button affects the visibility of elements only within the Animate workspace; it has no effect on the final project viewed with a browser.

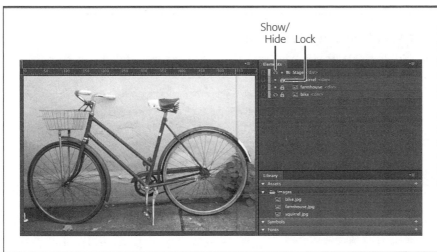

Show/
Hide Lock

FIGURE 2-14

The Elements panel has two tools to help you when you're working with elements on the stage. The eye toggle button shows and hides elements on the stage. The padlock button locks elements into position to keep you from accidentally selecting and moving them.

When Animate imports artwork, it automatically puts the upper-left corner of the image in the upper-left corner of the stage. So the Location properties for imported images are X=0, Y=0. In the case of the squirrel, farmhouse, and bike, this is exactly where you want your images for the Sliding Show project described next. However, the images are 600 × 400 pixels, which makes them a little wider than the standard 550 px stage. That's easy enough to fix. Select the stage in the Elements panel and set W to 600px.

The Sliding Show

Back in the olden days when photographs were recorded on film, there was an event called the *slideshow*. It was called a slideshow because the projector slid the images on and off the screen. These days, slideshows take the form of PowerPoint presentations, or they're used to display photos on a website. You can use a slideshow to show products. If you're selling cars, maybe you want to display all the color options. If you're selling home theater amplifiers, maybe you want customers to zero in on the different panels with controls and connectors.

In this next exercise, you create your own automated, sliding show. Each image is displayed for a period of time, and then it fades away as it slides offstage. You can use the three imported images from the previous exercise, or you can use as many of your own images as you want. Your show will look best if the slides are the same size and have the same portrait or landscape orientation.

Vector, Raster, and Your Favorite File Formats

The world of 2D computer graphics offers two systems for storing and displaying images: bitmaps (technically called *raster* graphics) and vector graphics.

Computer programs store bitmaps as a bunch of pixels, identified by color and position. The term *Bitmap graphics* doesn't refer to just files with the Windows bitmap (.bmp) extension; it refers to all images stored in bitmap format, including .gif, .jpg, .tiff, and .png. The good thing about bitmap graphics is that they let you create super-realistic detail with complex colors, gradients, and subtle shadings. On the downside, uncompressed bitmaps typically take up a whopping amount of disk space, and they're not particularly scalable. For example, suppose you have a bitmap image of a car, and you tell a program to increase the size by 500 percent. The program has to create new pixels for the bigger image, so it duplicates the pixels (colored dots) already in the image. The results

aren't always pretty. The entire image is likely to appear blurry. The curved edges may become blocky or *pixelated*.

Computers store vector graphics as a bunch of formulas. Compared to raster graphics, vector graphics are relatively modest in size, and they're scalable. In other words, if you draw a tiny car and decide to scale it 500 percent, your scaled drawing will still have nice, crisp details.

The strengths and weaknesses of each format are important when you're working with images. Bitmaps are better for photorealistic images with lots of colors and shades. Vector graphics are better for line art, charts, diagrams, and images that you're going to scale to different sizes. Animate can import four types of graphics files—JPG, GIF, PNG, and SVG—however, there are a couple of gotchas that might surprise you. See page 38 for details on the different file formats.

1. Import your photos using File→Import.

   Animate places the images on the stage and automatically creates an *images* folder for your project. Copies of the photos are placed in the *images* folder. In the Library panel, you'll see the three images listed under Assets. As the Tip on page 40 explains, you can also import graphics by dragging them from Windows or Mac OS X folders and dropping them directly onto the stage.

2. Select the stage in the Elements panel, and then set the stage dimensions and background color. Set the Overflow to hidden.

   Give the stage the same dimensions as your images. With overflow set to hidden, the images will disappear when they move off the stage.

3. Arrange your images so the first image is at the top of the Elements panel.

   In this project, the Z-order of the images determines when an image is displayed. It's as if you have a stack of snapshots on a table and you remove the top photo to see the next.

4. Shift-click to select all the images in the Elements panel, and then in Properties, click the Add Keyframe button next to X and Y, as shown in Figure 2-15.

   Left and Top keyframes are created for each of the images at 0:00 on the timeline. This locks in the starting position for each of the images.

5. With all the images still selected, in Properties make sure the opacity is set to 100 percent and then click to add keyframes for Opacity.

All the images will have an opacity of 100 percent until they begin to move off the stage.

6. Drag the playhead to 0:02, and then with the top image selected, add keyframes for X, Y, and Opacity again.

This locks in the position and opacity of the top image for the first 2 seconds of the slideshow. In the next steps, the photo will start to move and change. Make sure that the pin moves with the playhead to the new location. If necessary, press P to toggle the pin.

7. Make sure Auto-Keyframe Mode and Auto-Transition Mode are turned on.

With these two timeline buttons turned on, keyframes and transitions are created automatically when you make changes to the composition.

TIP　If the Auto-Keyframe Mode button is clicked on, Animate will automatically create the Location property keyframes when you move the photo. If Auto-Keyframe Mode is not on, you can create keyframes by clicking the Add Keyframe button next to X and Y in the Properties panel.

---

8. Drag the playhead to 0:03, and then drag the top slide completely off the stage.

You can have your slides move off the stage in any direction. Right movement imitates the old-fashioned slide projectors. Hold the Shift key as you drag if you want the image to slide along a vertical or horizontal axis.

FIGURE 2-15

Click the diamond-shaped Add Keyframe buttons to create X, Y, and Opacity keyframes in the timeline. You can set the value for each property independently. If you select more than one element, you can add keyframe properties for them all. When more than one element is selected, no ID is displayed at the top of the Properties panel.

9. With the image completely offstage, change the opacity to 20 percent.

This creates a nice fading effect for each image as it moves offstage.

10. Drag the playhead down the timeline another 2 seconds.

This gives your audience time to admire your next photographic masterpiece.

11. Select the next slide that's visible on stage and then in Properties click the Add Keyframe buttons for X, Y, and Opacity.

   This locks in the position and opacity for the slide that's showing. Like the previous slide, it will move and fade after this point.

12. Move the playhead another second down the timeline and drag the photo off-stage, and set the opacity to 20 percent.

   This completes the process for the second image in the slideshow.

13. Repeat steps 10–12 for each of the images in your slideshow.

14. When the last slide is removed from the stage, display a message to viewers.

   If you want, you can fade a message like "Thanks for watching!" on and off the stage to signal the end of the show.

You can preview your slideshow in Animate (Figure 2-16), or you can view it in your favorite web browser. You're probably already thinking of ways you can tweak and customize a slideshow like the one described in this exercise. Naturally you can change the timing for the appearance and disappearance of each slide. If you want a fancy pseudo-3D effect, you could use Skew and Size properties to make the slides look as if they are blowing away one by one. In future exercises (page 115), you'll see how to give your audience click controls for the slideshow.

■ On/Off: Another Way to Show and Hide Elements

So far this book has shown you a few ways to show and hide elements. For example, if you want to show and hide elements while you're working in Animate, you can use the visibility eyeball-icon in the Elements panel. That tool doesn't change the way your final animation looks; it merely hides elements while you're working in Animate. You've also seen how you can hide elements using their Opacity property. Set Opacity to 0 and presto-change-o—it disappears. Opacity is particularly good for animated effects like the one in the Sliding Show. Using Opacity, it's easy to make elements fade in and fade out. Still there's some work involved in controlling the opacity over the course of an entire Animate composition.

There's another, more fundamental way to show and hide elements on the stage: You can turn elements on and off. In the Properties panel, directly under the ID box (Figure 2-15), there's a drop-down menu that is initially set to Always On. So far, that's the option used in the exercises in this book. There are two other items on the menu: On and Off. Suppose you want to redo the Sliding Show so that images changed instantly without any motion or fading effects. That's a perfect job for the On/Off switch. Import your images as described on page 38. With all your images in place on the stage, set one image to On and set all the other images to Off. In the timeline move the playhead to the two second mark (or any other interval that suits you). Turn the displayed image off and turn another image on. In this case, the stacking order of the images (the Z-order) doesn't matter because only one image is visible at a time. If you want to review a working example of this method, check out *02-4_On_Off_Elements_done* from the Missing CD at *www.missingmanuals.com/cds/animatemm*.

FIGURE 2-16

Here in mid-slide, the squirrel is leaving the stage and the farmhouse is revealed underneath. The movement and opacity of the slides is controlled by property keyframes in the timeline.

There's one other thing to note: Once you use the On/Off menu in Properties, Animate adds an On/Off toggle button in the timeline for that element. See Figure 2-17. This makes it quick and easy to set the playhead to a particular point in time and turn your elements on or off.

FIGURE 2-17

You can turn elements off until you need them and then turn them on. The initial control is in the Properties panel and elements are set to Always On. Once you turn an element on or off there, you'll see Display On/Off settings in the timeline.

Adding and Formatting Text

In spite of the old saw about a picture being worth a thousand words, often words are the right tool for the job. When you want to label a button, build a menu based navigation system, or provide how-to instructions for a particular task—it's time for text.

Animate is rooted in HTML5, so it gives you the same properties and text-handling features that you'd find in other web-building tools like Adobe Dreamweaver. That means you won't have all the typographic features that you'd find in a page layout program or a more complex graphics program like Flash. As you'll learn in this chapter, you do get your choice of fonts, and you can set the size, color, and alignment. If Animate doesn't have the special font that you need, you can use *web fonts*. For example, this chapter shows how to link to Google's web fonts. In addition, you'll learn how to apply transforms and effects just like those used with graphics and photos. Along the way, you'll learn how to animate your text, giving it a little bounce. Links are important to any web page. This chapter explains how to import and manage HTML text that includes links on specific words. HTML has a number of tags that are used to identify the content of text, such as block quotes from other sources and computer code used for examples. You'll learn which tags Animate uses and how to apply those tags to text.

Adding Text to Your Project

There are three ways to add text to your Animate project:

- **Use the text tool.** In the Tools palette, click the big T (or use the shortcut key T), and then in your document, click and drag to create a text box. Initially, you don't have to worry too much about positioning or sizing the text box. You can manage those details later. Just go ahead and start typing. Try the phrase "ON the EDGE." The text you enter appears on the stage, as shown in Figure 3-1. If you want to create multiple paragraphs, just press Enter (Return) as you would in your word processor. When you're done, you can close the text window by pressing Esc or clicking the X button in the upper-right corner.

- **Copy and paste.** If you're working with large blocks of text, you may have already worked up a draft in a word processor or some other source. In that case, you can copy the text in your word processor, and then in Animate create a text box and press Ctrl+V (⌘-V) to paste it into your project. It won't be formatted exactly as it was originally, but the text will be there. This process maintains some of the major formatting, such as paragraph breaks.

- **Open HTML with text.** Perhaps you have a web page already created in an HTML editor or some other web-building tool. You'd like to add some animation excitement to the static page. You can open that page in Animate using File→Open and then use Animate to make the elements move. You're limited in what you can do with text imported in this way. You can't edit it or change its formatting. In essence, it's just another graphic element you can use in an animation. One significant advantage to this method is that links within the text are maintained.

FIGURE 3-1

As you enter text in the lower box, it's displayed on the stage in the upper box. The box with the blue border is the text box, which remains on stage when you're done typing. The lower box is sometimes called an IME for "input method editor." When you're through entering text, click the X in the upper-right corner to close the IME.

About Text Containers

Once you've added text to your project, its location and size are managed by a text container called a text box. You can reposition your text by dragging it or by changing the Position properties. To move text manually, click the Selection tool (it looks like an arrow) or press the shortcut key V. As with other elements, the X and Y properties position the upper-left corner of the text box, so you can position text with precision by typing X and Y values in Properties. To reshape the text box, drag one of the handles or change the W or H properties. Keep in mind you need to delink the size properties to change W and H independently. Initially, Animate displays all your text whether it fits in the box or not, so if your text doesn't fit within the height of the box, it extends out the bottom. If that's not the behavior you want, you can use the clipping tools (page 38) to trim the bottom of the text box. For that matter, you can trim the top or sides, too.

■ Changing Text-Specific Properties

Once you have text in your Animate project, there are several text-specific properties that you can use to change its appearance, as shown in Figure 3-2. These properties appear in the Text subpanel. Initially, some of the less-used options may be hidden. Click the button in the lower-left corner of the subpanel to show and hide additional properties. The names for each of these tools follow CSS (cascading style sheet) naming conventions, so they are lowercase with hyphens between words. There are more details about CSS on page 160.

- **font-family.** You can choose from several different typefaces. You might not find all the same fonts that you have on your computer. In web design, you're limited to fonts that are available to your audience unless you have a way of providing the font with your project. For more details on fonts and typefaces, see the next section. For a way to find and use additional fonts, see page 54.

- **color.** Click the swatch, and the standard color picker appears where you can set the color for your text.

- **font-size.** Dial in font size by number. Next to font-size you see a button called Text Property Units. Click this to change the method for specifying font-size.

  Animate uses three different units for specifying font-size: pixels (px), ems (em), and percentage (%). Pixels are equivalent to a single dot on a monitor. An em is roughly the size of the letter M. Most web browsers give users the ability to adjust the size of text, so an em is a unit that changes according to the browser setting. Percentage is a useful option when designing web content that may be viewed on mobile devices as well as desktop computers. There are more details about using text in responsive designs in Chapter 10.

- **font-weight.** Gives you several options such as Thin, Extra Light, Normal, and Extra Bold. The order of options and their accompanying numbers give you hints for comparing the different weights.

- **font-style.** Slants the text so it looks like italics.

- **text-decoration.** Use this button to underline text.

- **text-align.** Just like your word processor, Animate lets you align text right, center, or left. Alignment affects all the text in the text box. So if you want to create one paragraph aligned right and one paragraph centered, they must be in separate text boxes.

- **text-indent.** Indents the first line within a text box. You can change the value in pixels. It doesn't accept negative numbers to create hanging indents.

- **line-height.** Use to set the space between lines of text.

- **letter-spacing.** As the name implies, you can adjust the space between letters. Often used to create distinctive headlines or company logos, this effect should be used sparingly for normal body text.

- **word-spacing.** Varies the distance between words. Use carefully or you may end up with awkward, hard-to-read text.

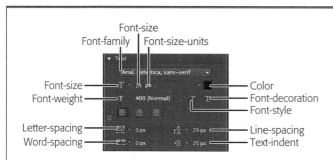

FIGURE 3-2

Animate provides the standard text formatting options, including choice of font, style, size, color, and alignment. In addition to these properties, you have access to the same properties available to graphics, such as size, location, rotate, and skew. If you're not sure what one of these widgets does, hold the cursor over it. A tooltip appears with the tool name.

About Typefaces and Fonts

Choosing a typeface for your project should be fun—just not too much fun. Make your typeface decisions based on the job at hand, and you can't go wrong. Think about what you expect your type to do, and then help it do that job by choosing the right typeface, style, size, color, and alignment. Beginning designers often treat text as yet another design element and let the desire for a cool look override more practical concerns. Designers sometimes talk about a text block as if it's just another shape on the page. But cool type effects can torture your readers' eyes with hard-to-read backgrounds, weird letter spacing, or hopelessly small font sizes. (For more advice on readability, see the box on page 53.)

When you specify type for a web page, you have to take into consideration which fonts are available to your audience. If you specify a font that your audience doesn't have, the web browser will supply a substitute. Sometimes that substitute is close to your spec, and other times not so much. This has always been a challenge for web designers. In the past, designers could expect different fonts on Mac, Windows, and Linux computers. That situation has improved over the years, but most web designers always specify a list of two or three fonts, such as Arial, Helvetica, sans-serif.

When a web browser sees the list, it uses Arial (originally a Windows font), if that's available. Next, it tries Helvetica—a font that was most common on Macs. If neither is available, the browser looks for some other sans-serif font. All of Animate's font specs use this multiple-choice method. In addition, the fonts listed are very likely to be available to your audience. Your choices are:

- **Verdana, Geneva, sans-serif.** Verdana (see Figure 3-3) was developed for Microsoft and is widely available on both Windows and Macs. The goal was to create a typeface that's readable on a computer screen in small sizes. Geneva was designed for the Apple with the same goal and was available on the original Mac. Both of these typefaces are good for long paragraphs of text. The term *sans-serif* is borrowed from the French and means without serifs. Serifs in ty-pography are the extra bars and strokes at the ends of letters that you see in some typefaces. In print, experts feel that serifs help make type more readable and lead the reader's eye along a horizontal line. Type isn't quite as sharp on computer screens, so the serifs' helpfulness isn't quite as obvious. (The text in this book is a sans-serif font.)

- **Georgia, Times New Roman, Times, serif.** Times was a typeface developed for the New York Times newspaper way back when. It's a very readable typeface and works well for long paragraphs of text. Times New Roman and Georgia are similar to this much-imitated font.

- **Courier, Courier New, monospace.** Back in the old days, when office workers used typewriters, everything looked like Courier. The term *monospace* means that every character is provided the same space horizontally. This creates notice-able gaps to accommodate narrow characters like "i," which get just as much space as "M". Monospace fonts are a little harder to read compared to a typeface like Times, but they do make a primitive kind of statement. Monospaced fonts are often used to display computer code.

- **Arial, Helvetica, sans-serif.** The monarchs of the sans-serif world, Arial and Helvetica, are used all over the place. They're also widely available to most computers. These typefaces can be used for body text or headlines. If you want a bolder typeface for a heading, choose Arial Black, Gadget, sans-serif.

- **Tahoma, Geneva, sans-serif.** Tahoma was designed for Microsoft and Geneva for Apple. Tahoma is a little narrower than its counterpart Verdana, which means you may be able to get more characters per line at a small sacrifice in terms of readability.

- **Trebuchet MS, Arial, Helvetica, sans-serif.** Trebuchet MS is a font that's more distinctive than Arial and Helvetica and not nearly as ubiquitous. A good type-face for headings of all sizes. It was also developed by Microsoft and widely distributed along with Office and other Microsoft applications.

- **Arial Black, Gadget, sans-serif.** Arial Black and Gadget are both heavy fonts, meaning they have very thick lines. Use these typefaces when you're creating big, bold headlines.

- **Times New Roman, Times, serif.** The Times fonts are very versatile. Often used for body text, they can also be used for headings at large sizes. Times adds a sort of "old school" elegance to projects.

- **Palatino Linotype, Book Antiqua, Palatino, serif.** Palatino is a typeface that's been widely available on computers since the Mac first adopted it. An attractive and readable font, the Palatino family of typefaces has grown over the years. This specification refers to the original serif font.

- **Lucida Sans Unicode, Lucida Grande, sans-serif.** Lucida Sans Unicode was designed to supply a font that supported the most commonly used characters in the large Unicode standard. (The Unicode computer standard was developed to handle and display text used in most of the world's writing systems.)

- **MS Serif, New York, serif.** These are basic serif fonts provided by Microsoft and Apple, respectively.

- **Lucida Console , Monaco, monospace.** Lucida Console and Monaco are mono-spaced, sans-serif typefaces, as shown in Figure 3-3. These are a good choice for menus or other user interface elements. In general, they won't work as well in large blocks of text.

Sometimes you may want to use a special or decorative font that's not included in Animate. Perhaps it's a company logo or a special heading style. In those cases, you might want to turn the text into a graphic. Create the text in a word processor or page layout program, and then take a screenshot to turn the text into a JPEG image. At that point, you can import the JPEG into Animate just like any other graphic element (see page 38). The downside of this technique is that your text can't be edited within Animate. Another alternative for displaying unique fonts is to use a web font as explained in the next section.

NOTE If you want to be technical in a Gutenbergian fashion, typefaces are families of fonts. Times Roman is a typeface, while "Times Roman, bold, 12 point" is a font. Somewhere along the line, as type moved from traditional typesetters to computer desktops, the meaning of the word "font" came to be synonymous with "typeface." That's OK, but knowing how the terms originated makes great cocktail party banter.

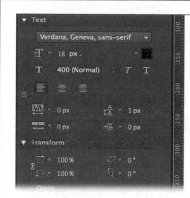

On the EDGE in Verdana

On the EDGE in Times New Roman

On the EDGE in Arial Black

On the EDGE in Palatino Linotype

On the EDGE in Lucida Console

FIGURE 3-3

Changing a typeface is as easy as selecting a font from the drop-down menu. However, it's important to choose the right typeface for the job. Arial Black is great for headings and bold statements, but it would be painful to read multiple paragraphs of the stuff. That job is better suited to Times New Roman or Verdana, which are very readable at small font sizes.

FREQUENTLY ASKED QUESTION

Small Is Beautiful

How can I use small type and make sure it stays readable?
For most people, reading text on a computer or iPhone screen is more difficult than reading it off a piece of paper. If your Animate project includes text with small font sizes (12 px or less), there are a few things you can do to keep your audience from straining their eyes. Actually, the fact of the matter is, people simply won't read text if it's too hard to see.

- If possible, bump the type up to a larger size. At small sizes, a single pixel makes a big difference.

- Black text on a white background is easiest to read. If you don't want to use that combination, opt for very dark text on a very light background. If you have to use light text on a dark background, make sure there's a great deal of contrast between the colors.

- Use sans-serif type, like Verdana, Arial, or Tahoma for small sizes. Sans-serif type looks like the text in this book;

it doesn't have the tiny end bars (serifs) you often find in type. Computer screens have a hard time creating sharp serif type at very small sizes.

- Use both upper- and lowercase type for anything other than a headline. Even though all-caps type looks bigger, it's actually less readable. The height differences in lowercase type make it more readable. Besides, too much uppercase type makes it look like you're shouting.

- Avoid bold and italic type. Bold and italic are often hard to read at small font sizes. It varies with different typefaces, so it doesn't hurt to experiment.

It never hurts to get second and third opinions. If you've got eyes like an eagle, you may want to get some opinions from your less-gifted colleagues when it comes to readability. You want your Animate project to be accessible to as wide an audience as possible.

■ Using Web Fonts

There's another way to increase the number of typefaces you use in your Animate animations. For years, web designers have been using *web fonts*. For programs, including web browsers, to display a specific font, they need to have access to the font description. Usually, that description resides on the same computer as the program—sometimes called the *client*. Web fonts work a little differently. For example, with Google's web fonts (*www.google.com/webfonts*), the definitions for the fonts are stored on Google's servers. As a web designer, you can use these fonts by adding code to your pages that tell browsers where to find the font descriptions.

NOTE In web-speak, the computer with the browser is called the client; the computer serving up the web pages is the host.

First, find the web font you want to use. Google web fonts are free and surprisingly easy to use, so they're a great candidate for your first attempt. Here are the steps to selecting a Google web font and grabbing the code you need to identify it in your project:

1. In your web browser, go to: *www.google.com/webfonts*.

   You see a page displaying font samples. There are hundreds, so the widgets on the left help you filter the fonts. The buttons at the bottom of the page direct you to the three steps for a successful web font hunt: Choose, Review, and Use.

2. On the left, below the word Filters, click the drop-down menu. Choose from Serif, Sans-Serif, Display, and Hand Writing.

   The menu uses checkboxes, so you can choose a combination of characteristics. For example, you could use Sans-Serif and Display.

3. If necessary, use the Thickness, Slant, and Width sliders to narrow your font search.

   With so many choices, it helps to thin the crowd of fonts displayed on the screen.

TIP At first, the Search box isn't much use to you because Google web fonts don't have the familiar names. After you use them a bit, you'll probably find a few favorites that you use repeatedly. If you remember their names, then you can use the Search box to quickly find that needle in the haystack.

4. Use the tabs at the top of the font window to change the display to Word, Sentence, or Paragraph.

   If you're looking for a font for headings, the Word or Sentence tab is the best choice. If you're choosing a font for body text, make sure you check its appearance with the Paragraph option.

5. Click the blue "Add to Collection" button.

   You can have more than one font in a collection, but for page-rendering speed and good design, you'll want to limit the number of fonts you use.

6. Click Review.

This step may not always be necessary, but as the name implies, on this page you can take a closer look at your font in use as a headline or paragraph.

7. Click Use.

A new page loads with instructions for using the fonts on your website. Part way down the page is a blue box with the heading "Add this code to your website"; see Figure 3-4.

FIGURE 3-4

Google provides several different code samples for using their web fonts on your website. The shortest and easiest one to use is under the Standard tab shown here.

8. Click the Standard tab and then select and copy the code displayed.

With the code stored on your Clipboard, you're ready and loaded for the second part of the process: adding the location for the font description to your Animate project.

Adding Web Fonts to Your Composition

Once you've chosen a Google or other brand web font and copied the code that identifies it, adding to your project easy in Animate. Here are the steps:

1. In the Library panel, on the bar that says Fonts, click the + button, as shown in Figure 3-5.

The Add Web Font dialog box opens.

2. Paste the code that identifies the location of your font in the lower "embed code" text box.

This code is provided by the same organization that hosts the web font. If you followed the previous steps, the code is stored on your Clipboard.

3. Type the name of web font in the upper Font Fallback List along with the fonts that should be used if the web font isn't available.

If the client computer isn't connected to the Internet, then the web font won't be available.

4. Click the Add Font button.

The font now appears in the Font Name drop-down menu when you're working with text.

There are a few of things to keep in mind when you expand your font toolbox by using web fonts:

- It takes browsers a little longer to find, download, and use web fonts compared to fonts stored on the local computer.

- Web fonts won't be available to computers or mobile devices that aren't connected to the Internet.

- Just because you have access to a bunch of new fonts, that doesn't mean you have to use them all. Don't sacrifice readability for novelty.

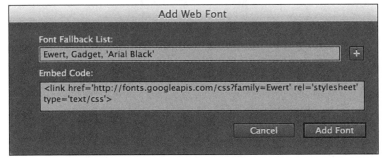

FIGURE 3-5

Three steps for adding fonts to your project.

Top: Click the Add Web Font button.

Middle: Paste in the code that identifies the location for the web font description.

Bottom: Choose your new font from the Font Name box.

NOTE Google web fonts have the significant advantage of being free to use, but they aren't the only game in town. As this book went to press, Adobe announced Edge Web Fonts, a free service similar to Google Web Fonts. See Figure 3-6. In fact, the choice of fonts include many that were originally commissioned by Google. For details go to *http://www.edgefonts.com.* You'll find other options at *http://typekit.com, http://webfonts.fonts. com*, and *http://fontsquirrel.com.*

FIGURE 3-6

Adobe's Edge Web Fonts work much the same as Google fonts. You choose your typeface, see an example, and then you can copy the code to add the font to your web page.

■ Changing Other Text Properties

Like any other element in Animate, you probably don't expect your text to be static all the time. Fortunately for you, the designer, you don't have to learn new tools to make your text dance around the screen. The X/Y Position properties determine where your text appears, and the W/H Size properties determine the dimensions of the text box. Keep in mind that the Size properties change the size of the text box, but they don't change the size of the letters. To change the size of the letters, you can use the font-size properties or the Scale properties. For the readable text, it's best to use the font-size properties; however for special visual effects scale may do the trick. As with drawings and photos, you can create property keyframes in the timeline to make text properties change over time. For example, page 11 showed how to use the Opacity setting to make text fade in and out.

Remember those fold, spindle, and mutilate tools? You can use the Transform properties on text, too. Go ahead and rotate or skew blocks of text for special effects as you add or remove them from the web page. Use the Scale properties to make the text box and the text inside bigger or smaller. Scale works on text the same way it works on a JPEG image: Dial in a percentage, and everything grows or shrinks. Keep in mind that text gets a bit blurry when it's enlarged using the Scale property.

> **NOTE** Animate anticipates how you want your text to move. With this in mind, it automatically puts the transform origin in the middle of the text box. That makes it a cinch to create a headline that spins like a pinwheel. Naturally, you can reposition the Transform Origin at any time using the X/Y transform origin properties.

Clipping Text Around the Edges

As with other graphic elements on the stage, you can use Clip properties to hide the edges of a text box. It's a lot like cropping the edges of photograph. Suppose you want to animate a text box so that at first only a pinpoint in the middle is visible, then it grows to display an entire block of text. Select your text and then look near the bottom of the Properties panel. Click the triangle button to expand the Clip subpanel. In the upper-right corner of the subpanel, click the button to turn clipping on. Edge Animate provides four controls that represent the top, bottom, left, and right edges of the element (Figure 3-7, bottom). Type or scrub in values in pixels (px). As you make changes, you see the effect they have on your text box. Want to remove clip properties after you've applied them? Just right-click (Control-click) the clipped element and choose Remove Clip from the shortcut menu.

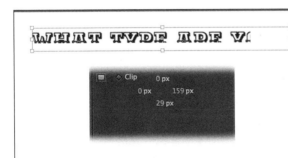

FIGURE 3-7

Clip properties give you an easy way to crop a text box.

Top: The right and bottom edge of the text box are hidden.

Bottom: That effect was created by increasing the values of the right and bottom clip properties.

Making That Headline Drop In

In most cases, the purpose of text is to communicate a message, so it's counter-productive to subject your audience to constantly moving and changing text. That doesn't mean you can't have a little bit of fun. For instance, you may want to have the heading on your web page drop down or bounce into place when the page first loads. Check out *03-01_Heading_Drop_done* if you want to see an example.

In this project, you create a banner at the top of the stage. When the web page loads, three words—"ON the EDGE"—drop into place. In this case, you're animating the phrase "ON the EDGE." You break the words into three separate text boxes, so that you can move each word independently. In other cases, you may want to animate all the individual letters in a word or phrase. The toughest part of the trick is to get the letter or words to line up properly once they're in place. You want letter spacing to look natural, and you want the text to sit evenly on a horizontal line. Often, when you're animating words or letters like this, it helps to create a positioning template, and that's exactly what you do in this project. The positioning template (Figure 3-8) is visible at design time to help you align those moving words and letters. When you're done building the animation, you can remove the template.

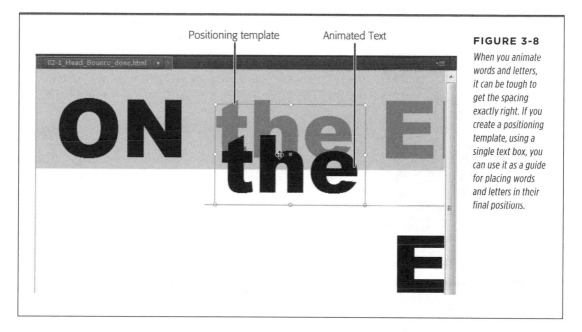

FIGURE 3-8

When you animate words and letters, it can be tough to get the spacing exactly right. If you create a positioning template, using a single text box, you can use it as a guide for placing words and letters in their final positions.

Here are the steps to create a drop-in heading:

1. Create and save a new 550 × 400 document with a white background color.

   As usual, create a new folder to hold the HTML and JavaScript files for your project.

2. With the Rectangle tool (M), create a rectangle 550px × 100px and place it at X=0, Y=0. Set the background color to R=200, G=210, B=250, and A=100%. Set border color to *none*. Give the rectangle the ID *BannerBG*.

   The quickest way to make a rectangle to spec is to drag out a quick box that's any old shape and then type in the values in Properties. Make sure you click the link next to the W/H Size properties so you can enter nonproportional values.

3. In the Elements panel, click the Lock Element button next to *BannerBG*.

   A padlock appears next to *BannerBG*. Now, you can't accidentally select or move the blue box on the stage.

4. Select the text tool and drag out a text box. Then type *ON the EDGE*. Set the font to Arial Black; the size to 72 px; and the alignment to Centered.

This text will serve as a positioning template for the animated text.

5. In Properties, give the text box the name *OnEdgeTemplate*.

As with your graphics, you want to be able to identify different blocks of text in the timeline and the Elements panel. At this point, the properties for the text look like Figure 3-9.

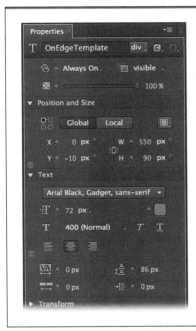

FIGURE 3-9

Arial Black is the thickest, boldest typeface in your text toolbox. It's well-suited to massive headings and titles. Using the 72 px font size and the Center Align property makes this banner fill the stage.

6. Set the text box's size and location to match the colored rectangle, with the size to 550px x 100px and the location to X=0, Y=0.

When you're done, the top of the Animate stage should look like Figure 3-10. If for some reason the text is behind the blue box, you can change the Z-order in the Elements panel. Just drag *OnEdgeTemplate* so that it's above *BannerBG*.

7. Select *OnEdgeTemplate* and then press Ctrl+D (⌘-D).

This duplicates the text, though you might not notice right away because it is placed right on top of the previous text. However, you can see *OnEdgeTemplateCopy* in the Elements panel.

8. Drag *OnEdgeTemplateCopy* down to the middle of the stage.

In the next steps, you'll use this to create individual text boxes with separate words: "ON," "the," and "EDGE." Before that, it's a good idea to finish setting up the positioning template.

FIGURE 3-10

The blue box and your text box have identical Size and Location properties. That means the text appears centered over the blue box, making an attractive page banner.

9. Select the original *OnEdgeTemplate* and then set the Text Color to red (#ff0000).

   As advertised, this text is being used for a positioning template. Later, the bright red color will make it easier to see if the text is correctly positioned.

10. In Elements, click the Lock Element button next to *OnEdgeTemplate*.

    This locks your positioning template in place so you can't accidentally select or move it.

11. Select *OnEdgeTemplateCopy* and press Ctrl+D (⌘-D) twice.

    This creates two more copies of the entire banner text.

12. Double-click the first *OnEdgeTemplateCopy*. In the text edit box, delete everything except the word "ON." Then in Properties, rename the text *ON*.

    It's best to eliminate extra spaces when you're animating single words or letters and you should reduce the width the text box to fit the edited text.

13. Repeat step 12 to make text elements for *the* and *EDGE*.

    You now have three properly labeled words that you can identify and animate independently. You may want to resize the text boxes' width to match the words, as shown in Figure 3-11.

14. Drag the word "ON" up so that it is above and slightly to the left of the stage. Drag the word "EDGE" so that it is above and slightly to the right of the stage. Drag the word "the" straight up so that it is above the stage.

    These are the starting positions for each of the words. They should be completely offstage.

15. Select "ON" and change the Rotate property to -30. Select "EDGE" and set the rotation to 30 degrees.

    These two words will appear to drop in at an angle from their respective sides.

16. Select all three words and click the Location and Rotate Add Keyframe buttons.

    The starting positions for each word are duly recorded in keyframes.

17. Drag the playhead to the half-second mark: 0:00.500.

    The entire animation will take a second, which is plenty of time for a simple animation like this. You don't want to bore your audience. Each word will take a half-second to complete its move. Each word will start at a different moment.

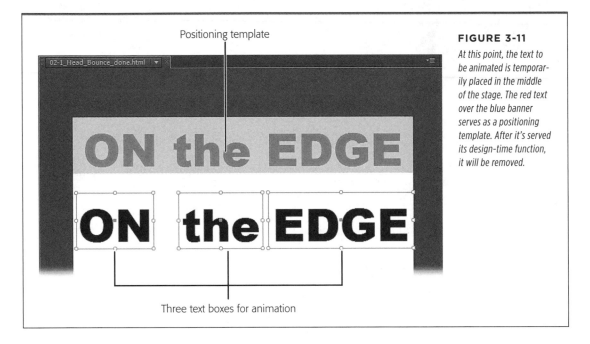

Positioning template

Three text boxes for animation

FIGURE 3-11

At this point, the text to be animated is temporarily placed in the middle of the stage. The red text over the blue banner serves as a positioning template. After it's served its design-time function, it will be removed.

TIP This animation uses fractions of a second in the timeline, like 0:00.500 and 0:00.250. If you don't see those numbers on the timeline, you can use the slider in the lower-right corner of the timeline, as shown in Figure 3-12.

---

18. Select "ON" and set the Rotate property back to 0, and move "ON" over the same word in the positioning template.

    If you want to review the motion, drag the playhead back and forth. If necessary, you can readjust the start or end point. Just move the playhead into position and tweak the word's position.

19. Move the playhead to 0:00.250. Then select the word "the" and click the Location Add Keyframe button.

    The plan here is to start the word "the" moving before "ON" has finished its movement. However, you want the word "the" to remain motionless for the first quarter-second, so you must create two location keyframes with identical values at 0:00.000 and 0:00.250.

20. Drag the playhead to 0:00.750, and then move "the" over the same word in the positioning template.

   No rotation is used for "the", so this word will appear to drop straight down.

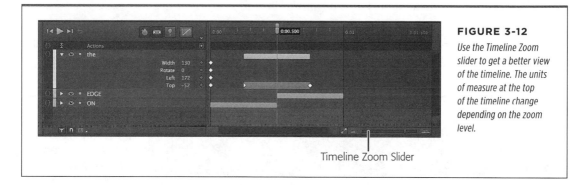

Timeline Zoom Slider

FIGURE 3-12

Use the Timeline Zoom slider to get a better view of the timeline. The units of measure at the top of the timeline change depending on the zoom level.

21. Move the playhead to 0:00.500. Select "EDGE" and click the Location and Rotate Add Keyframe buttons.

   This keeps "EDGE" in place for the first half-second of the animation.

22. Move the playhead to 0:01, and then drag "EDGE" into place over the positioning template.

   At the 1-second mark on the timeline, the words have finished their journey, and the first version of the animation is complete, except for removing the positioning template.

Before you remove the red positioning template, you probably want to preview the animation. Press Home and then the space bar to get a look. If necessary, you can continue to tweak the starting and ending points for the animated words. For example, you might prefer it if "ON" and "EDGE" drop in first and the word "the" is added last. If you'd like to add a little bounce to the words' entrance, see page 64.

▉ Dealing with the Template

The red positioning template isn't meant to be a permanent part of the animation. So if you're happy with everything, you can remove it. First turn off the Lock Element button to make the Template selectable. Then you can select the template in either the Elements panel or on the stage and press Delete. As an alternative, you could turn the template into a drop shadow (Figure 3-13) or glow effect for the text.

* For a **drop shadow,** set the text to a mid-gray tone and then adjust the opacity to taste. Something around 30 percent usually works well. You might want to keep the drop shadow hidden until the three words have finished moving. If that's the case, set the opacity to zero until that point in the animation, and then bring it up.

- For a **glow effect,** choose a yellow or orange color. Use the Scale control to make the text slightly larger than the text that drops in place. Again, you'll probably want to use opacity to control the timing and appearance of the glow text. You might want the glow effect to fade in and then fade out, adding momentary emphasis on the heading.

NOTE Animate has the ability to create even slicker shadow and glow effects through the drop shadow properties described on page 36.

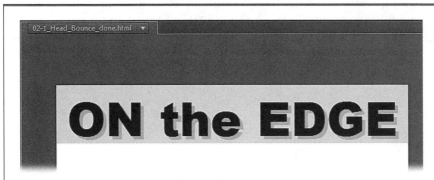

FIGURE 3-13
You can turn the positioning template into a quick and easy drop shadow for your drop-in heading. Apply a gray text color and some opacity and you're ready to go.

Adding Some Bounce

If the previous example, where text drops into place, is too sedate for your web page, you might want to consider adding a little bounce to the action. Bounce makes it seem like your web page adheres to the laws of physics. Like a basketball, your text can start with a big bounce and then one or two smaller bounces until it settles into place. You can create your own bounce by adding position keyframes, or you can create a bounce using the Easing properties that are part of the transition in the timeline. Chapter 4 covers the timeline and all of its features in much greater detail. This section will quickly cover some bounce basics.

Creating a Bounce Manually

You can take a crack at creating a bounce manually using the *03-2_Word_Bounce* project. Open the file and examine the Elements panel—you'll see the stage with three other elements. "BOUNCE" is the word that you'll animate. "BounceTemplate" (red text) is the positioning template. As in the previous example, this marks the final position for the animated text. The ground element is a gray rectangle that's positioned at the bottom of the stage. You can think of this as the ground on which the text will bounce.

A bouncing motion is created in the timeline by adding keyframes with alternating up and down locations (Figure 3-14). With the playhead still at 0:00, select BOUNCE and click the "Add Keyframe for Y" button in Properties. This sets the starting point. For the next leg of the journey, drag the playhead to 1:00 and move BOUNCE so that it covers BounceTemplate. Click "Add Keyframe for Y" to add new location keyframes. Drag the playhead to 1.75 and then move BOUNCE up near the middle of the stage. Move the playhead to 2.25 and then move BOUNCE back over the template. You can create a few more bounces using a shorter period for the motion—half a second, then a quarter second. With each bounce up, shorten the distance.

When you're done, your project will look something like *03-3_Word_Bounce_done*. When you get tired of a straight up-and-down bounce, you can always add a little rotation to the movement, making it look like the word is bouncing back and forth off of the lower corners. If you reduce the vertical scale property when the text hits the ground, you can create a cartoon-like smooshing action, as if the text were compressing on impact with the ground.

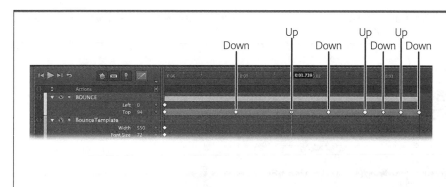

FIGURE 3-14

You can make just about anything bounce in Animate, including text boxes. It's simply a matter of creating position keyframes that alternate an element's position. Here the up-down motion is created using the text box's Y property.

Using Animate's Prebuilt Bounce

First, a little background about transitions and the concept of easing. When you animate an element on the stage, by changing properties and creating keyframe properties in the timeline, you create transitions. Those transitions are shown visually as bars in the timeline. Like the elements on the stage, transitions have properties, too. One of the properties is called Easing. In the real world, when objects move, they accelerate and decelerate. You never see a car begin to move at full speed or come to a stop instantly. The Easing properties help you create more realistic movement by automatically controlling an element's transition. It just so happens that one of the easing options helps you to create a bouncing motion.

Here are some steps to explore transition properties:

1. Open *03-4_Easing_Bounce* in Animate.

   The stage looks suspiciously similar to the Word Bounce exercise.

2. Drag the playhead to 0:01, and then drag BOUNCE down so that it covers BounceTemplate.

   Animate creates a transition in the timeline.

3. In the timeline, click the transition lane next to BOUNCE.

   The transition in the timeline is highlighted.

4. At the top of the timeline, click the Easing button.

   The easing panel appears above the timeline. Initially, the tooltip for this button says Easing: Linear, because that is the easing method that's applied. With linear easing, the transition is applied at a steady rate from beginning to end.

5. On left side of the Easing panel, click Ease Out. Then, on the right, click Bounce, as shown in Figure 3-15.

   When you click Ease out, the panel displays a number of Ease Out methods. The graph gives you a visual representation of the easing method.

6. Click outside of the Easing panel.

   The panel closes and your easing method is applied to the selected transition.

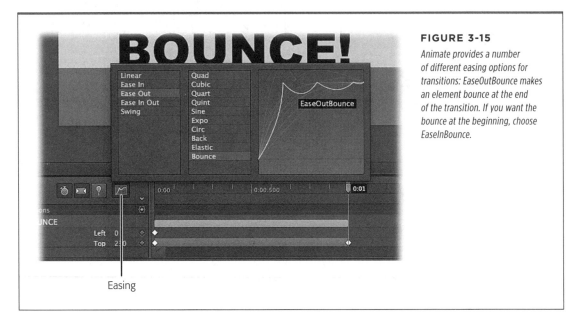

FIGURE 3-15

Animate provides a number of different easing options for transitions: EaseOutBounce makes an element bounce at the end of the transition. If you want the bounce at the beginning, choose EaseInBounce.

Easing

7. Press Home and then the space bar.

   When the animation plays, you'll notice some nice bouncy action at the end of the motion. If you'd applied EaseInBounce, the bouncing motion would have occurred at the beginning of the transition.

The easing properties for transitions can be a real timesaver. Animate includes a number of different transitions, but sometimes the names are a little cryptic. The best way to learn the different easing characteristics is to create a practice animation and apply different eases to identical elements and transitions.

■ Adding Links to Text

As you'll see in Chapter 5, you can add links to the elements you place on the stage using Animate's triggers and actions. Often you'll want to have a link on one or two words within your text. The simple way to handle that is to create your web page in your favorite web builder and then save it as an HTML file. Then, using Animate you can open that HTML file. Once the HTML text is in your composition, you can animate the text box just as if you'd created it in Animate.

> **NOTE** There's another way to create clickable links within text using JavaScript and jQuery. For those details, jump ahead to page 211.

In this exercise you can use the file *03-6_Outside_Text.html* from the Missing CD (*www.missingmanuals.com/cds/animatemm*), or you can use one of your own files. The missing CD file is just about the simplest HTML document that you could create, which makes it easier to find the line of text once you've imported it into Animate. The code looks like this:

```
<!DOCTYPE html>
<html>
<head>
</head>
 <body>
    <p>You can learn everything in a <a href=
    "http://www.missingmanual.com"> Missing Manual.</a></p>
 </body>
</html>
```

You'll learn more details about HTML in upcoming chapters. At this point it's help-ful to know that HTML code uses pairs of tags. Tags are identifiable by their angle brackets: <tag_name>. For example, in this code there is a paragraph of text that says, "You can learn everything in a Missing Manual." The paragraph is placed inside two tags. The <p> tag marks the beginning and the </p> marks the end of the paragraph. Inside the paragraph is a hyperlink, which also uses a pair of tags, <a> and </a>. When you're specifying a link, you need to provide an address for the link. That is done within the first tag, so it reads like this: <a href="*http://www. missingmanual.com*">. The *href* stands for hyperlink reference. It's followed by the assignment operator (=) and then the address is placed within quotes.

1. While you're in Animate, choose File→Open and open *03-6_Outside_Text.html*.

   When the file is open, the Elements panel lists two items matching the tags in the document: <p> and <a>. Note that the <a> tag is inside the <p> tag, just as the hyperlink is inside the paragraph. Click the triangle button to expand and collapse the <p> element in the Elements panel. You can check to make sure the link works by going to File→Preview In Browser.

2. Select <p> in the Elements panel.

   A text box appears around the text on the stage, and the properties are displayed in the Properties.

3. Create a simple drop-and-bounce animation for the text, using the techniques described on page 65. Use the Transformation tool to double the size of the paragraph. Skew the text slightly at the beginning if you want it to appear to fly in from an angle.

   You can animate and change any of the properties for the <p> element just as you'd animate other graphic elements inside your composition.

4. Go to File→Preview In Browser and click the hyperlink.

   The text dances around the page, and through the whole process the hyperlink is active and clickable. If you're connected to the Internet, it takes you to the Missing Manuals website.

As shown in the example, you can change the properties for the elements you loaded from an HTML file. The one thing you can't do is edit the text in the <p> or the <a> elements from within Animate. If you need to fix typos or make other changes, you can do that by editing the HTML file in a text editor like Notepad++ (Windows) or BBedit (Mac). Just make sure you save the file as HTML and reload it in Animate.

> **TIP** You can add Animate text (and other elements) to an HTML document that you open in Animate. So, for example, you might have body text that was originally in the document, with hyperlinks throughout. Then, you can create some animated headings using Animate's text tool.

■ HTML Tags in Animate

As shown in the previous example, Animate speaks HTML and makes use of some of the standard HTML tags. You can apply tags to the text you create in Animate, as shown in Figure 3-16. One of the major advantages of doing this is to help you format text consistently. For example, all your paragraphs may be displayed in a serif font at a font size of 12 px. Your major heading <H1> might use the 24 px font size, while the next heading <H2> uses 18 px.

All of these tags come in pairs, and the closing tag includes the slash character, like so: <div>This is the content inside.</div>

- **<div>** The div tag is used to define a section within a document. You can think of it as dividing the document into parts. The div tag is particularly popular in Animate because you use it to define any element you want. Once the element is defined with div, you can make it move.

- **<address>** The address tag is used to identify the author of the document and to provide contact details.

- **<article>** The article tag is new in HTML5. It is used to specify content that may be from another source.

- **<blockquote>** The blockquote tag is used to define a long quotation.

- **<p>** The paragraph tag has long been one of the most common tags in HTML.

- **<h1>** through **<h6>** These tags define headings, each of which can have distinctive formatting.

- **<pre>** The pre tag designates preformatted text. Usually HTML ignores extra white space; however when text is within the pre tags, it is displayed with its original formatting.

- **<code>** The code tag defines computer code, making it available for special formatting such as monospaced fonts.

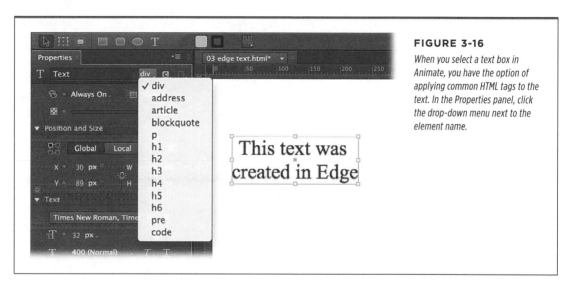

FIGURE 3-16

When you select a text box in Animate, you have the option of applying common HTML tags to the text. In the Properties panel, click the drop-down menu next to the element name.

Animation with Edge Animate

Learning Timeline and Transition Techniques

The art of animation is all about images changing over the course of time in a natural, pleasing, and entertaining manner. It's the same whether you're creating a cartoon with a long-eared rabbit or you're developing a presentation for the next quarterly sales meeting. Elements move, change shape, and change color. In Animate, that means that the properties that define an element change over the course of time. Those properties and their changes are tracked on the timeline through the use of *keyframes*—those little diamond-shaped markers.

The previous chapters involved some timeline manipulation. This chapter provides more complete details on timeline basics and controls. You'll learn how to create timeline labels and how to set, move, and remove keyframes. And of course you'll explore transitions, learning how to tweak them to do your bidding. When you're through, you'll know how to operate every button and widget the timeline has to offer.

■ Introducing the Timeline

Master the timeline, and you'll be an Animate Jedi. You'll have a jump on the learning process if you've used a timeline in a video editor, Adobe After Effects, or Flash. If you tackled any of the exercises in the earlier chapters, you're not a complete stranger to the timeline. When you work in Animate, you use three panels to create your animation: Elements, Properties, and the timeline. Usually you jump back and forth among them, using their features as necessary. It's no surprise that the timeline is the panel that's devoted to working with time—selecting specific moments in your animation and making something happen.

When you first look at the timeline, it seems to be quite complicated with all its buttons and widgets. Create a couple of transitions, and things don't get any simpler down there in Animate south. Don't be intimidated. Think of the timeline simply as a ruler that measures time in your animation. See Figure 4-1. The playhead lets you select a certain moment in time. For example, drag it to 0:02 on the timeline, and the stage displays the elements as they appear 2 seconds into your animation. As explained in the earlier chapters, elements' position on the stage and their appearance is controlled by properties: Location properties, Color properties, Size properties, and so on.

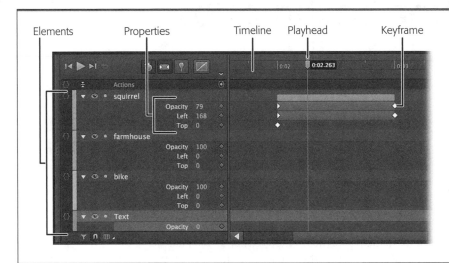

FIGURE 4-1

The timeline lists elements in your animation and their properties. The playhead lets you select a certain moment during the animation. Keyframes mark a point in time when the value of a particular property changes.

Initially, the timeline displays numbers like 0:01 and 0:02, with minutes on the left side of the colon and seconds on the right. As you're working, you'll want to zero in on a particular portion of the timeline and the property keyframes it holds. You can zoom in and out of the timeline; however, doing so changes the tick marks and numbers displayed. The controls for zooming in and out of the timeline are in the lower-right corner, as shown in Figure 4-2. When you zoom in on the timeline, you'll begin to see fractions of seconds displayed, like 0:00.500 and 0:00.250, as shown in Figure 4-2.

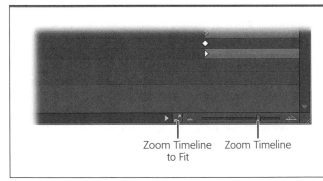

FIGURE 4-2

Want a better view of a particular segment of the timeline? Drag the slider to zoom in and out of the timeline. Click the Zoom Timeline to Fit button to see the entire active portion of the timeline.

Zoom Timeline to Fit   Zoom Timeline

Choosing a Moment in Time

To select a particular moment in time, drag the playhead along the timeline. The playhead and its red marker line selects a point in the animation's run time. As you move the playhead, the time counter to the right of the playhead changes to display the selected time in numbers (Figure 4-3). The three playback buttons in the upper-left corner of the timeline work just like the ones on your iPod or Blu-ray player. The left button jumps to the beginning of your animation, and the right button jumps to the end, wherever that may be on the timeline. The big triangle in the middle plays your animation in real time. If the animation is playing, the same button works as a pause button. You won't always want to play your entire animation. Sometimes, you're just interested in a segment. The play button starts to play your animation from the playhead's position. After you've watched your animation, click the return arrow next to the playback controls to move the playhead back to its previous position.

> **TIP** If you can see the point in time you want to select, but the playhead is missing in action, click the timeline. The playhead will jump to that spot.

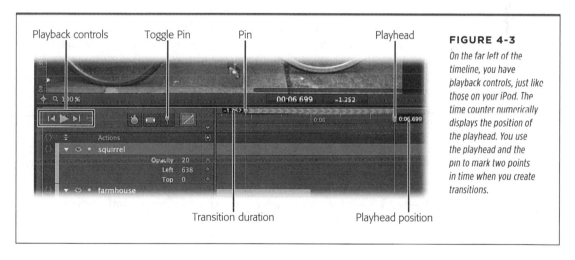

FIGURE 4-3

On the far left of the timeline, you have playback controls, just like those on your iPod. The time counter numerically displays the position of the playhead. You use the playhead and the pin to mark two points in time when you create transitions.

If you want some additional help dividing time into little pieces, check out the Grid, which displays subtle vertical lines over the timeline at regular intervals. You can turn the grid on and off with the Timeline→Show Grid tool. Once it's displayed, use the Timeline→Grid submenu to set the time increments. As you can see in Figure 4-4, you can choose from 1 per second through 30 per second. Even though Animate doesn't work in film frames, you can emulate the cinematic frame-per-second rates with settings of 24 fps or 30 fps. The standard frame rate for film is 24 fps while the video rate is usually 30 fps. The grid is more than just a visual aid; as you'll see in the next section, you can use snapping to assist marking a point in time.

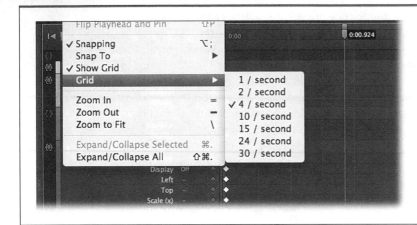

FIGURE 4-4
When you turn on the timeline grid, the vertical lines displayed are faint but visible. You can use the Timeline→Grid submenu to choose just the right incremenet for your project.

As you drag the playhead around, you may notice some snapping action as the playhead jumps to a particular tick mark on the timeline's ruler or jumps to a keyframe. That snapping action is deliberate, but you're in complete control over how it works. Go to Timeline→Snapping to turn the feature on or off, as shown in Figure 4-5. (That's right. The timeline is important enough to have an entire menu of its own.) To fine-tune snapping behavior, you can choose the things that the playhead snaps to. Go to Timeline→Snap To and then turn on or off a snapping feature. These are your choices:

- **Grid.** The playhead snaps to the grid lines displayed when turn on the grid (Timeline->Show Grid). You can choose increments such as half-second, quarter-second, or 24 frames per second.

- **Playhead.** The playhead comes in two parts, top and bottom. With this feature turned on, the two parts snap to each other when they're moved. For more details on using the bottom portion of the playhead while making transitions, see the note on page 83.

- **Keyframes, Labels, Triggers.** You manually add keyframes, labels, and triggers to the timeline. That means they have significance to the timing of your composition. Often, you'll want to change multiple properties at a single point in time, which means you'll want this Snap To option turned on most of the time.

The Snap To options work when you're moving the playhead, but that's not the limit of their assistance. Later on, as you edit and fine-tune animations, you'll find snapping handy for lining up keyframes and the edges of transitions.

FIGURE 4-5

With snapping on, the playhead jumps to specific things in the timeline, and you don't have to be such a mouse marksman. With snapping off, you're in complete control to move the playhead as you wish.

Adding Labels to the Timeline

Computers like numbers more than most human beings do. People appreciate the precision of numbers, but often the descriptive value of a word like *BOUNCE* or *ChangeSlide* trumps something like 0:03.720. You can add labels to the timeline to mark important points in your animation. They appear right beneath the number scale, giving you the benefit of both a word and a number.

Drag the playhead to that special point on the timeline that you want to label. Then go to Timeline→Insert Label (or press Ctrl+L or ⌘-L). A label appears on the timeline with a less-than-helpful name like Label 1 or Label 2. See Figure 4-6. It's up to you to give the label a useful name. Just start typing after you create a label. When you're done, that label serves as a meaningful bookmark for you in the future. What's more, as you'll see on page 112, labels are extremely useful when it comes to creating triggers and actions that control your animation.

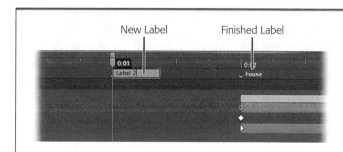

FIGURE 4-6

Use timeline labels to mark the important points in your timeline. As you'll see on page 112, you can also use labels in JavaScript when you want to jump to a point in the timeline or to trigger an event.

TIP   There's one more way to create a label. Just to the left of the timeline's time scale, there's a down arrow button. Clicking it adds a label to the timeline at the playhead position; type a descriptive name.

Editing Labels

Labels aren't chiseled in stone once you create them. Change the name of a label by double-clicking on the label and typing in a new name. Unlike elements, labels can include the space character, so they can be more than one word. On the timeline, labels display about 20 characters; still it's often best to keep them short and sweet.

You can move labels to a different point on the timeline by clicking and dragging them to a new spot, as shown in Figure 4-7. To delete a label, click to select it. Once it's highlighted, press Delete or Backspace (just Delete on a Mac).

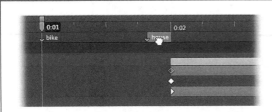

FIGURE 4-7

Click to select a label. When it's highlighted you can delete it or move it, as shown here. If you're moving a label along the timeline, don't worry about the other labels. They won't bump into one another. Simply drag the selected label past any others on the timeline.

■ Understanding Elements' Timeline Controls

The busiest part of the timeline is over on the left side, where the elements are listed. Elements are the objects displayed on the stage. Actually, even the stage itself is considered an element, as you can see in Figure 4-8. As explained back on page 16, each element has a number of properties that you use to control it. For example, text has a Color and a Size property. Rectangles have Width and Height properties. All visible objects, except the stage, have Position properties: X and Y. These properties are listed in in "lanes" under the element's name in outline fashion, with properties subordinate to their element. Click the triangle button to show or hide the property lanes under an element. You can also use the Timeline→Expand/Collapse Selected option as long as you have an element selected in the timeline, or its related shortcut key Ctrl+period (⌘-period for the Mac). There's also a handy command that expands and collapses all the elements at once. Use Timeline→Expand/Collapse All. The shortcut for that command is Ctrl+Shift+period (Shift-⌘-period on the Mac).

TIP To the left of each element name, there's a small color bar. Animate automatically labels each element with a specific color that you see in the timeline and the Elements panel. The same color appears on the transition bars in the timeline. This color coding of elements makes it a little easier to quickly identify them. The colors don't serve any other function.

Even though you're building an animation, that doesn't mean every single element in your animation is going to change over time. Perhaps you have several background elements that remain static through the whole show. In that case, there's no need to clutter up the timeline with elements that aren't animated. Click the Only Show Animated Elements button (Figure 4-8) to filter out the lazier elements in your animation. When necessary, you can always toggle them back on.

In the timeline to the right of each property name, you see the value for that property based on the current playhead position. You can create new property keyframes by changing the values. If the playhead is already over a keyframe, you can change the value of that keyframe.

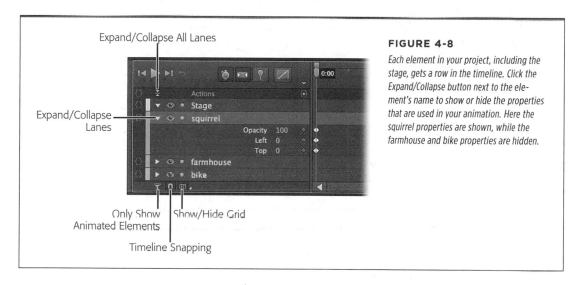

Expand/Collapse All Lanes

Expand/Collapse Lanes

Only Show Animated Elements

Show/Hide Grid

Timeline Snapping

FIGURE 4-8

Each element in your project, including the stage, gets a row in the timeline. Click the Expand/Collapse button next to the element's name to show or hide the properties that are used in your animation. Here the squirrel properties are shown, while the farmhouse and bike properties are hidden.

Showing, Hiding, and Locking Elements

When you're working with a lot of elements and a complex animation, you tend to have some of those "can't see the forest for the trees" moments. You need to hide some elements on the stage so you can focus on others. That's the job of the show/hide toggle buttons next to each of the element's names in the timeline. See Figure 4-9. When the button looks like an eyeball, the element is visible. When it looks like a period, the element is hidden. Keep in mind that this affects elements' visibility only while you're working in Animate. It doesn't affect your finished animation when it's viewed in a web browser. To control the visibility in the finished animation, you need to use the On/Off property, the Alpha property, or the JavaScript show/hide methods, as explained on page 193.

Accidentally moving an element while you're working is another design-time problem. Perhaps you want to select some text but accidentally grab a background photo, and now you've dragged it out of position. To avoid these problems, you can lock elements in place. When they're locked, you can't move them—you can't even select them in the Elements panel or on the stage. The Lock button looks like a lock when it's enforcing the no-move, no-select rules. When an element is unlocked, the button looks like a period (Figure 4-9).

Show/Hide Lock/Unlock

FIGURE 4-9

The elements part of the timeline is very busy with buttons and toggles. Many of these controls duplicate controls elsewhere. For example, the show/hide and lock/unlock buttons work exactly as they do in the main Elements panel.

Using Timeline Keyboard Shortcuts

Like most applications, Animate gives you several ways to do the same thing. When it comes to managing the timeline, you may be able to perform the necessary acts using the menus, buttons, or keyboard shortcuts. The good thing about keyboard shortcuts is that they give you a quick way to trigger a command, such as "create a label" or "turn on Auto-Keyframe Properties." The bad thing about keyboard shortcuts is that you have to remember the key combinations. That means you'll probably learn just a few shortcuts for the things you do the most.

NOTE Forgot the keyboard shortcut for one of your favorite commands? You can usually find keyboard shortcuts listed next to commands in the menu.

Here's a quick cheat list for common timeline tasks, along with their menu commands and keyboard shortcuts:

ACTION	MENU COMMAND	WINDOWS KEYBOARD SHORTCUT	MAC KEYBOARD SHORTCUT
Play or Pause the animation	Timeline→Play/Stop	Space bar	Space bar
Go to the beginning	Timeline→Go to Start	Home	Home
Go to the end	Timeline→Go to End	End	End
Go to previous keyframe	Timeline→Go to Previous Keyframe	Ctrl+Left Arrow	⌘-Left Arrow
Go to next keyframe	Timeline→Go to Next Keyframe	Ctrl+Right Arrow	⌘-Right Arrow
Zoom in on timeline	Timeline→Zoom In=	=	=
Zoom out on timeline	Timeline→Zoom Out	-	-
Show all active time	Timeline→Zoom to Fit	\	\
Toggle snapping on or off	Timeline→Snapping	Alt+;	Option-;
Add a label to the timeline	Timeline→Insert Label	Ctrl+L	⌘-L
Add trigger to timeline	Timeline→Insert Trigger	Ctrl-T	⌘-T
Toggle Auto-Keyframe Mode	Timeline→Auto-Keyframe Mode	K	K
Toggle Auto-Transition Mode	Timeline→Auto-Transition Mode	X	X
Expand or collapse a selected element's properties	Timeline→Expand/Collapse Selected	Ctrl+. (period)	⌘-. (period)
Expand or collapse all elements' properties	Timeline→Expand/Collapse All	Ctrl+Shift+. (period)	Shift-⌘-. (period)
Activate the pin portion of the playhead	Timeline→Toggle Pin	P	P
Switch pin and playhead positions	Timeline→Flip Playhead and Pin	Shift+P	Shift-P

■ Creating Transitions

Transitions have been part of this book since the first exercise in Chapter 1, so chances are you've created a transition or two by now. This section examines transitions and highlights some of the ways you can tweak and modify them. If you want to experiment along with the discussion, go ahead and create and save a new Animate document. Turn off Auto-Keyframe and the other buttons on the top of the timeline. Draw a rounded rectangle that's about 100 to 140 px—no need to be too precise. Drag the playhead away from the starting point 0:00. Now, move the element. As expected with Auto-Keyframe Properties turned off, no keyframe or transition is created. This is simply the new location for the element along the whole timeline. Scrub the playhead a bit, and you can confirm this.

Creating Instant Transitions

A traffic light changes from red to green. A headline says "98 Degrees in the Shade" and then flashes "It's HOT!" Those are instant transitions; there's no gradual change over the course of time. Here's a quick experiment you can perform with the Missing CD project called *04-1_Instant_Transition* (*www.missingmanuals.com/cds/animatemm*). A simple traffic light graphic is made from a black rectangle and three colored circles. The elements are appropriately named: redLight, yellowLight, and greenLight. Initially the opacity for greenLight is set to 100% while the opacity for the other two lights is set to 30%, making them appear turned off.

1. At 0:00 on the timeline, click the Add Keyframe button next to Opacity for redLight, yellowLight, and greenLight.

    You can select all three lights in the Elements panel and then click Add Keyframe for Opacity once. The advantage of selecting elements in the Elements panel is that you won't inadvertently move them on the stage. After you click the button, Opacity lanes appear in the timeline for each of the elements, as shown in Figure 4-10. Next to the word Opacity, you see the value for the property and a second Add Keyframe button you can use to create new keyframes for that specific property.

2. In the timeline, turn on Auto-Keyframe (K) and turn off Auto-Transition Mode (X).

    These buttons work as advertised: Auto-Keyframe automatically creates keyframes when you change a property and Auto-Transition Mode automatically creates smooth transitions between property keyframes. That's not what you want for your traffic light: You want instant transitions so the light changes immediately.

3. Move the playhead along the timeline a second or two. Then change the Opacity value for greenLight to 30% and the value for yellowLight to 100%.

    You can change the Opacity property for each element in the Properties panel, or you can input the value in the property lane. When you change the value, new keyframes automatically appear in the timeline.

Test your animation and you see the instant transition as one light turns off and the other turns on.

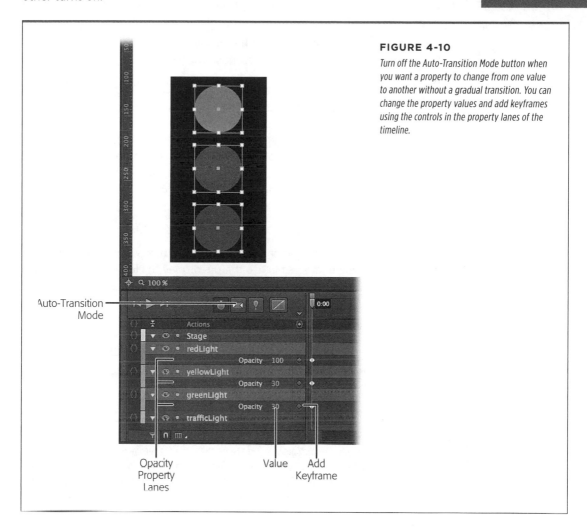

FIGURE 4-10

Turn off the Auto-Transition Mode button when you want a property to change from one value to another without a gradual transition. You can change the property values and add keyframes using the controls in the property lanes of the timeline.

Setting the Pin for a Smooth Transition

When you want to animate Newton's apple falling from a tree, Pinocchio's nose growing, or a car driving down the road, you need to create a smooth or gradual transition. Often you'll want to make these kinds of smooth transitions as the value of a particular property changes. Smooth transitions aren't limited to a location on the stage. You can smoothly change from one color to another—the element will pass through several shades of the two colors. You can smoothly change the size of an element, making it appear to grow gradually.

Here's a quick experiment you can do with a rounded rectangle or any other element:

1. Create a new Animate project, turn on Auto-Keyframe Mode (K), and turn on Auto-Transition Mode (X).

   When Auto-Keyframe Properties is turned on, Animate automatically creates keyframes when you change an element's properties.

2. Draw a rectangle, rounded rectangle, or some other element on the stage.

   Any old element will work for this quick experiment.

3. Turn on the Pin (P).

   When the pin is toggled on, you can move the playhead and the pin separately. This makes it easy to mark two positions on the timeline at once. More importantly, it makes it easy to mark the beginning and end point for a smooth transition.

4. Drag the playhead to 0:01 and move the pin to 0:00.500.

   A gold transition bar appears in the timeline with arrow pointing toward the playhead. The blue numbers next to the pin display the length of time for the transition. A negative number is displayed when the pin is to the left of the playhead.

5. Move the element to a new location on the stage.

   Animate creates keyframes; one at 0:00.500 marking the original location of the element and one at 0:01, marking the new location, as shown in Figure 4-11. Colored bars signal a smooth transition, and if you scrub the playhead over the transition, you'll be able to appreciate the smooth motion.

NOTE It's worth taking a moment to consider how the two-part playhead works. Both the top and the bottom portion create keyframes. The changes you make on the stage are recorded in the keyframes at the playhead position. The pin (top part) creates keyframes that match the property values before the change. Why are these keyframes that duplicate property values important? In the previous example, if you don't set the pin, the element's motion would begin immediately at 0:00. Setting the pin ensures that the rounded rectangle remains motionless between 0:00 and 0:00.500. The element's motion begins at the point of the pin, and it ends at playhead position 0:01.

In the timeline, there are numbers to the right of the Top and Left properties. These values are editable by typing or scrubbing. Select the transition in the timeline, and you'll see values next to each keyframe. These are quick references that you can use when you're working with multiple elements with lots of transitions.

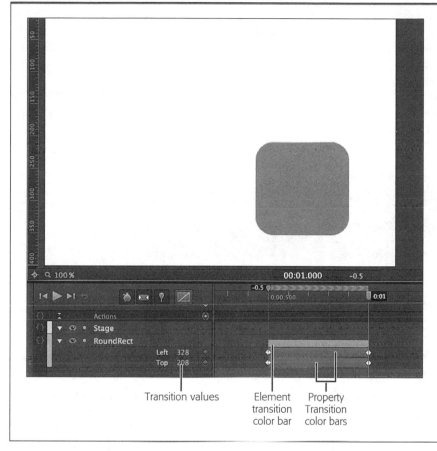

FIGURE 4-11

*Color bars mark smooth
transitions in the timeline.
The colors match the
identifying color of the
element. You can select a
single property transition by
clicking on the bar. You can
select all the transitions by
clicking the element's bar.*

Transition values   Element   Property
transition   Transition
color bar   color bars

Your transition has three colored bars: the two bars for the Position properties and one bar at the top for the element. For example, note RoundRect, as shown in Figure 4-11. If you collapse RoundRect to hide the properties, you still see the top bar as a signal that there's a transition.

It's worth noting that the pin doesn't always have to be positioned behind the playhead in the timeline. So, for example, in the current animation you can put the playhead at 0:01.500 mark and the pin at 0:20 and create another transition, by moving the rectangle again. Keep in mind the element's new location is marked by the playhead, while the pin retains the value prior to the move. The result is the rectangle moves to the new location (playhead) and then returns to the previous position (pin). This is a handy trick whenever you want to create a repeating or yo-yo kind of motion or if you want to an element to grow and then shrink back to its original shape.

Manually Adding and Removing Property Keyframes

Sometimes, you'll want to add keyframes manually. Exercises earlier in the book showed how to create keyframes with the Auto-Keyframe (K) button toggled off. Simply click the Add Keyframe button next to the property you want to add. To create a transition, you need to have two keyframes with different values—see the box below. If you want to remove a property keyframe, the process is similar to deleting a word in a document. Click to select the doomed keyframe. It shows a gold highlight (Figure 4-12). At that point, just press Delete (Mac or PC) or Backspace (PC). If you delete the two and only keyframes for your rounded rectangle, it still remains visible on the stage. You've deleted the keyframes that recorded its position, but you didn't delete the element.

FIGURE 4-12

Here the Left and Top properties each have a single keyframe in the timeline. As a result, there won't be a visible change. It takes two property keyframes with different values to make a change in the timeline.

Don't Forget the Starting Position Keyframe

Consider the following scenario: You've got Auto-Keyframe Mode turned on. You import a photo to your project. Animate automatically places the images on the stage with the upper-left corner at X=0, Y=0. You move the playhead down to the 2-second mark and then move the photo to another location. That's fine and good. But when you move the playhead back to 0:00, the photo is no longer in its original position: X=0, Y=0. What happened?

In short, you're missing a keyframe. Even with Auto-Keyframe Properties turned on, Animate doesn't create a keyframe when it imports a graphic. It creates keyframes only when properties change. When you're starting out with Animate, the previous scenario and similar gotchas occur every so often. Just keep in mind that when transitions or changes don't work as expected, it's very possible you're missing a keyframe at the beginning of the animation. It takes at least two keyframes for a transition or a change in an element to take place—one at the beginning and one at the end.

So the solution is to explicitly create a keyframe for the starting position of the element. If you remember to do this when you add elements to the stage, you'll avoid these problems.

Editing Transitions

In most animations, timing is critical. If you're animating a bouncing basketball, your audience will immediately notice if the ball hangs too long in midair. If you're syncing a slideshow to a music track, your audience will notice if you miss the beat. So don't be surprised if you don't get it right the first time you create a transition. Often, it'll need a little tweaking to get the timing just right. Fortunately, it's not hard to tweak transitions in Animate, and there are a few different ways to do it.

You can change the timing of transitions by dragging individual keyframes or the entire transition left and right along the timeline. For example, if you drag the keyframe on the end of a transition to the right, making the transition bar longer (as shown in Figure 4-13), you extend the time it takes for the transition to take place. If you're animating a car and you extend the transition, the car drives slower, taking more time to reach its destination. Want the car to go faster? Make that transition shorter.

When it comes to changing the duration of a transition, you don't have to edit each property separately. If you want to change all the properties at once, select the element bar. This selects all the properties below. Then you can drag the ends to change the duration.

In some cases, you'll want to move a transition without changing its duration. That's easy to do, too. Just select the transition you want to move and then move the cursor over the middle, until it changes to a hand. Then click and drag the transition to its new home.

FIGURE 4-13

You can change the duration of a transition by dragging the keyframe at the beginning or the end. Here, the keyframe at the end of the left property is being dragged down the timeline, extending the transition. RoundRect will continue to move horizontally after the vertical motion stops.

TIP The timeline displays your element's properties and the transitions visually. Often that's just the ticket for fine-tuning a particular effect. If you need numerical precision, you can see the time displayed on each end of the currently selected transition.

The Insert Time command can also be used to extend the length of a transition. Move the playhead to the point where you want to add more time, and then choose Timeline→Insert Time. As shown in Figure 4-14, a dialog box appears, where you can type or scrub in a time value in the usual 0:00.000 format. Bear in mind that the Insert Time command affects the entire timeline. If three transitions are taking place at that point in time, Insert Time extends them all. It also adds to your project's overall running time.

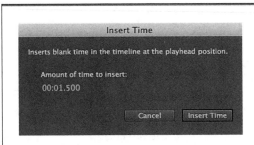

FIGURE 4-14

You can insert time at any point in the timeline by moving the playhead to a position and then using the Timeline→Insert Time command. Dial up the amount of time you want to add and click the Insert Time button shown here.

Adding Easing, Reversing Motion, and Fine-Tuning Transitions

Want to practice fine-tuning a transition? Here's a project that will give you a little exercise. You can find *04-3_Basketball_Bounce* with the Missing CD folders at *www.missingmanuals.com/cds/animatemm*. The goal is to make the basketball bounce with a realistic motion. As the ball bounces on the big letter B, it squashes the letter against the ground. When the ball comes back up, the letter re-inflates to its natural stature. See Figure 4-15. Along the way, you'll apply some easing to the basketball bounce, and copy and paste a transition. Most likely, you'll want to adjust the timing a bit by shortening or lengthening the transition bars.

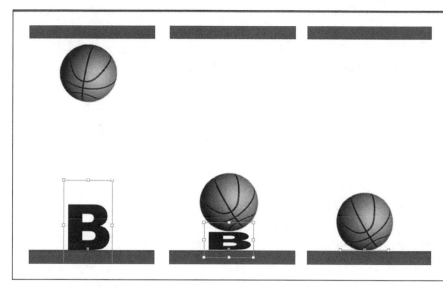

FIGURE 4-15

In this animation, the basketball drops from above (left). When it meets the letter B, it squashes the letter (middle). By the time it hits the ground, the letter is flat (bottom). As the ball bounces up, the letter springs back into shape.

Here goes! Follow the bouncing ball.

1. Open *04-3_Basketball_Bounce.edge* in Animate.

   There are two elements on the stage: a basketball image and a text box with a big bold letter B sitting at the bottom of the stage.

2. Press K to turn on Auto-Keyframe Mode; press X to turn on Auto-Transition Mode; finally, press P to toggle the pin.

   The shortcut keys give you a quick and easy way to toggle these features on and off. As an alternative, you can click the buttons on the timeline or use Timeline menu commands.

3. Drag the playhead to 0:01 and leave the pin at 0:00.

   With the playhead and pin in this position, you can create a transition that lasts 1 second—a good first try for the basketball's downward motion.

4. Drag the basketball down so its bottom edge is at the bottom of the stage.

   The basketball should hide the letter B, for the most part. The bottom of the basketball graphic should snap to the bottom of the stage. If you drag the ball straight down, only one property is added to the timeline: the basketball's Top property.

5. Press P to toggle the pin off. Click to select the basketball's Top transition and press Ctrl+C (⌘-C).

This copies the transition. You can now paste it back into the timeline. You can paste it into a different timeline location, or you can paste the transition in the timeline for a different element.

6. With the playhead still at the end of the transition, go to Edit→Paste Special→Paste Inverted.

This handy command not only pastes the transition into the timeline, but it also reverses the action. So the basketball will go from the bottom of the stage back to its original position. You now have both motions for the bounce.

7. Press Home and the space bar to test the animation.

The ball goes up and down, but you wouldn't call it realistic animation. It feels a bit wooden. Time for some easing.

8. Select the first section of the Top transition. Then, in the timeline, click the Easing button. When the Easing panel appears, choose *Ease in* and then choose *Cubic*.

When you first see the transition panel, Easing is set to linear. That makes the ball travel at the same speed the whole length of the motion. With the *Ease In, Cubic* applied, the ball moves more slowly at the beginning of the journey, picks up speed, and is moving faster by the time it hits the ground. If you're curious, go ahead and test some of the other easing options.

9. Select the second section of the Top transition and apply the *Ease Out, Cubic* easing.

This easing option is the reverse of the first one. That means the ball will slow as it reaches its highest point on the stage.

10. Press Home and the space bar to test the animation.

The motion feels better. The ball seems to react to hitting the ground, and with the slowing down at the top, it feels like gravity is in play.

11. With the playhead at 0:00, click the Add Keyframe button (next to Rotate in the Properties panel).

This step locks sets the ball's Rotate property to zero when the animation begins.

12. Move the playhead to the 0:01 point where the ball hits the ground. Then select the ball and set its Rotate property to 40 degrees.

The ball rotates rather lazily as it drops. Realistic enough. You can give it more or less spin by changing the Rotate value.

13. Move the playhead to 0:02 and set Rotate to 80 degrees.

This makes the ball continue to spin in the same direction. If you prefer, use a negative number to make the ball spin back when it hits the ground. At this point, the ball is doing pretty well. Time to focus on that letter B.

14. Drag the playhead to the point where the ball first touches the top of the letter B, then select the letter B, as shown in Figure 4-16.

The Properties panel shows B's properties, including Transform Origin and Scale. The transform origin is the point around which transformations such as rotate and scale take place. For more details, see page 24. When B is selected, the transform origin is shown as a blue square. It starts out centered in the text box.

15. Adjust the Transform Origin Y property so that the transform origin is at the bottom of the letter B.

With the transform origin at the bottom of the character, that point will stay in place when you apply transformations like Scale. Click the link next to Scale (x) and Scale (y).

FIGURE 4-16

Here the transform origin (blue square) for the text box is positioned at the bottom of the stage. Now the bottom of the letter will stay positioned at the bottom of the stage when transformations are applied.

16. In Properties, with B selected, click to break the link next to the horizontal and vertical scale properties. Then click the keyframe diamond next to the vertical value.

Animate creates a keyframe where B is scaled at 100 percent. You're breaking the link between X and Y because you want to scale Y independently.

17. Drag the playhead to the point where the basketball hits the bottom of the stage. Then set B's vertical scale to 0 percent.

This makes it look like the basketball is squashing the letter.

18. Select the letter B's Scale (y) transition bar and press Ctrl+C (⌘-C).

The transition is copied, and now you can paste it back into the timeline at a different point.

19. With the playhead at the end of the transition, and B still selected, go to Edit→Paste Special→Paste Inverted.

As with the basketball motion (step 6), this reverses the scale transition. So, as the basketball bounces up, the letter bounces back to its regular size.

At this point, the basketball bounce is pretty good. If you want to compare your work to another example, check out *04-4_Basketball_Bounce_done*. Naturally, there's a lot more you can do. For example, if you don't find the motion realistic enough, you can speed it up or slow it down by adjusting the length of the transitions. To adjust everything at once, Shift-click to select both the basketball element and the B element. Then drag the end of the basketball transition. Don't like the results? A simple Undo (Ctrl+Z or ⌘-Z) puts everything back the way it was. If you're ambitious, you can have the basketball bounce out an entire word. (LeBron, anyone?) Or you can apply the bounce-squish to some of your own artwork. Experimentation is an artist's best tool.

Animating a Filmstrip

Here's another way to create a slideshow, one that's based on a filmstrip metaphor. (Hope you like slideshows...you'll see several increasingly complex slideshows as you work your way through this book.) In this example, a single .jpg file has five photos of flowers arranged horizontally, as shown in Figure 4-17. Each flower pic is 500 pixels wide and 375 pixels tall. So, the entire .jpg file is 2500 × 375 pixels. If you set the stage to be 500 × 375 pixels and set the stage's overflow property to Hidden, you create a viewer that shows one image at a time. Then you can create timeline transitions that slide the filmstrip left or right, to view different photos.

FIGURE 4-17

Here's a zoomed out view of the stage with the filmstrip in place. The daisy picture in the middle is directly over the stage, so it's the one currently displayed. Slide the filmstrip 500 pixels in either direction to show a different picture.

1. Open project *04-5_Film_Strip*.

   The project is empty except for a single image called *flowerStrip375x2500.jpg*. The stage is already set to dimensions of W = 500 and H = 375.

2. Drag *flowerStrip375x2500.jpg* on to the stage, and then, in Properties, change the ID to *flowerStrip*.

   It doesn't matter exactly how you place flowerStrip on the stage, you position it in the next step.

3. Set the location to X=0 and Y=0.

   This puts the first image directly over the stage.

4. Set the stage's Overflow property to Hidden.

   If the Overflow isn't set to Hidden, the entire filmstrip is visible when viewed in a web browser.

5. On the timeline, turn on Auto-keyframes (K) and Auto-Transition (X).

   These settings ensure that Animate creates smooth transitions, making the filmstrip's sliding action visible as it moves from one picture to the next.

6. Drag the playhead to the 1 second mark.

   The first image will be visible for a second before the transition to the next picture begins.

7. Press P to toggle the pin.

   You can create transitions quickly when the pin and the playhead move independently. The playhead marks the current position, so when you change a Property, the new value (keyframe) takes place at the playhead. The pin marks the other end of the transition. It creates a keyframe with the previous property value.

8. Drag the playhead to the right so there's one quarter of a second between the playhead and the pin.

   The cyan-colored time display next to the pin will read -0.250 when there's a quarter second between the pin and playhead.

9. Change flowerStrip's location X property to -500px.

   The filmstrip moves, placing a new flower picture over the stage. Animate creates a smooth transition to animate the motion as shown in Figure 4-18. The entire transition, sliding the filmstrip to expose a new picture, takes a quarter of a second.

10. Repeat steps 6 through 9 to create transitions to display the rest of the images in the filmstrip.

    Each photo is 500 pixels wide, so keep subtracting 500 to reposition the filmstrip: -1000px, -1500px, -2000px. This timing displays a photo for a second, with a quarter second for the transition, but you can use whatever timing suits your project. If a photo deserves a better look, let it stay on the stage a little longer.

11. Optional: At the end of the filmstrip, you can create a transition that returns to the first image. Just set the X value back to 0.

    In the next chapter, you'll see how to use a timeline trigger to loop an animation. Looping is a perfect fit with this project.

FIGURE 4-18

The filmstrip is in mid-transition, with the rose moving offstage and the daisy moving on. The motion for the entire filmstrip is created by changing the Left property of the flowerStrip image. You can choose whether or not the audience sees the sliding action. Don't want the animated motion? Turn Instant Transitions off and don't bother with the pin when you create the value of the Left property.

There's a certain logic behind the filmstrip concept that might not be apparent at first. A single large image travels the web and loads faster than several small images. Early computer game designers took advantage of this when they animated characters or gaming action. Want a walking villain? Designers created multiple frames that showed Murderous Mike walking and stored them all in a single graphic called a *sprite*. Then, when it was time for Mike to walk over to the hatchet, the animation displayed different portions of the sprite to show his walking action. At the same time, they'd move Mike across a pre-designed background. Once a computer has loaded an entire sprite into memory, it can quickly jump from one image to the next, which makes for a smooth, hesitation-free animation.

▪ Dealing with Timeline Claustrophobia

If you're working on a computer with modest screen real estate, the area available to the timeline is probably minimal. That becomes a problem when your projects get bigger and more complex. The best long-term solution is to move up to a larger monitor or add a second monitor. Many computers, including laptops, let you run two monitors at once. With that kind of a setup, you can devote an entire monitor to your timeline and stage. Then you can move the Properties, Elements, and Library panels to a separate monitor. That gives you room to see all of the elements and their properties at a glance. It will definitely cut down on that constant scrolling to find a new moment on the timeline. If your time is valuable, a large monitor or a second monitor will pay for itself.

An alternative short-term solution is to set up and save a special workspace that maximizes the area devoted to the timeline. Go to the Windows menu and turn off everything except the timeline and tools, as shown in Figure 4-19. That leaves just the stage and the timeline visible. Drag the top edge of the timeline up, giving it as much space as you need. You can hide the stage entirely if you want. Go to Window→Workspace→New Workspace and save your new layout with a name like *Timeline Max*. Now you can quickly jump from one space to another using the workspace menu.

> **TIP** You may have similar claustrophobia issues when you're working with elements on the stage. There's a built-in solution to this problem. Click the menu in the upper-right corner of the stage panel and choose Maximize Frame. At that point the frame fills the workspace. Use the same menu to jump back to the previous workspace layout; choose Restore Frame Size.

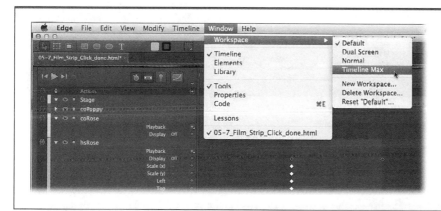

FIGURE 4-19

When the timeline seems too small for serious work, create your own Timeline Max workspace like the one shown here. In the Windows menu, turn everything off except the timeline and Tools panel.

Triggering Actions

The great beauty of the World Wide Web is that it's interactive. Unlike a static newspaper or magazine, with a mouse click or a finger swipe, you can make something happen. Perhaps you're flicking your way to the next photo in a slideshow. Or maybe you're jumping to view a new segment of an animation or movie. When you're building websites, the best way to hold your audience's attention is to put them in control of their experience. Let them turn features on and off. Let them quickly access the content that's most important to them. Let them control the speed of the slideshow, viewing each image just as long as they want.

This chapter shows you how to give your audience interactive control over their web experience. As a developer, Animate gives you tools called triggers and actions. You get to choose which events act as triggers. It might be a mouse click, or it might be the playhead reaching the end of the timeline. Then you can specify the actions that take place. For example, you can change the size, color, or transparency of a clicked element, or you can jump to a new point in the timeline. As always, Animate translates your project into JavaScript/jQuery code, but it makes development easy for you. In some cases, adding a trigger and an action is as easy as choosing items from a menu. In other cases, you'll need to tweak the code a bit to make it work according to your needs. This chapter walks you through the process. You'll learn how to use triggers and actions to do things like showing and hiding elements on the stage. You'll see that the timeline has some special features when it comes to triggers. Near the end of the chapter, you'll revisit the slideshow project from Chapter 2, learning how to make it interactive.

■ Elements, Triggers, and Actions

If you're building interactive web pages, you'll love triggers and actions. The very words "trigger" and "action" describe how they work. Some event takes place (the trigger), and that makes something happen (the action). Triggers are attached to elements like the stage, the timeline, a rounded rectangle, a car graphic, or a box of text. That means you have different triggers for different elements, as shown in Figure 5-1. A mouse click, for example, is an obvious trigger for an element on the stage. However, you can also create a trigger in the timeline. For example, when the playhead reaches the end of the timeline (complete), you can specify an action like going to another point in the timeline to start playing again ("Play from").

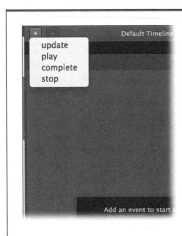

FIGURE 5-1

As you can see here, different elements have different types of triggers. The timeline (left) has triggers like play, complete, and stop. A graphic like a rectangle (right) has triggers like click, mouseover, and touchmove.

Building this Animate-style interaction or automation involves three major steps:

1. Choose an **element**.

2. Set the **trigger**.

3. Specify the **action**.

Notice the icons that look like curly brackets in Properties, Elements, and the timeline (Figure 5-2). Animate calls these Open Actions buttons, and by design, they are already attached to specific elements. See how each element in the Elements panel has Open Actions buttons? The timeline, even though it's not included in the Elements panel, has its own Open Actions button. Click one of those buttons, and a panel opens with the name of the element in the panel's title bar. You're immediately prompted to choose a trigger, like *click* or *dblclick*. Once you've done that, you're two-thirds of the way home. The last thing you need to do is specify the action, which you can do by choosing from the buttons on the right side of the Actions panel. These pre-built actions pop the necessary code into your project and display it in the panel, where you can fine-tune it when necessary.

TIP At a glance you can tell whether an element has any triggers and actions attached. If the element has none, the brackets are empty and appear grayed out. If there are triggers and actions attached to an element, the brackets are bright white and there's a dot filling the inside.

Action Button   Action Button

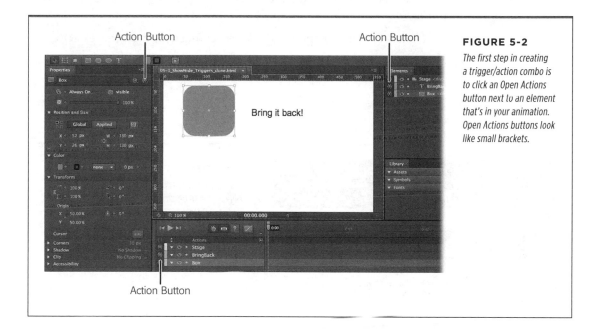

FIGURE 5-2

The first step in creating a trigger/action combo is to click an Open Actions button next to an element that's in your animation. Open Actions buttons look like small brackets.

Action Button

NOTE When Animate adds triggers and actions to your animation, it's actually writing JavaScript/jQuery code. You view this code from the comfort of a panel with buttons. This arrangement shields you from some of the nitty-gritty details, but if you want to roll up your sleeves and make changes to the code, you can do that, too. Wondering why Animate uses curly brackets for the Open Actions icons? It's appropriate because JavaScript uses curly brackets to enclose the methods and functions that provide action.

Trigger Your First Action

The easiest way to understand how to use triggers and actions is to put them to work. Here's a bare-bones exercise that shows how to attach a trigger and an action to an element on the stage.

1. Go to File→New to create a new Animate project. With the stage selected, in the Properties panel's Title box, enter the name *Action Packed*.

   You don't have to name the stage element for your animation to work; however, the stage title is displayed as the page title in web browsers. If you don't specify a title, you see *Untitled* in the tab for the page.

2. Choose File→Save and save your project as *Action Packed* in an empty folder.

   Now you can save the file quickly with a simple Ctrl+S (⌘-S).

3. With the Rounded Rectangle Tool (R), create a rectangular object and give it the ID *Box*.

   Size, color, and other properties don't matter much for this quick exercise.

4. Right-click (or Control-click) on Box and choose Open Actions for "Box" as shown in Figure 5-3.

   The Actions panel for Box opens with the triggers menu displayed, as shown in Figure 5-4.

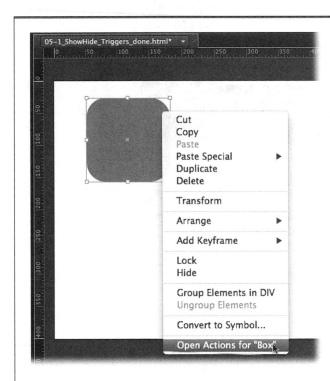

FIGURE 5-3

The quickest way to add a trigger to elements that are visible on the stage is to right-click the element and then choose the Open Actions option, as shown here.

5. From the Triggers menu, choose *click*.

   The *click* trigger is the first option on the triggers menu. If the triggers list closes before you select a trigger, click the + button to show the list again, as shown in Figure 5-6. After you choose *click*, the menu disappears, and some text is automatically added to the Box actions. It reads:

   ```
   // insert code for mouse clicks here
   ```

   This text is Animate's way of prompting you, explaining what you should do next. It's actually a comment. Comments in JavaScript code don't make anything happen; they're used to provide information. Edge Animate comments are a different color from the actual code, making it easy to tell them apart. For more details, see the box on page 103.

TIP   If you'd rather not see Animate's comments, you can turn them off by clicking the button in the upper-right corner of the Actions panel and turning off "Include Snippet Comments." The other options in that menu let you change the size of the text used in the Actions panel and show or hide line numbers. (The line numbers to the left of the code give you a handy reference if you're working and communicating with a team of developers.)

---

6. On the right side of the Actions panel, click Hide Element.

   The JavaScript/jQuery code to hide an element is displayed in the Actions panel. As explained in the box on page 103, comments are displayed in a different shade of text. That means the only line of active code in the panel is the line that reads:

   ```
   sym.$("Text1").hide();
   ```

   The word "Text1" is automatically selected, because you need to change this word for your code to work. You need to tell Animate exactly which element you want to hide.

7. Replace "Text1" with *"Box"*.

   Make sure that the word Box remains inside the quotes, like so:

   ```
   sym.$("Box").hide();
   ```

   When you're finished, the Actions window looks like Figure 5-4.

8. In the upper-right corner of the Actions panel, click the X button.

   The Actions panel for Box closes.

9. Press Ctrl+S (⌘-S) to save your work. Then press Ctrl+Enter (⌘-Return) to preview your project in a browser.

To test your triggers and actions, you need to preview the project in a browser. Animate's workspace doesn't respond to clicks and other triggers.

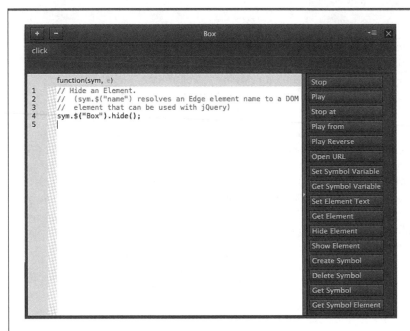

FIGURE 5-4

When you've finished tweaking the code for the Box element, the Actions window looks like this. You use the buttons along the right side of the Actions window to add actions (JavaScript/jQuery code) to your project.

When you test this first trigger and action project, you see your web page called Action Packed. Your rectangle is displayed on the page, and when you click it, the rectangle disappears from view. If your version isn't working as advertised, go back and double-check that single line of code (step 7). Make sure the spelling and capitalization are correct. JavaScript and jQuery pay attention to capitalization.

Even when it works properly, the project at this stage is a little underwhelming, but it does hold promise for the future. In the next section, you'll add another element and more triggers. You'll see how a trigger in one element can affect another element.

NOTE At this point, don't worry too much about parsing the JavaScript/jQuery code. Chapter 8 provides more complete details.

Many Ways to Comment

CSS and JavaScript use a common method to add comments to code. The system is also used by C and other programming languages. There are two types of comments: line comments and block comments. The comment shown in step 5 on page 101 is a line comment. When CSS or JavaScript code interpreters see two slashes (//) they ignore the remainder of that line. That means you can add descriptive text or anything else at the end of the line. For example:

```
sym.$("Box").hide(); //hides "Box"
```

Animate often places // at the beginning of a line, meaning that the whole line is ignored. Usually these comments prompt you on what to do next or explain the purpose of code inserted using the action buttons. When you come back to the code months later, you'll have a handy explanation about how it works. Animate uses a different color of text for comments. This makes it easier for you to quickly differentiate between active code and comments.

When you want to add several lines of comments, you can use block comments. Block comments begin with /* and end with */. Everything in between these markers is considered a comment. JavaScript and CSS ignore any text that appears between these marks. Often, block comments are used at the beginning of a document to provide details about the project and perhaps information about the person or company that developed the code.

There's another popular use for comments among coders. Comments are frequently used to turn chunks of code on and off, while developers test and work on a project. Suppose you have a line of code that hides *Box* when you click on it. You're testing another part of your program and temporarily you don't want the box-hiding function to work. You don't want to delete the code, because you'll want to turn it back on when you're done testing. The solution is to place // in front of the line to turn it into a comment. In coder-speak, you're "commenting out" the line. When you're ready to bring it back, just delete the // marks. If you've got a big chunk of code you want to turn off, you can use the block quote marks.

■ Triggering Actions in Other Elements

The exercise on page 99 provided a bare-bones example for attaching a trigger to an element and then specifying an action that changed that element. In that case, the *click* trigger was attached to a rectangle named Box. Then the action code made the box *hide*, so Box was no longer visible on the stage. Fine as far as it goes, but that leaves the audience with an empty stage and nothing left to do. For a next step, you can add another element to the stage—a text box that appears when the box disappears. With a little trigger/action magic, the text can make the hidden Box element reappear. The obvious difference in this example is that the trigger in one element makes a change to a different element.

This exercise continues the Action Packed project started on page 99.

1. If necessary, go to File→Open to open the *Action Packed* project.

   The elements in this project are the stage (named Action Packed) and a rectangle (named Box). A *click* trigger and Hide action are already defined for Box.

2. With the text tool (T), create a text box and type *Bring it back!* Name the text box *BringBack*.

   Like the rectangle, the text box is an element. It's listed in the Elements panel and has a number of properties. You can create triggers and actions for a text box.

3. Right-click the text box named BringBack and choose Open Actions for "Bring-Back."

   The Actions panel for BringBack appears, and you're prompted to choose a trigger, as shown in Figure 5-5.

4. Choose the *click* trigger.

   The triggers menu disappears, and you see the actions listed on the right side of the Actions panel.

FIGURE 5-5

The "Bring it back" text shown here is about to get a click trigger of its own. The action attached to this trigger will change the visibility of the rectangle. Even though triggers are attached to an element, the actions can affect other elements and aspects of your animation.

5. Click the Show button.

   Comments and code appear in the Actions box. Again, the word "Text1" is preselected. This is Animate's subtle hint that you need to edit the code at this spot. You need to tell Animate what you want to show.

6. Replace Text1 with *Box*.

   You want the hidden Box to reappear when someone clicks "Bring it back!" Remember that "Box" needs to remain inside the quotes like this:

   ```
   sym.$("Box").show();
   ```

7. Go to File→Save. Then press Ctrl+Enter (⌘-Return) to preview your progress.

If all goes according to plan when you test Action Packed in your browser, Box disappears when you click it. Then when you click on the *Bring it back!* text, the Box graphic reappears.

Now, at least, there's a way to bring Box back after it disappears. The example also proves that a trigger in one element (the text box *BringBack*) can make changes to a different element (the rectangle *Box*). The technique followed the same development process: Choose an element, set the trigger, and specify the action. Still, there's something a little odd about this animation, as simple as it is. It's strange to have the text saying, "Bring it Back!" while the box is visible. It would be better if the text was hidden when the box was visible and vice versa. That's the task for the next section, where you'll also learn how to use the timeline and stage to trigger actions.

◼ Triggers and Actions for the Stage and Timeline

The two earlier examples showed how to attach triggers and actions to elements on the stage. Even though they're different types of elements, the rectangle and the text box used very similar triggers and actions. Not so with the two objects next up for discussion: the *stage* and the *timeline*. The stage shows up in the Elements panel, but because it is a container for the other elements, it has different properties from a graphic or text box. The same is true when it comes to triggers for the stage. You open the stage's actions by clicking the bracket-shaped Open Timeline Actions button next to the stage in Elements, Properties, or the timeline. You'll see a list of triggers, including some that weren't displayed for the rectangle and text box.

- **compositionReady:** Triggers when the various parts of the Animate composition are read by the browser.

- **scroll:** Triggers when the page scrolls.

- **keydown:** Triggers when a key on the keyboard is pressed down.

- **keyup:** Triggers when a pressed key is released.

The timeline also has its own unique triggers. Technically, the timeline isn't even an element. It's not listed in the Elements panel. On the other hand, the timeline does generate events, and those events can be used to trigger actions. To review the triggers for the timeline, click the bracket-shaped Open Timeline Actions button next to the word "Actions" in the timeline. You'll find these triggers:

- **update:** Triggers when the stage changes.

- **play:** Triggers when the timeline begins to play.

- **complete:** Triggers when the timeline reaches the end.

- **stop:** Triggers when the timeline stops playing, even if it's not the end of the timeline.

In the case of the Action Packed project, you want Box to be visible at the start, but not the "Bring it Back!" text. Reviewing the stage and timeline actions, there seem to be two likely candidates for hiding something at the start. The stage's compositionReady trigger runs at the start of an animation. Likewise, the timeline's play trigger runs when an animation begins to play.

Spoiler alert! compositionReady is the better choice; however, you can see why if you try the timeline's play trigger first. Not only that, but you'll also learn how to remove an unwanted trigger from your project. Follow these steps to test the timeline's play trigger. With the Action Packed project open in Animate, follow these steps:

1. In the timeline, next to Actions, click the Open Actions button.

    The Default timeline Actions panel opens, and the menu shows four triggers: "update," "play," "complete," and "stop."

2. Choose the play trigger from the list.

    If the list disappears before you make your choice, click the + button in the upper-left corner.

3. From the list of actions on the right, click Hide Element.

    The generic code to hide an element is displayed in the Actions panel. The word "Text1" is preselected, because you need to change this text to indicate the element that is to be hidden.

4. Replace "Text1" with *BringBack*.

    BringBack is the ID or name for the text box that says, "Bring it Back!"

5. Click the X button in the upper-right corner of the Actions panel.

    The Default Timeline Actions panel closes.

6. Press Ctrl+S (⌘-S) to save your project. Then press Ctrl+Enter (⌘-Return) to preview it.

When you preview your animation, you may see a little flicker at the beginning where the BringBack text appears briefly on the stage before it's hidden. This is one of the reasons why it's not the best option for this job. The other reason is that play trigger goes into action whenever the timeline begins to play—not just at the beginning of the timeline. The compositionReady trigger works differently. It triggers when the Animate project is first loaded into a browser. That means it triggers once at the start. As an added benefit for this job, the text is less likely to be displayed and then hidden.

Deleting Triggers and Actions

Removing a trigger or action from your project is as easy as clicking a button. In the case of the Action Packed project, you want to remove the *play* trigger and its related action from the timeline. Here are the steps:

1. In the timeline next to Actions, click the Open Actions button.

   The Default Timeline Actions panel opens. The title bar of the Actions panel names the element. In this case, it says Default Timeline. Tabs near the top of the panel show triggers that are attached to the element. In this case, there's only one trigger in use: "play."

2. With the Play tab selected, click the minus button (–) in the upper-left corner (Figure 5-6).

   Unless you have more than one trigger attached to the timeline, the Play tab is already selected. When you click the minus button (–), the entire tab is removed and the Actions panel is empty.

3. Click the X button in the upper-right corner.

   The Actions panel closes.

Animate doesn't give you a warning or an alert when you delete a trigger and its accompanying actions. Just whoosh and everything's gone. However, if you make a mistake, you can bring the trigger and actions back as long as you do it right away. Just use your good old friend Edit→Undo (Ctrl+Z in Windows or ⌘-Z on a Mac).

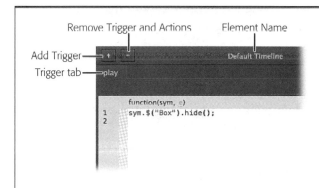

Remove Trigger and Actions   Element Name

Add Trigger

Trigger tab — play

FIGURE 5-6

Use the plus button (+) to add triggers to an element. Use the minus button (–) to remove them. Each trigger that's attached to an element is shown in a separate tab. Click the tab to see the actions code that runs when the trigger is pulled.

Adding Triggers to the Stage

Having tried and removed a timeline trigger to hide the BringBack text box, it's time to try the stage's *compositionReady* trigger. *compositionReady* runs once when the HTML code is read by a web browser. It sounds like the perfect tool to hide an element at the start. Then you can use another trigger to show the element at the right moment. By now you probably know the drill for adding a trigger and the Hide action; however, here are the steps as a reminder:

1. In the Elements panel, click the Open Actions button next to the stage.

   The many triggers for stage appear in the open menu. Fortunately, *compositionReady* is at the top of the list.

2. Click *compositionReady*.

   The *compositionReady* trigger tab is created in the Actions panel, and you're ready to code.

3. On the right, click the Hide Element button.

   The code for the generic Hide Element action appears in the panel.

4. Replace "Text1" with "*BringBack*".

   BringBack is the ID for the text box. Remember to leave the quotes around "BringBack."

5. In the upper-right corner, click the X button.

   The Actions panel closes.

6. Press Ctrl+S (⌘-S) and then press Ctrl+Enter (⌘-Return).

   The first command saves your project. The second previews the project in your browser.

Now the text box is hidden at the beginning of your animation. However, when you click Box, the box disappears and there's no way to bring it back. You need to tell Animate exactly when you want the text box to show up.

Editing an Action

It just so happens, you've already created the proper trigger to make the BringBack text appear. It's Box's *click* trigger, the same trigger that makes Box disappear. All you need to do is add code to show the BringBack text box. You can tell that Box already has at least one trigger and action, because the bracket-shaped button is next to it in Elements and the timeline is bright white and not grayed out. Here are the steps to open the actions and make some changes:

1. In Elements, click the Open Actions button next to Box.

   The Box Actions panel opens. In this case, you're not prompted to choose a trigger because Box already has a trigger: *click*.

2. In the *click* actions code, click to put the editing cursor on an empty line at the bottom.

   The actions code pane is a workplace. You can add more actions using the buttons on the right, or if you're comfortable speaking jQuery, you can add your own code.

3. On the right, click the Show Element button.

   As usual, the generic Show code appears, and you need to specify what element is to be shown.

4. Replace "Text1" with *"BringBack"*.

   "Text1" is placeholder text. BringBack is the ID of the text box that says, "Bring it Back!"

5. In the upper-right corner, click the X button.

   The Actions panel closes.

6. Press Ctrl+S (⌘-S) and then press Ctrl+Enter (⌘-Return).

   The first command saves your project. The second previews the project in your browser.

Now, when you preview the animation, it's behaving better. When it begins, the BringBack text is hidden. A click on Box performs two actions. It hides Box and displays BringBack. It's clear to the viewer what must be done. Click on the text, and the box comes back. Just one issue: The text should hide when Box shows. Time for another quick edit.

1. Right-click (Control-click) the text box BringBack and choose Open Actions for "BringBack."

2. With the Click tab selected, place the editing cursor at the bottom of the code.

3. Click the Hide Element actions button.

4. Replace "Text1" with *"BringBack"*.

5. Save and preview your project.

It may not be as complex as Google Docs or Netflix's movie queue, but this time, your project works well. Elements are showing up and disappearing as they should. It's a pretty simple trick, but you'd be surprised how many interesting web pages are based on making elements show and hide. What's more, as you'll learn on page 193, it's easy to substitute those show and hide methods with something a little more interesting, like fade in and fade out or other effects.

NOTE Want to compare your project to a completed version of this exercise? Download *05-1_ShowHide_Triggers_done* from the Missing CD at *www.missingmanuals.com/cds/animatemm*.

Just to recap, here are some of the trigger/action concepts discussed in the exercise that began back on page 99:

- There are three main steps to interactivity: Choose an element. Attach a trigger. Specify an action.

- A trigger is an event, like a mouse click, that's attached to an element.

- Actions are defined using JavaScript/jQuery code.

- Actions can affect elements other than the one with the trigger.

- A single trigger can lead to more than one action.

- The stage and the timeline have triggers unique to their role in an HTML document.

- You can add, remove, and edit triggers from the Actions panel for each element (Figure 5-7).

- You need to preview your project in a browser to test triggers and actions.

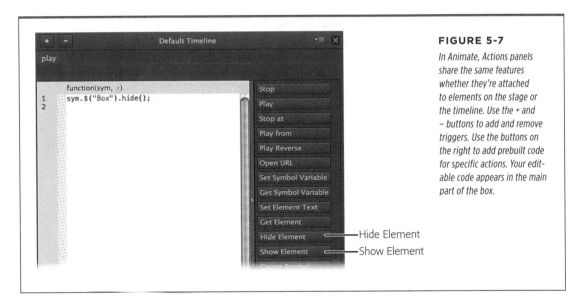

FIGURE 5-7

In Animate, Actions panels share the same features whether they're attached to elements on the stage or the timeline. Use the + and – buttons to add and remove triggers. Use the buttons on the right to add prebuilt code for specific actions. Your editable code appears in the main part of the box.

Timeline Triggers and Tricks

When you work in Animate, you've always got that timeline down there at the bottom of the screen. It's keeping track of the elements, their positions on the stage, and any visual changes that you want. In some projects, the timeline is less relevant. For example, consider the previous exercise, where the playhead never leaves the 0:00 mark. In that case, changes are entirely controlled by triggers and actions. It's also worth noting that it means change and timing are, for the most part, controlled by the audience. Earlier projects like the slideshow (page 41) and the filmstrip (page 92) used the timeline to control changes and timing. There were no triggers and actions. Naturally, you're not forced to choose one method or the other. You can create masterpieces when you combine the strengths of timeline animation with triggers and actions.

Adding a Trigger to Loop Your Animation

As gatekeeper to your animation's timing, the timeline has special triggers like "play," which fires when the animation starts playing. One of the most-used timeline triggers is "complete," which fires when the playhead reaches the end of the timeline. So if you want to make an animation loop back to the beginning, you use the complete trigger and add code to send the playhead back to 0:00. Want to give it a try? Roll up your sleeves and grab the files and folders in *05-2_Timeline_Trigger*.

Open the web page, *05-2_Timeline_Trigger.html*, in a browser, and you see that it's a simple counter. Every half-second, a new number appears on the stage. If you dig into the Animate project, you see that the appearance and disappearance of the numbers are controlled by keyframes that toggle the opacity properties of each number. In other words, it's a simple animation, and at this point there's no trigger/action magic involved. That's about to change. Here are the steps to add a timeline trigger that makes the animation loop continuously:

1. Open *05-2_Timeline_Trigger.edge* in Animate.

   There are five elements placed on the stage. They are named num_1 through num_5.

NOTE   Element names can't begin with a number, so you need to place at least one letter at the beginning.

---

2. On the timeline, next to the word "Actions," click the Open Timeline Actions button and choose the complete trigger.

   The complete tab appears in the Actions panel, and a comment prompts you to "Insert code to be run at the end of the timeline."

3. On the right, from the list of actions, choose "Play from."

   Animate inserts a comment and a line of code:

   ```
   // play the timeline from the given position (ms or label)
   sym.play(1000);
   ```

   The code isn't too hard to parse here: "sym" is short for symbol. In Animate, the initial stage and timeline are considered a symbol. In Chapter 6, you'll learn all about symbols and how one symbol can be nested in another. For this example, it's enough to know that "sym" refers to the timeline itself; "play" is a method that tells the timeline to run or play. The number inside of the parentheses tells the timeline where it should start playing. Animate pops the "1000" in there simply as a placeholder. The unit of time measurement is one one-thousandth of a second. So 1000 is equivalent to the 1-second mark. If you preview your animation at this point, after playing once, the animation jumps to the 1-second mark and displays the number 3. Then it continues looping by always jumping back to the 1-second mark.

4. Change the 1000 inside the parentheses to *0*, as shown in Figure 5-8.

   This command sends the playhead back to the 0:00 mark on the timeline:

   ```
   sym.play(0);
   ```

5. Press Ctrl+S (⌘-S) to save and Ctrl+Enter (⌘-Return) to play.

   Your animation loops continuously.

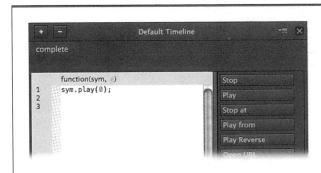

FIGURE 5-8

The code shown here in the Actions panel was inserted using the "Play from" button. Originally, the placeholder text "1000" was in the parentheses. By changing that to 0, the code sends the playhead to the beginning of the timeline.

By using the complete trigger on the timeline and adding the simple line of code shown in step 4, you can make any of your Animate animations loop. As you saw at the start, you can send the playhead to any point on the timeline using the thousandth-of-a-second unit of measurement. Want the playhead to go to the 6-second mark? Just pop *6000* in between those parentheses.

Using Labels in Your Timeline Code

You're not limited to specifying timeline locations by thousandths of a second. A far easier way to identify a point on the timeline is to use a label, as described back on page 77. A label is a word that appears on the timeline ruler, and for most human beings, labels are more descriptive and easier to remember than numbers representing fractions of a second. Suppose you want to add labels to the counters' timeline for each spot where the number changes. Start by moving the playhead to 0:00, and then press Ctrl+L (⌘-L) to insert a label. Type a name, perhaps the word *one*. For the next number, move the playhead half a second down the timeline where the number on the stage changes and repeat the process. Once you're done with all five labels, the timeline looks like Figure 5-9.

Now, using the same timeline trigger ("complete") and action ("Play from"), you can send the playhead back to any of the labels. For example, to send the playhead to the label "two," edit the action so it looks like this:

```
sym.play("two");
```

Notice that the label is inside the quotation marks. When you reference a label, it must always be inside quotes. When you're developing larger and more complex Animate projects, you'll find plenty of opportunities to use timeline labels as destinations for actions.

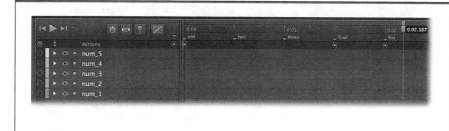

FIGURE 5-9

Labels on the timeline mark each point where the counter changes from one number to the next. You can use labels in your actions to move the playhead to a specific position.

Adding Triggers to a Point in Time

You can add triggers to a specific point along the timeline and then specify an action for that point in time. Suppose you want to briefly display a caption in the middle of your animation. You can place a trigger in the timeline that "shows" the caption, and then a moment later, you place another trigger that hides the text box with the caption. If you want to try this experiment, you can use the Timeline Trigger exercise beginning on page 111. Here are the steps to display a caption for half a second in the middle of the counter. Suppose you're overly fond of the number 4, and you want to display the message "Great Number" while the 4 is displayed. Here are the steps:

1. With your Timeline Trigger project open, use the text tool (T) to create a text box that says, "Great Number." Name the text box *Great*.

    Format the text so that it looks good with your counter numbers. For text formatting details, see page 49.

2. Make sure that Auto-Keyframe Mode and Auto-Transition Mode are toggled off. Drag the playhead to 0:00.

    At this point in the animation, you want the text box hidden.

3. Go to Timeline→Insert Trigger.

    An Actions panel titled "Trigger" opens. You see a panel like this each time you add a timeline trigger, but each trigger has its own panel.

4. Click the Hide Element action button. Then, in the Hide Element code, replace "Text1" with *"Great"*. Close the actions box.

    As shown in the earlier exercises, this code hides the text box named Great. The action should read:

    ```
    sym.$("Great").hide();
    ```

When you close the actions, check the timeline under the "one" label, and you see a trigger icon (Figure 5-10). This particular trigger is only half visible because it's positioned at the start of the timeline.

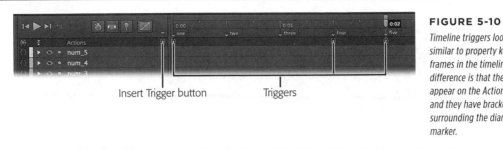

FIGURE 5-10

Timeline triggers look similar to property keyframes in the timeline. The difference is that they all appear on the Actions row, and they have brackets surrounding the diamond marker.

5. Drag the playhead to the "four" label and press Ctrl+T (⌘-T).

   Another trigger actions box opens. Ctrl+T (⌘-T) is the shortcut key to create timeline actions.

6. Click the Show button, and after you see the new code, replace "Text1" with "*Great*". Close the actions box.

   This trigger shows the caption "Great Number." Another action keyframe appears in the timeline.

7. Move the playhead to 0:02, the point with the "five" label. Press Ctrl+T (⌘-T) to create a timeline trigger. Add hide code just like the code in step 4.

   At the three points in the timeline triggers, you see triggers ready to perform their accompanying actions.

8. Press Ctrl+S (⌘-S) to save and Ctrl+Enter (⌘-Return) to play.

   Your animation plays. While the number 4 is displayed, the caption also shows with the words "Great Number."

Keep in mind that you need to preview and test your work in a browser when you're using triggers and actions. Even something as simple as Show and Hide actions require a browser to read and interpret the JavaScript/jQuery code. The finished project can be found with the Missing CD files. It is named *05-3_Timeline_Trigger_done*.

TIP Want more practice with timeline triggers and actions? Try rebuilding the counter so triggers control the numbers' visibility. First remove all the opacity keyframes. Then add triggers and actions to the timeline to take over the Show and Hide duties.

■ Sliding Show Revisited

The exercise back on page 41 showed how to create a slideshow that automatically swapped images using transitions that included changes in locations and transparency. Each slide faded away and actually slid off the stage. Using the same images, you can create a different type of slideshow. Suppose you want the viewer to be in control. Each time she clicks the mouse, the slide changes instantly, moving to the next slide. If she's on the last image in the show, a mouse click takes her back to the beginning. You can find the files for this project on the Missing CD at *www.missingmanuals.com/cds/animatemm*. Find *05-4_Click_Show* for the folders and files for this exercise. If you want to see the finished project, check out *05-5_Click_Show_done*.

Follow these steps to create a clickable slideshow:

1. In Animate, go to File→Open and then select *05-4_Click_Show.edge*.

   The Elements panel for this project shows a stage and three images: squirrel, house, and bike. All three images are already positioned on the stage. Each image is 600 × 400 px, the same size as the stage.

TIP You can examine each of the images by toggling the show/hide buttons for the elements, as explained on page 40.

---

2. Turn off Auto-Transition Mode (Timeline→Auto-Transition Mode).

   The button in the timeline appears pushed in when this feature is turned on.

3. In Elements, select the squirrel, house, and bike elements. Then in the Position and Size subpanel in Properties, click the Add Keyframe button next to X and Y.

   This adds Top and Left property keyframes to the beginning of the timeline to lock in the initial position for all the photos.

4. With the playhead at 0:00, press Ctrl+L (⌘-L) to create a label named *squirrel*. At 0:01, create a label named *house*. At 0:02, create a label named *bike*.

   When you're done, the timeline should look like Figure 5-11.

5. Move the playhead to 0:00. Then click the Insert Trigger button shown in Figure 5-10, and choose Stop from the available actions.

   When you click the Insert Trigger button, a panel opens where you can add and edit the JavaScript/jQuery code that controls your animation. The button on the Actions row opens the code window for the timeline trigger, shown in Figure 5-12.

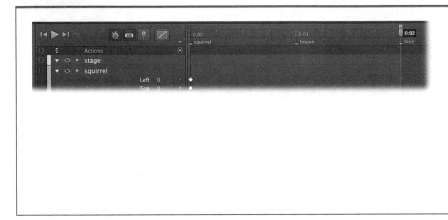

FIGURE 5-11

In this case, it doesn't really matter how far apart you place the labels on the timeline, because there will be no transition. JavaScript/ jQuery code will make the playhead jump from label to label. Just give yourself enough space to separate the labels for easy reading.

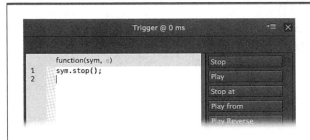

FIGURE 5-12

The code in this Trigger window controls the main timeline at a specific point in time. In effect, it stops the animation from running at the very start. That way the first image stays on the stage until the viewer clicks on it.

6. Right-click (Control-click) the squirrel photo on the stage, and then choose Open Actions for "squirrel."

   The actions panel labeled "squirrel" opens, where you can write or insert JavaScript/jQuery code. Initially, several trigger options, like *click, dblclick,* and *mouseover,* are displayed. If you move the box, the list may disappear. You can always bring it back by clicking the + button in the upper-left corner.

7. Choose "click" from the triggers list.

   The panel changes, displaying the actions that can be associated with the click trigger, as shown in Figure 5-13.

8. Choose "Stop at."

   The code for the "Stop at" method is added to the squirrel actions panel. It reads:

   ```
   // stop the timeline at the given position (ms or label)
   sym.stop(1000);
   ```

The first line is a comment describing the "Stop at" method. The second is the code that sends the playhead to a particular point in the timeline and stops playback. The 1000 inside the parentheses is a numerical reference to a point on the timeline. In the next step, you'll replace that reference with a reference to one of the labels you created earlier.

9. Replace "1000" in the code with *house.* When you're done, click the X button in the upper-right corner of the box to close it.

   Don't forget to include the quote marks (") as shown in Figure 5-13. When you reference a label, you must put the label in quotes.

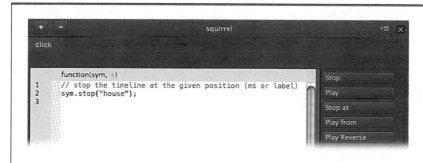

FIGURE 5-13

You can associate prebuilt actions with a trigger. It's simply a matter of clicking a button. The code is then automatically added to the Actions panel. In this exercise, you use the "Stop at" action to control your slideshow.

10. In Elements, click the show/hide button (eyeball) next to squirrel.

    The squirrel picture is hidden from the stage, and the house picture is visible.

11. Repeat steps 5–8 for the house image, creating a *click* trigger and a "Stop at" action. In step 8, instead of replacing "1000" with the *house* label, use the *bike* label.

12. Hide the house photo. Then repeat steps 5–8 for the bike photo. In the "Stop at" method, use the *squirrel* label.

    The method now sends the playhead back to the first label on the timeline: *squirrel.* Next, you'll set up the timeline to display the proper image at each label.

13. In Elements, click the show/hide buttons to make the squirrel and farmhouse visible.

    Keep in mind that the show/hide buttons affect the elements only during design time. They have no effect on what your audience sees when they view your project in a browser. You'll fix that in the next few steps.

14. Move the playhead to the *house* label. Then drag the squirrel photo off the stage completely.

    It doesn't matter where you drag the photo. The audience won't see its movement because there's no transition. The playhead just jumps from label to label. At this point in the animation, the audience will see the house photo.

15. Move the playhead to the *bike* label. Then drag the house photo off the stage completely.

   At this point in the animation, the audience will see the bike photo.

16. In Elements, select the stage. Then, in Properties, make sure the Overflow property is set to hidden.

   If Overflow is set to "visible," your audience will see the photos that are offstage.

17. Choose File→Preview In Browser to see your slideshow in action.

   You need to view the slideshow in a browser to check the clicking action. If you press Play to view the slideshow within Animate, you won't get the benefit of the JavaScript code that controls the playhead.

At this point, you're probably thinking of different ways you can create a slideshow for your own photo library. You can tackle the project in a number of ways, and the example above is just one solution. For example, using timeline labels, triggers, and actions, you can create a button interface for your slideshow. Buttons could advance the show forward and backward. Other buttons could jump to the beginning, end, or special sections of your slideshow. You could combine timeline animation effects with timeline trigger controls, creating a slideshow that has animated effects and gives the audience control over the experience.

■ Non-Linear Thinking and Design

Up to now, most of the projects in this book have been fairly linear, moving along the timeline in a natural left-to-right fashion. When you start using labels, timeline triggers, and the other tools covered in this chapter, you aren't limited to a simple linear timeline. Suppose you're developing a graphic novel for the Web. The novel has three alternate endings, and at some point you let your audience choose one of the endings. See Figure 5-14. All you need to do is stop the timeline at a certain point. Create three buttons or some other type of widget representing the three different endings. Then connect triggers and actions to the buttons that lead to different labeled points on the timeline. Want to get more elaborate? You could develop an entire adventure-style game, where the player's decisions lead to different challenges. In that case, the action could branch out in all different directions. Certain user actions could make the game loop back to a previous point.

For these kinds of projects, you need to think of the timeline as a kind of random access storage device, like a computer hard drive. Using triggers and actions, you access the parts of the storage that you need at a given moment. One portion of the timeline might hold a single text box, like the answer to a quiz question. Or it might contain an entire animated sequence for a graphic novel. After you've used (or read) that portion of the timeline, use timeline triggers to send the playhead back to another point in the timeline.

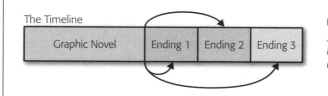

FIGURE 5-14

Just because it's called a timeline, that doesn't mean you have to play an animation in a linear fashion. Here's a diagram of a graphic novel with alternate endings.

Timeline Button Controls

As mentioned at the beginning of this chapter, the best way to keep your audience engaged is to put them in control. Take the example from the previous chapter: A filmstrip with images of different flowers was animated using the timeline and smooth transitions (page 92). You, the creator, arbitrarily set the timing. But you can give power to the audience by adding buttons that let them control the playback: play, stop, and play in reverse.

1. From this book's Missing CD (*www.missingmanuals.com/cds/animatemm*), open the project *05-6_Film_Strip_Click*.

    The project looks very much like the filmstrip project from Chapter 4, except three buttons appear at the bottom of the stage. They sport the universal symbols for play, stop, and reverse. If you preview the project at this point, you see that it shows the five flower photos, with sliding animation between each. When it reaches the end of the film strip, it appears to rewind back to the beginning. As you may recall from the earlier filmstrip project, that rewind animation is at the end of the timeline. This filmstrip is a great candidate for some looping action, so that's the first task.

2. Under the stage where the time is shown, type *7.5* and press Enter (Return).

    The playhead quickly moves to 0:07.500—the seven-and-a-half second mark—which is the end of the animation.

3. Press Ctrl+T (⌘-T), the command to insert a Timeline Trigger.

    The Trigger actions panel opens. At the top, it displays the point in time when the trigger will fire: 7500 ms.

4. On the right of the actions panel, click "Play from."

    This code is inserted into the actions panel:

    ```
    sym.play(1000);
    ```

    As you may recall from page 111, that moves the playhead to the 1000 ms (1 second) mark and then starts playing the timeline from there.

5. Change the 1000 to *0*.

   When you're done, the command looks like this:

   ```
   sym.play(0);
   ```

   This code, when placed at the end of the timeline, will loop any animation. If you test your animation now, you see that at the end, the filmstrip rewinds and then the animation begins playing again from the first picture. Now, it's time to add audience controls.

6. At the bottom of the stage, right-click the left button and choose Open Actions for "btnReverse."

   The actions panel for btnReverse appears, and the trigger menu is displayed. If you don't see the trigger menu, click the + button in the upper-left corner.

TIP These three buttons were deliberately designed to be a bit oversized. While they may seem a tad big on a desktop computer screen, they work quite nicely on a phone or tablet.

---

7. Choose the "click" trigger.

   The actions panel opens displaying a click tab. Action buttons are shown on the right.

8. Click the Play Reverse button.

   As shown in Figure 5-15, this code appears in the actions panel:

   ```
   sym.playReverse();
   ```

   That's the complete code to make the animation play backward. You don't have to add anything.

TIP In the playReverse example shown here, there is nothing inside of the parentheses, so the animation reverses from the current playhead position. As an alternative, you could place a number or a label inside the parentheses to move the playhead to a new position before it reverses. For numbers, use milliseconds where 1000=1 second. If you use a label, don't forget to place it in quotes.

---

9. Hit Esc to close the actions panel.

   You can also close the panel by clicking the X button in the upper-right corner.

10. At the bottom of the stage, right-click the middle button and choose "Open Actions for btnStop."

    The action panel for btnStop appears.

11. Choose the "click" trigger.

    The tab for click is displayed in the actions panel.

12. On the right side of the panel, click Stop. After examining the code, close the actions panel.

The code to stop the timeline from playing is inserted into the panel. You don't need to make any changes to it.

```
sym.stop();
```

FIGURE 5-15

The Play Reverse snippet makes your animation run backwards. It will continue until it reaches the beginning of the timeline or another trigger and action.

13. Open the actions panel for btnPlay and choose the "click" trigger.

The drill is the same for all three buttons.

14. When the click tab appears, click the Play button.

You can probably guess what the code for play looks like:

```
sym.play();
```

Congratulations! You programmed three buttons—reverse, stop, and play—without writing a bit of code. Animate did almost all the heavy lifting.

When you test your animation, you should be in complete control, able to stop the film strip and play it in either direction. If your project isn't working as expected, compare it to *05-7_Film_Strip_Click_done*.

Triggers for iPhones and Androids

So far, the activities in this chapter have focused on just a few common triggers and actions. When you get into developing your own projects, you're likely to do the same. The simple click is probably the most used trigger on the planet, because it's the simplest form of interaction. Showing and hiding elements and jumping to spots on the timeline are all natural actions for a development system like Animate. However, time marches on, and we all browse the Web using iPhones, Androids, and tablets of all kinds. One of the great benefits of HTML5 is that it's been designed with the handheld revolution in mind. That's true of Animate, too.

When you open the triggers menu for an element like a rectangle, you might notice that they are divided into groups (Figure 5-16). At the top, you have standard desktop, mouse-like triggers, like *click* and *dblclick*. As a developer, you'll be glad to hear that these commands work on touchscreens as well as mouse-operated computers. As you might guess, the mouse commands like mouseover and mouseout are exclusive to mice, because there aren't any related touchscreen triggers. Next, you have three triggers that are used with touchscreens: *touchstart, touchmove,* and *touchend*. At the bottom, there are special triggers that respond to mouse events and cursor focus.

If you want to reach the widest audience, you may as well go ahead and start thinking about developing apps that work equally well for mobile devices and traditional computers. These days you never know whether someone will be viewing your work on a 30-inch widescreen monitor or a 4.5-inch iPhone.

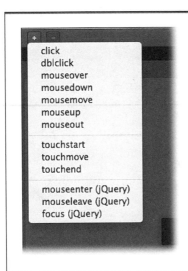

FIGURE 5-16

The triggers at the top of the list work for computers, but some—like click and double-click—work for phones and tablets, too. The group of three triggers in the middle are touchscreen-specific.

Working Smart with Symbols

There's one trait that animators, web builders, and programmers all share. They hate to do the same job more than once. In each of these crafts, there are tools and techniques that help you minimize the grunt work and maximize the time available for creativity. In Animate, *symbols* work that way. You build an element once, and then you can use it many times. Symbols make your web page more efficient, too. If you're building a scene with a couple hundred raindrops, all you need is one definition of a raindrop in order to fill the sky with them. You can even change the size, rotation, and opacity of the individual instances to add variety to your scene.

As you begin digging deep into symbols, you may be surprised at how much they have to offer. Symbols aren't just a way to clone an individual element: You can also group several different elements into a symbol. So, if you're creating a Stop sign, you can combine an octagonal shape with a text box to make one symbol. Furthermore, symbols aren't just static elements—each has its own stage and timeline. Want to animate a horse running? Create a horse symbol with animated leg motion. Then you can place that symbol on top of a background of Monument Valley. Using triggers and actions from the previous chapter, you can even stop and start the galloping.

This chapter gives you all the details about creating, using, and editing symbols. You'll also learn some tricks for working with Animate's Library panel—the storage barn for symbols and other project assets.

■ About Symbols

Copying and pasting is the most obvious way to reuse something you've created, but while that time-honored technique saves time, it doesn't save *space*. Say, for example, you need to show a swarm of cockroaches in the Animate advertisement you're creating for New and Improved Roach-B-Gone. You draw a single cockroach and then copy and paste it 100 times. Congratulations: You've got yourself 101 cockroaches...and one big, slow page download.

Instead, you should take that first cockroach and save it in Animate as a *symbol*. Symbols give you a way to reuse your work and keep your animation's finished file size down to a bare minimum. When you create a symbol, Animate stores the information for the symbol, or master copy, in your document as usual. But every time you create a copy (an *instance*) of that symbol, all Animate adds to your file is the information it needs to keep track of where you positioned that particular instance and any modifications you make to it on the stage.

So, to create the illusion of a swarm of roaches, you drag instances of the symbol onto the stage. Neither you nor Animate has to duplicate the work of drawing each roach. You can even vary the roach instances a little for variety and realism (so important in a pesticide ad) by changing their opacity, position, size, and even their skew. If symbols offered only file optimization, they'd be well worth using. But symbols give you additional benefits:

- **Grouping.** Keeping certain elements together, so you can operate on them all at once, helps you save time and stay organized. For example, in the case of those roaches, you can keep the body, legs, and antennae together in one discrete unit, making it much easier to move each insect around the stage.

- **Consistency.** By definition, all the instances of a symbol look pretty much the same. You can change certain instance characteristics—opacity and position on the stage, for example—but you can't redraw them without changing all instances of the symbol. Animate simply won't let you. (You can't turn one roach into a ladybug, for example.) For situations where you really need basic consistency among objects, symbols help save you from yourself.

- **Instantaneous update.** Suppose you want to change the roach color from brown to black. Edit the "master" roach stored in your Library, and Animate automatically updates all the instances of that symbol. So, for example, say you create a symbol showing the packaging for Roach-B-Gone. You use dozens and dozens of instances of the symbol throughout your animation, and then your boss tells you the marketing team has redesigned the packaging. If you'd used Copy and Paste to create all those boxes of Roach-B-Gone, you'd have to find and change each one manually. But with symbols, all you need to do is change the symbol in the Library. Animate automatically takes care of updating all the symbol's instances for you.

Does that mean you can't make changes to *one* of the roaches already on the stage? No, not at all. You can change an instance without affecting any other instances or the symbol itself. (You can turn one roach light brown using opacity, for example, without affecting any of the dark brown roaches.)

- **Nesting.** Symbols can contain other symbols. Sticking symbols inside other symbols is called nesting, and it's a great way to create unique, complex-looking images for a fraction of the file size you'd need to create them individually. Suppose you've drawn the perfect bug eye. You can turn it into a symbol and place it inside your symbols for roaches, ladybugs, and any other insect you want.

■ Building with Symbols

Here's a mad scientist experiment. Build a roach using as few parts (symbols) as possible, using Edge Animate to create all the elements. That means you're limited to Animate's primitive drawing tools: the rectangle and its cousins, the rounded rectangle, and the ellipse. You're going to have to be a little creative. Need some guidance? Here are the steps for creating three symbols, using only Animate's drawing tools. Then you assemble those parts into a fairly respectable roach (if there actually is such a thing).

1. Create and save a new Animate project called Build-A-Roach.

   Make sure you save it in its own folder. After all, you don't want roaches all over the place.

2. Use the rounded rectangle tool to draw a roach body that's 200px long and 100px wide.

   Pick an ugly brown color for your bug—something like R=70, G=60, B=30 will do the trick.

TIP   Even if your ultimate plan is to have lots of little roaches in your project, it's easier to build one large master roach. Working bigger gives you more mouse control over control handles and other objects you need to manipulate. You can always scale the roaches down when you add them to your project.

---

3. Use the border radii tools in Properties or the Transform Tool to make your rounded rectangle oval shaped and somewhat pointed on the ends—like a roach body.

   Roaches vary, so your bug body doesn't have to match this book's roaches.

TIP   Sometimes when you're trying to draw, it works best if you turn off the smart guides (Ctrl+U or ⌘-U). You can avoid some unwanted snapping as you position elements and bounding box control handles.

---

4. Right-click (Control-click) the body and choose Convert to Symbol from the shortcut menu.

The Create Symbol dialog box, shown in Figure 6-1, appears. It has a Symbol Name text box and an "Autoplay timeline" checkbox.

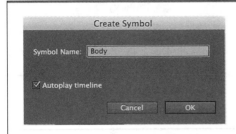

FIGURE 6-1

Every time you create a new symbol, you need to give it a name. That name appears in the Library panel under Symbols. When you create instances of a symbol, you can give each instance a different Element ID. That way you can control instances independently.

5. Into the Symbol Name text box, type *Body*. Leave "Autoplay timeline" turned on. Press OK.

You've transformed the simple rounded rectangle into a symbol, with all the rights and privileges that accrue to that new lofty status. How do you know it's a symbol and not just a run-of-the-mill rectangle? When it's selected, take a look at the icon next to its name in the Properties panel. The gear-shaped icon indicates Body is a symbol.

6. With the Body on the stage selected, in the Properties panel type bugBody in the ID box.

You're going to use more than one instance of the Body symbol as you build your bug, so it's best to give each instance an appropriate ID.

7. Drag one more instance of Body to the stage and give it an ID of: bugHead. Then resize and reshape the instance into a bug head.

You can drag the handles around the bugHead bounding box to reshape it or you can use any of the controls in the Properties panel shown in Figure 6-2.

Building a Multipart Leg Symbol

At this point your roach consists of two parts made from one symbol. If you want to, you can continue to enhance your roach using the Body symbol. For example, you can make roach wings from the body symbol and ID them as leftWing and rightWing (no political puns intended). Then, use the Opacity, Size, and Skew properties to make the rounded rectangles look more wing-like. Wings aside, what your roach really needs is legs—six of them, so it can scurry across the floor when the light comes on.

The trick is to create a single leg symbol that you can use in all the positions: left, right, front, back, and middle. Here's one solution:

1. Draw a long skinny leg-like rectangle. Set the background color to black.

   At this point, the limit of Animate's drawing tools becomes apparent—there's no line tool. You could turn to your favorite drawing program and import some artwork. But to meet the current Animate-only challenge, you can use skinny rectangles for your lines.

2. Add two more skinny rectangles to create a crooked roach leg.

   As you build the perfect roach leg, consider the different positions it'll appear in. A somewhat symmetrical leg may be best for all front/back and left/right purposes.

FIGURE 6-2

Note that the available properties are different for a symbol than they are for a rounded rectangle. For example, you can control Opacity, but you can't change the basic color. As shown at the bottom of the Properties panel, you can control playback actions because each symbol has its own timeline.

3. Select each of the three leg parts, then go Modify→Create Symbol.

   Modify→Create Symbol is simply another way to open the Create Symbol dialog box and turn a selection into a symbol. You could just as easily use the right-click (Control-click) method or press Ctrl+Y (⌘-Y).

4. In the Symbol Name box, type *Leg*.

   You now have a Leg symbol and one instance of that symbol is on the stage.

5. Move the leg into position on your roach and change its ID to match its position.

   For example, the ID might be legLeftFront or legRightMiddle.

6. Add the rest of the legs to your roach.

   With a little creativity, you can provide six decent bug legs. If you want to give the front legs a look that's different from the others, try spinning them around 180 degrees.

Creating a Curved Line with a Rounded Rectangle

Your roach is now looking mobile. It still needs some antennae to feel its way around. If you want to really be economical, you can use the Leg symbol to make antennae. For example, you can hide most of the leg under the body so that only one or two of its rectangles show. You can use size and skew properties so the antenna doesn't look leg-like. In reality though, most roaches have graceful, long curved antenna. So, for the sake of entomological realism, here are the steps for creating a curved line when your only drawing tool is a rounded rectangle.

1. Draw a long narrow rounded rectangle. Make the rectangle's background color black.

   Keep your goal in mind. You want a long antenna-like curve on one side of your rounded rectangle.

2. Using the Border Radii controls (Figure 6-3), click the top-left and bottom-left buttons.

   This makes the rounded rectangle flat on one side and rounded on the other.

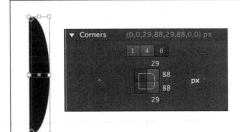

FIGURE 6-3

The Border Radii controls give you a rough idea of the shape your rounded rectangle will take. Here, the left buttons are pressed in, making that side of the element flat instead of curved.

3. Select the rectangle and press Ctrl+D (⌘-D).

   The duplicate rounded rectangle is directly above the original.

4. Change the background color of the duplicate to white.

   The assumption here is that the stage is white. If your stage is a different color, use that color for the duplicate rounded rectangle.

5. Drag the white element to the left, revealing enough of the lower rounded rectangle to form an antenna as shown in Figure 6-4.

   If possible, make sure that your antenna is symmetrical and slightly pointed on both ends.

FIGURE 6-4

Animate doesn't give you an easy way to draw a simple curved line like this bug antenna. This was created with two rounded rectangles: one black and one white. The white one placed over the black creates a pseudo-mask so only a portion of the black rectangle is visible.

6. Select both the black and white rounded rectangle and then right-click (Control-click). Choose Convert to Symbol from the shortcut menu.

   The Create Symbol dialog box appears.

7. In the Symbol Name box, type *Antenna*.

   There's an instance of the newly created Antenna on the stage.

8. Attach two antennae to your roach.

   You can use the one on the stage and drag another antenna from the Library. At this point, your roach should look something like Figure 6-5.

TIP In cases where you want lines of uniform thickness, you may want to create a rectangle or rounded rectangle with a border. Then, set the background color to none. At that point, you can create a mask, as described in steps 3 to 5, to hide portions of the border. The method described here is better for creating lines with a more organic look.

■ Nesting Symbols Within Symbols

So far your roach consists of three discreet symbols: Body, Leg, and Antenna. Each symbol is used more than once and they look like they're connected because they're placed on top of each other. As far as Animate is concerned, these symbols aren't really a single unit—they're just elements on the stage.

Animate lets you place symbols inside of other symbols. The technique is called *nesting,* and it's perfect for bug building. You want to be able to move your roach around the stage without having to reposition each leg and antenna individually. The solution? Select all the bug parts on the stage and then right-click (Control-click). A shortcut menu appears; choose "Convert to Symbol." When the Create Symbol dialog shows up, name your masterpiece *Roach,* and then click OK. Now that you have a Roach symbol in your Library, you can create as many as you want. As you see, the process is like the one used to create the legs.

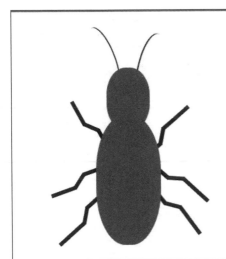

FIGURE 6-5

This roach is made from only three symbols. In the Library, they are named Body, Leg, and Antenna. Instances of symbols can be altered by changing their properties so they can perform multiple duties.

Working with Symbol Timelines

Your roach isn't intended to be a still life, so you need to add some action. Specifically, it needs leg action. Now that your roach is a symbol, you can drag multiple roaches from the Library and place them on the stage. Wouldn't it be great if each roach came with moving legs? With Animate symbols, you can accomplish that. Animate once in the master roach, and all the instances that you add to the stage will have the same moving parts.

Each symbol has its own timeline, which is helpful in many ways. First of all, it cuts down on clutter in the main timeline. Every single element and property keyframe doesn't have to be in the main timeline. Secondly, you can start and stop symbol timelines from playing. For example, you can use the symbol timeline to control whether the roach's legs are moving, as you'll see on page 214.

The first step is to animate the legs; the start and stop business will be handled later. Follow these steps:

1. In the Library, right-click (Ctrl-click) the Roach symbol and choose Edit from the shortcut menu.

   The stage disappears, and the Roach remains on a white background: The Roach symbol is open for editing. In the upper-left corner you see the words: "Stage / Roach," as shown in Figure 6-6. When you have symbols inside of symbols, you can use these "breadcrumbs" to remember exactly where you are. You can also click them to close the symbol you're editing and jump up to a parent symbol.

For example, if you click Stage, you close the Roach symbol and return to the stage and the main timeline.

FIGURE 6-6

Right-click (Control-click) a symbol in the Library and choose Edit, and you see an editing space devoted to that symbol. No other elements are visible. To return to the stage and main timeline, click the word Stage.

2. Go to the Elements panel and click the show/hide eyeball next to bugBody.

   The bugBody is now hidden. This gives you a full view of all the legs, making it easy to edit them.

3. Select one leg.

   In addition to the handles on the bounding box around the symbol, there's a blue square in the center. That's the Transform Origin. When you use the Rotate property, the symbol spins around this point.

4. With the Transform Tool (Q), drag the Transform Origin from the middle to the end of the leg that is usually hidden by the body as shown in Figure 6-7.

   You can't move the Transform Origin with the Select Tool; you have to use the Transform Tool. Once the Transform tool is selected, the Transform Origin changes to a crosshairs symbol as shown in Figure 6-7. It will be easier to position the legs and to create more realistic motion if the legs rotate around an end point rather than the center.

5. Move the Transform Origin for all the legs.

   Each leg symbol will be able to move independently around its Transform Origin. This might be a good time to reposition the legs a bit if you think it's necessary.

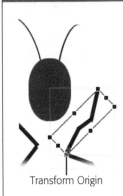

FIGURE 6-7

Here, bugBody is temporarily hidden. The Transform Origin has been moved to the left end of the selected leg. Now when the leg is positioned using the Rotate property, it will rotate around that point.

Transform Origin

The emphasis should be on getting the end with the Transform Origin into just the right spot for the most realistic leg movement.

6. In Elements, click the eyeball next to bugBody.

   All parts of your roach are visible again. The legs are partially hidden by the bug's body.

7. Make sure the Auto Keyframe (K) and Auto-Transition (X) are on. Then, create a starting pose for your roach.

   Animation within a symbol is just like animation on the stage. Move the playhead to a position and then arrange the elements the way you want them at that point in time. To pose a leg, select it and then use Rotate in the Properties Panel to move it into position. Use this method to create a starting pose for each leg.

TIP To create the complete leg motion, you set several different leg positions in the symbol's timeline. You want the last position to match the first position. That way, if you loop the animation, it will appear smooth. To remember the original position of the legs, mark those first positions with small rectangles, as shown in Figure 6-8. You can use these rectangle markers when you set the last leg position. When you're done, just delete the rectangle markers.

---

8. With the playhead at 0:00.000, select all the legs and then in Properties, click the diamond-shaped button next to Rotate.

   Animate creates Rotate property keyframes for each leg's starting pose.

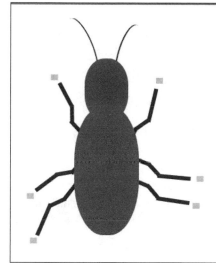

FIGURE 6-8

Temporary position markers are handy tools. Here, small rectangles mark the starting pose for each of the legs. That makes it easy to recreate the pose for the final frame of the animation.

9. Drag the playhead down the timeline to the 0:00.250 mark. Move all the legs to a new position.

   For skittery roach action, it's best if the legs don't all move in unison like marching soldiers. Front legs may be using a pulling motion while back legs push. The left rear and right rear legs may be moving in completely different directions. Use your best guess now; you can always fine-tune the leg motion later.

10. Create new leg positions for the 0:00.250, 0:00.500, and 0:00.750 marks. Lastly, move the playhead to the 0:01.000 mark and put the legs back in the starting position.

    With the legs in the same position in 0:00.000 and 0:01.000, you'll be able to loop the animation smoothly. See the note on page 132 for help marking the leg position. Naturally, if you want faster leg action, shorten the time span. If you want slower action, use a longer time period for your four new leg poses.

11. With the playhead at the 0:01.000 mark, click the Add Trigger button on the timeline.

    The Trigger box opens, where you can add an action that takes place at this point in time.

12. On the right of the Trigger panel, click Play from.

    Animate adds a line of code that sends the playhead to the one second mark:

    ```
    sym.play(1000);
    ```

13. Replace the 1000 with 0.

    The zero moves the playhead to the beginning of the timeline.

14. In the upper-left corner of the workspace, click the word Stage.

    The Roach symbol is closed. You're no longer editing it. The workspace you see is the stage. Your animated roach rests peacefully on the stage.

15. Press Ctrl+S (⌘-S) to save your project. Then press Ctrl+Enter (⌘-Return).

    Your animation opens in your web browser for previewing. You should see some good leg action even though your roach isn't moving anywhere. On page 214, you'll learn how to start and stop the roach timeline. That's a job for JavaScript/ jQuery code.

Just to recap what's taken place so far in the Build-A-Roach project. You drew three elements: Body, Leg, and Antenna. You turned each into a symbol and then used multiple instances to build your roach. Then you selected all the parts and turned that into your master roach symbol. Lastly, you used the timeline in the roach symbol to animate the legs.

- You can turn any element or group of elements into a symbol using the Modify→Convert to Symbol (Ctrl+Y or ⌘-Y) command.

- You can modify an existing symbol by right-clicking (Control-clicking) its name in the Library panel and then choosing Edit.

- You can place symbols inside of other symbols, a technique called *nesting*. (Perhaps not the most pleasant term when you're discussing roaches.)

- Symbols have their own timelines, so you can animate the elements within a symbol.

◼ Animating a Symbol on the Stage

To create a respectable roach, you not only need to have legs that move, you need to move the roach around the stage. In the previous exercise, you opened the Roach symbol for editing and then used its timeline to animate the legs. Now that the legs move back and forth, you'll want to make the roaches move around the screen as shown in Figure 6-9. That's a job for the stage and the main timeline. If you've been working through the exercises so far in this book, that's a cinch. It's the same old animation two-step. Move the playhead to a point on the timeline, and then position the element where you want it at that point in time.

Here are some tips and suggestions for creating a satisfying roach animation:

- Think about the route that you want your roach to travel. If you intend to loop your animation, you want your roach to circle back around to the starting position.

- Two or three seconds should be enough time to scurry around an average size stage of 550 × 400 pixels.

- Make sure the Auto-Keyframe (A) and Auto-Transition (U) are turned on before you reposition your bug.

- Use the Position and Rotate properties to move and pose your roach. Consider using some erratic movements both in direction and speed.

- To view leg motion while you position your roach and work with the timeline, select the symbol, then turn on Properties→Playback Actions→Scrub.

- To create a multi-roach animation, just click on Roach in the Library and drag another instance onto the stage. Use the scale properties to make roaches in different sizes (Figure 6-9).

NOTE Want to compare your Build-A-Roach project to some finished code? Get *06_1_Build_A_Roach_done* from the Missing CD at *www.missingmanuals.com/cds/animatemm*.

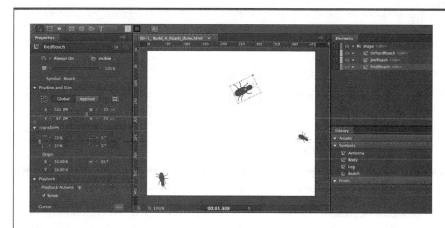

FIGURE 6-9

After you've built one roach, complete with moving legs, you can drag several more roaches out from the Library's Symbol panel. You can size each instance of the roach symbol independently. You can also send them scurrying around the stage on different paths.

Duplicating and Renaming Symbols

Chances are you'll put in a lot of work when you create a complex symbol. Suppose you're creating a street scene with several different cars. You don't want your cars to all look alike. So, you create your first car: a Prius. Then you right-click (Control-click) the car name in the Library and choose Duplicate. A new item appears in the list of symbols: Prius Copy 1. This car is a new, separate symbol; right now it just happens to look like a Prius. That can change when you open and edit the symbol. Right-click (Control-click) and choose Edit from the shortcut menu. Perhaps you turn it into a Chevy Volt. It's still work, but it's a lot easier making changes to an existing car than creating a new one from scratch. When you're done editing, you'll want to change the name to match the new vehicle. So...you guessed it. Right-click (Control-click) the name in the Library and choose Rename from that same shortcut menu.

Deleting or Undoing a Symbol

There may come a time when you want to delete a symbol that you created. If you no longer need the symbol and want to get rid of all the instances of that symbol, it's easy. Just right-click (Control-click) the symbol name in the Library and choose Delete. A warning appears that reminds you that you have instances of the symbol on the stage and that asks: "Are you sure you want to delete the selected symbol?" Say yes, and the symbol is removed from the Library, and all the instances on the stage are deleted.

NOTE If you accidentally delete a symbol and all the instances of that symbol in your project, you can always bring it back with an Undo command (Ctrl+Z or ⌘-Z).

What if you want to keep the elements inside, but remove the symbol definition? For example, you want to break a symbol back into the elements it was made from. That requires a couple of extra steps:

1. Open the symbol for editing by right-clicking (Control-clicking) its name in the Library.

2. Choose Edit from the shortcut menu.

3. Press Ctrl+A (⌘-A) to select all the Elements in the symbol. Then, to copy, press Ctrl+C (⌘-C).

4. In the upper-left corner of the workspace, click the word Stage to close the symbol and return to the stage.

5. Choose Edit→Paste to paste the elements onto the stage. When that's done, they aren't part of a symbol. They're just individual elements.

6. Right-click (Control-click) the symbol name in the Library and choose Delete. The instances of the symbol will be removed from the stage, but the elements you copied will remain.

■ Create a Button Symbol with Rollover Action

One of the most common tools on the web is the lowly button. Many buttons include some sort of *rollover* action. That is, when someone moves her mouse over the button, the button changes to indicate it's clickable. When she clicks the button, it may change appearance again. If you're developing a navigation system for a website, you usually want some uniformity when it comes to buttons. That's a perfect job for a symbol. You can use the symbol's timeline to create different looks for normal and mouseover states.

1. Open and save a new Animate project with the folder name and filename *Button*.

   Make sure you save your project in an empty folder.

2. With the Rounded Rectangle tool, draw a button-sized rectangle.

   You don't have to worry about making adjustments now. You can make changes after you've converted the rectangle to a symbol.

3. Right-click (Control-click) the rectangle and choose "Convert to Symbol" from the shortcut menu, as shown in Figure 6-10.

   A box appears prompting you to name the new symbol.

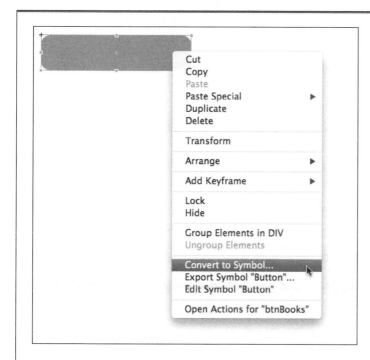

FIGURE 6-10

You can turn any element into a symbol. Just right-click (Control-click) and then choose "Convert to Symbol" from this shortcut menu.

4. Type the name *Button*, turn Autoplay off, and click OK.

   You've transformed the simple rectangle into a symbol. Look in the Library panel under Symbols→Library. If it's not already open, choose Window→Library and click the triangle button next to Symbols. The Library panel opens with three expandable lists: Assets, Symbols, and Fonts. Button is in the Symbols list. With Autoplay turned off, the button's timeline will stop at 0:00 until a trigger tells it to do something else.

5. Double-click the unmodified instance of Button on the stage.

   The stage and all the other elements darken except for the unmodified instance of Button, which is available for editing. This technique is called "editing a symbol in place." It gives you the opportunity to see your symbol's relationship with other stage elements while you make changes. The timeline displayed when you're editing a symbol is the timeline for that symbol.

6. With the playhead at 0:00, press Ctrl+L (⌘-L) to create a label named *normal*. Create a second label at 0:01 named *over*.

You'll use these labels, shown in Figure 6-11, to control the color of the button.

7. Turn Auto-Keyframe Mode on and turn Auto-Transition Mode off. With the playhead at 0:00, choose a background color for the button's normal state. Then, in Properties, click the Add Keyframe button next to Background Color.

The button will display this color most of the time, when it has no mouse-attention.

8. Move the playhead to the "over" label. Choose a backgroud color for the button's over state. Add a property keyframe.

The chosen color is displayed when someone moves the mouse cursor over the button.

9. Right-click (Control-click) the rounded rectangle and choose Open Actions for "RoundRect" from the shortcut menu. Choose the *mouseover* trigger.

The Actions panel appears, ready for you to add actions to the mouseover event.

FIGURE 6-11

Each symbol has a timeline all its own. Here the button has labels in its timeline to mark the "normal" and "over" state of the button.

10. On the right of the Actions panel, click "Stop at."

The code to go to and stop at a point on the timeline appears in the actions.

11. Replace the argument in the *stop()* function that reads "1000" with *'over'*.

Now the line of code reads:

```
sym.stop('over');
```

Don't forget to include the quotes when you use a label as the argument for a function.

12. In the upper-right corner of the Actions panel, click the + button. Then choose *mouseout* from the list of triggers.

A new tab appears in the Actions panel, ready for your mouseout code.

13. On the left side of the Actions panel, click "Stop at."

The code to go to and stop at a point on the timeline appears in the actions.

14. Replace the argument in the *stop()* function that reads "1000" with *'normal'*.

Now the line of code reads:

```
sym.stop('normal');
```

15. While your symbol is still open for editing, in Properties, deselect the Autoplay box.

This step prevents your button from automatically playing the timeline. (If it did so, the button would flash both colors whether the mouse was over it or not.)

16. In the upper-left corner of the work stage window, click Stage.

You leave the symbol editing space and return to the stage. Now the timeline displayed is the main timeline for your project.

17. Save (Ctrl+S or ⌘-S) your project. Then press Ctrl+Enter (⌘-Return) to preview it.

Your button behaves as advertised. Initially, it shows the normal state. When the mouse is over the button, it changes color. Remember, when you have triggers and actions, you need to preview your composition in a browser.

Most buttons have some sort of label that identifies the button and the expected action when it's clicked. For example, you may drag an instance of button out of the Library and then place text over it to create, say, a Home button or a Contact Us button. There's one slight problem with this method, though. When the mouse is over the text box, the button doesn't change color. That's because the text box is over the button, blocking its rollover behavior. There are a few different solutions to this conundrum. In Chapter 9, you'll see how to fix it with JavaScript/jQuery code. For now, you'll learn a graphic workaround, which is to place the text beneath the button and then dial down the Opacity of the button. The color is softer but at least the text shows through; see Figure 6-12.

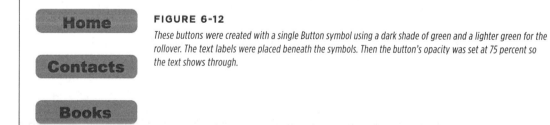

FIGURE 6-12

These buttons were created with a single Button symbol using a dark shade of green and a lighter green for the rollover. The text labels were placed beneath the symbols. Then the button's opacity was set at 75 percent so the text shows through.

In this example you saw how you can change the color of a button using a symbol's independent timeline, labels, and a couple of "Stop at" actions. If you'd like to have snazzier animated buttons, you could use "Play from" actions. On *mouseover* and *mouseout*, the symbols' timelines would play a section of the timeline. You'd need to have some sort of triggers at the end of each sequence to either stop the Timeline from playing or to move the playhead back to the "normal" state.

Grouping Elements Without Symbols

You've seen in the previous examples how symbols can group elements into a single unit, making it easy to keep all the bits and pieces together. That's not the only reason for using symbols, but it's a good one. As you work at Animate, there will be times when you want to group things, but you don't need or want the other features that symbols provide.

In the button example, the symbol feature provides a great way to create consistent button behavior with different background colors for the "normal" and "over" button states. You need text labels for your buttons, but if you try to put text inside of the symbol, all your buttons end up with the same label. You don't need three Home buttons! So, you created text labels that were outside of the symbol. Still, it would be great to group the text labels and the button symbol together, so you can easily position them as a single unit. The solution is the Group Element in DIV command (Figure 6-13). When you group elements, you want to:

- Make sure the elements you want to group are positioned properly.

- Select the elements you want to group.

- Right-click (Control-click) the grouped elements.

- Choose "Group Elements in DIV" from the shortcut menu.

> **NOTE** If you're wondering about that DIV business, Edge Animate groups elements using bits of HTML code called a DIV tag. There are more details about HTML, the language that describes web pages, in Chapter 7.

Once your elements are grouped you can position them as a single unit. Groups have properties like any other element. You can give groups an ID, animate their position, adjust their opacity, and apply triggers and action to them. If you ever need to break a group of elements back into their native bits and pieces, just right-click the group and then choose Ungroup Elements from the shortcut menu.

Adding a Click State to Your Button Symbol

Simple two state rollovers, like the one in the previous example, are good for a lot of situations, like swapping images or displaying callouts. Buttons can add a third state to provide feedback when they're clicked. Often they briefly show a brighter color for a fraction of a second before they perform their task. To create this type of third state for your button symbol, you simply add one more label to the symbol timeline. You then display a brighter color for a quarter of a second and then send the playhead back to the original, "normal" state. Using the project started on page 136, the following steps show you how:

1. Double-click one of the button symbols on stage.

   The symbol opens for editing in place. When you edit the symbol, the changes you make will appear in all the other instances of the symbol. For example, Figure 6-13 shows three buttons created with the same button symbol. Edit one in place, and they all change.

2. On the symbol's timeline, move the playhead to the two-second mark (0:02). Then press Ctrl+L (⌘-L).

   A new label appears at 0:02.

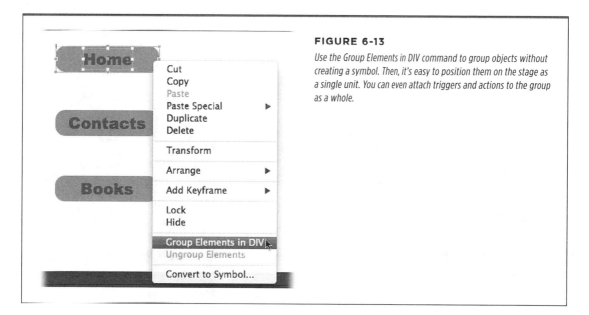

FIGURE 6-13

Use the Group Elements in DIV command to group objects without creating a symbol. Then, it's easy to position them on the stage as a single unit. You can even attach triggers and actions to the group as a whole.

3. Name the new label *down*.

   At this point the timeline should have three labels: normal, over, and down. Visual changes you create following the down label tell users that the button has been clicked.

4. Make sure that you toggle Auto-Keyframes (K) on and Auto-Transition (X) off.

   No gradual transitions for this button. It's all instant response.

5. Select RoundRect and then in Properties→background-color, click the swatch and change the color to a yellowish hue.

   Yellow works well for getting attention. It will only be visible briefly. If you aren't sure what values to use, try R=210, G=230, B=60, A=100. After you select your color, a new background-color keyframe for RoundRect appears in the timeline. If it doesn't, you probably don't have Auto-Keyframes turned on.

6. Move the playhead to the right, marking another quarter of a second (0:02.250). Then, press Ctrl+T (⌘-T).

   A trigger is added to the button's symbol timeline at 0:02.250 and the Timeline Trigger actions panel appears. Timeline triggers fire automatically when the playhead reaches that point. You want this trigger to stop the flash of yellow and send the button back to its "normal" state.

7. In the actions panel, click *Stop* at.

   Generic *Stop* at code is inserted into the actions panel:

   ```
   sym.stop(1000);
   ```

8. Change the 1000 to '*normal*' as shown in Figure 6-14.

   When you're done, your timeline trigger code reads:

   ```
   sym.stop('normal');
   ```

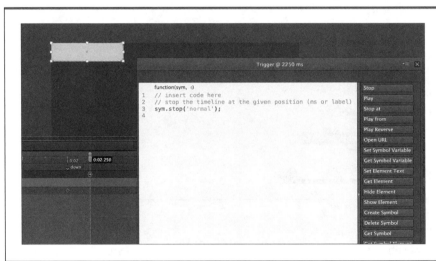

FIGURE 6-14

When someone clicks a button, the playhead is sent to the "down" label. The timeline plays for a quarter of a second, showing the yellow button highlight. The timeline trigger and its code sends the playhead back to the "normal" label, so that the button displays its normal, non-highlighted behavior.

9. Press Esc to exit the Timeline Trigger actions panel.

   When the actions panel closes, you're still in the symbol's edit-in-place mode. There's one more task to make your button work. It's time to create the clicking action.

10. Right-click the RoundRect in your button symbol. Choose Open Actions for "RoundRect" from the shortcut menu.

    The actions panel opens and the trigger menu appears. You've already created a mouseover and mouseout trigger.

11. In the upper-left corner of the RoundRect actions panel, click the + button, then choose the click trigger.

    A tab for the click trigger opens, ready for code.

12. On the right of the actions panel, choose "Play from."

    The generic "Play from" code appears in the actions panel:

    ```
    sym.play(1000);
    ```

13. Change the 1000 to 'down'.

    Don't forget the quotes around 'down'—when you're done the code reads:

    ```
    sym.play('down');
    ```

14. Press Esc to exit the actions panel. Then, in the upper-left corner of the stage, click the word Stage.

    After you press Esc the actions panel closes, but you're still in the button symbol's edit-in-place mode. When you click Stage, you return to the project's main stage and timeline.

15. Press Ctrl+S (⌘-S) to save your project. Then, press Ctrl+Enter (⌘-Return) to preview the project.

If all works according to plan, your button has three states. It starts off in the normal state. Move your mouse over the button, and the color changes reflecting the over state. If you move the cursor back out, it changes back to normal. Click the button and for one quarter of a second it displays the yellow highlight of the down state before returning to normal.

You've got a button that does everything it should, except for actually doing something useful. The next section explains how to make your button open a web page. Now that's the start of a beautiful button and web designer friendship.

Making Your Button Open a Web Page

If you followed the previous exercise, you now have a button that behaves kind of like a button. If this were a button on a web page that displays a home page, you could add a trigger and an action to do that. Most of the time, you want to add actions to instances of your symbols. That way different buttons trigger different actions. If you open a symbol for editing and then add a trigger and action, that behavior will be part of every instance of the button symbol. In this case, you have a DIV group of elements with the ID and label "Books." Here are the steps to add an action that opens a web page.

1. Right-click (Control-click) the Books group on the stage, and choose Open Actions for Books. Then choose the *click* trigger.

2. On the left of the Actions panel, click the Open URL button.

3. Edit the *window.open()* function to use the desired web address.

When you're done, you should have a line of code that looks something like this:

```
window.open("http://missingmanuals.com", "_self");
```

Within the parentheses there are two bits of info sometimes called parameters or arguments. The first ("*http://missingmanuals.com*") is a complete web address. The second ("_self") tells the browser to replace the current page with this new page. If you used the argument "_blank" then the browser would open the new page in a new tab or window.

At this point, it's pretty clear that you can make a series of animated buttons that could serve as the navigation system for a website. You don't have to make each button from scratch, either. A single rollover button symbol is reusable. All you need to do to create distinct buttons is to add text for a label. After the buttons and labels are grouped, you can create distinct actions for each. For an example of the buttons described here, see *06-2_Rollover_Button_done* from the Missing CD at *www.missingmanuals.com/cds/animatemm*.

Moving Symbols Between Projects

Symbols are all about efficient reuse of the elements you build, so it's only natural that once you create an ideal symbol, you'll want to use it in another composition. With that in mind, Animate offers an easy way to move a symbol out of your project and import it into a new one. On both ends, the action takes place—where else?—in the Library→Symbols panel. Right-click the symbol you want to reuse and then choose Export from the shortcut menu shown in Figure 6-15. A standard file window opens giving you the options to choose a folder and name your symbol file. Animate gives the file the .eglib extension.

On the receiving end, you want to open the Animate composition that will be the new home for the symbol. In the Library→Symbols panel, click the + button in the upper-right corner, and then choose Import Symbols. Another file/folder window opens where you can find the symbol file you created, and click the Open button (lower-right corner) to slurp it up. Once you have the symbol in your Library, you can use it just as you would any other symbol.

Building a Drop-Down Menu System

Anyone who's built a website knows that the process is like building a brick wall. You start off by putting a couple of bricks down. Add some mortar and then add some more bricks. You can use that same technique to build a drop-down menu out of rollover buttons (Figure 6-16). The great thing about drop-down menus is that anyone who's used Windows or a Mac knows exactly what to do.

Think of your button groups as the bricks you use for construction. Create them using techniques similar to those described back on page 136. You can be creative when it comes to shape, color, and the actions that take place for mouseover, mouseout, and click triggers. You can make as many button groups as needed. If you're creating a website navigation system, it's best to position your buttons consistently. To build a drop-down menu, use one button to show and hide the other buttons that represent the menu items. Using Animate actions, those buttons can lead to a new web page as described in the previous section. Or they can display a different part of the timeline as done in the example: *06-3_Dropdown_Menu_done* from the Missing CD at *www.missingmanuals.com/cds/animatemm*.

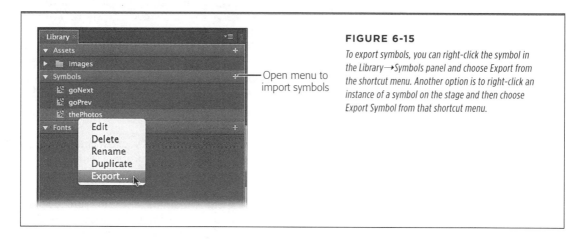

Open menu to
import symbols

FIGURE 6-15

To export symbols, you can right-click the symbol in the Library→Symbols panel and choose Export from the shortcut menu. Another option is to right-click an instance of a symbol on the stage and then choose Export Symbol from that shortcut menu.

TIP Chapter 9 provides details on controlling elements nested within symbols using JavaScript and jQuery. Those skills provide even better ways to show and hide the buttons in a drop-down menu.

FIGURE 6-16

The buttons on this drop-down menu display different pictures. Click the Photos button at the top to show and hide the submenu. As explained on page 143, they could just as easily open a new web page.

■ Creating Text Callouts with Rollover Action

When you use a program like Animate, you work with an interface that has lots of buttons and widgets; inevitably you come across a tool and you don't know what it does. Savvy computerist that you are, you move the cursor over the mystery widget and a text label appears describing the tool. The label is called a *tooltip*, and you can add similar callouts to your projects. An example back on page 92 showed a filmstrip that showed photos of five different flowers. Buttons controlled the filmstrip, giving viewers control to *play*, *stop*, and *play in reverse*. Most adults know the difference between a rose and a daisy, but suppose that filmstrip was created for second graders, and the lesson plan was to teach them how to identify flowers in their gardens. That's a perfect project for text callouts.

This project uses symbols and groups. First, you create hotspot symbols that you place over the flower pictures. Then, you create callouts (groups) with the name of each flower. When students point to a flower with the mouse, the flower's name pops up. The main hotspot trick is this: After you've created and positioned the hotspots correctly over the flowers (at the right moment in time), you set their Opacity to 0. The hotspots are still there and they'll trigger a mouseover action; but they're invisible, so they don't hide the flower. To get started on this project, get *06-4_Film_Strip_Callouts* from the Missing CD (*www.missingmanuals.com/cds/animatemm*).

1. Open *06-4_Film_Strip_Callouts*.

   You see a photo of flowers on the stage with two buttons underneath. Scrub the playhead, and you see the filmstrip move horizontally, displaying different flower photos at different points in time. If you preview the composition at this point, you see that the buttons work as advertised. The "Next Flower" button advances the filmstrip to the next picture. The "Start Over" button rewinds the filmstrip back to the beginning. The mechanics behind these buttons are click triggers and play() actions. There are timeline triggers with stop() actions to keep the filmstrip from advancing until a button is clicked.

2. With the playhead at the start (0:00), select the rectangle tool, and then draw a rectangle over the yellow poppy.

   This rectangle is the hotspot. It's not exactly the shape of a poppy, but for callouts, close enough is good enough.

3. Right-click the rectangle you just created and choose "Convert to Symbol" from the shortcut menu. Name the symbol *hotspot*.

   On the stage, your rectangle is now an instance of the hotspot symbol and its ID has been changed to hotspot. You can verify this in the Properties panel. In the Library panel under Symbols, you see the hotspot symbol. You can use this to create new instances of the hotspot symbol.

   Why create a symbol for this job? You'll save time by making one hotspot symbol with the properties you want and then creating hotspot instances as needed. Each instance can trigger a different action. In this case, the instances will display different callouts.

4. On the stage, double-click the hotspot and then select the rectangle.

The symbol opens for editing in place. The rectangle properties appear in the Properties panel.

5. In the Properties panel, change the Opacity to 40%. Set the background-color to white.

A little transparency makes it easier to position hotspots over parts of the photo. Eventually, you'll make the hotspot invisible.

6. In the upper-left corner of the stage, click the word "Stage."

The symbol being edited closes and you're back at the main stage and timeline. Your hotspot is semi-transparent.

7. Change the ID of the hotspot on Stage to *hsPoppy*.

When you're dealing with multiple hotspots, you'll be glad to have unique IDs for all of them.

8. With the playhead at 0:00, change the Display property for hsPoppy from Always On to On.

The Display property is right under the ID. You want to be able to turn your hotspots on when the target flower is on stage and off when the flower is off stage. See Figure 6-17.

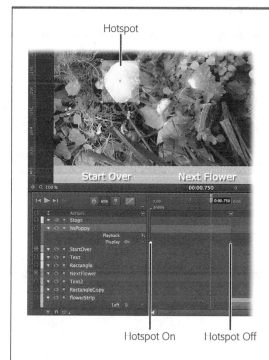

Hotspot

Hotspot On   Hotspot Off

FIGURE 6-17

The hotspot over the poppy is turned on while the poppy is on stage, and turned off when it's not on stage. While you are working, you can set the Opacity of your hotspot to about 40%. When you're ready to publish your project, you dial down the Opacity to 0, to make them entirely invisible.

9. Drag the playhead to 0:01 and turn Display *Off*.

   You can use the same drop-down menu in Properties or you can use the Display button in the timeline that's under the element's name.

10. In the time setting under the stage, type *1.5*.

    At this point, the filmstrip displays the rose.

11. Drag a new instance of the hotspot symbol from Library→Symbols onto the stage.

    A small semi-transparent rectangle appears on the stage.

12. Drag the corners and edges of the new hotspot so it covers the rose as shown in Figure 6-18.

    These dimension changes only affect this instance of the hotspot symbol.

FIGURE 6-18

You can change the width (W) and height (H) properties of instances of symbols independently. That means the hsRose instance of the hotspot symbol can be bigger than the hsPoppy hotspot. Here the rose hotspot is being resized on the stage; note the cursor in the lower-right corner.

Start Over   Next Flower

13. In Properties, change the ID for this hotspot to hsRose and resize it, as shown in Figure 6-18.

    As you create new hotspots and rename them, those instance names are used in Properties, the timeline, and the Elements panel.

14. Turn hsRose on at 0:01.500 and then off at 0:02.500.

    You can use the transitions in the timeline under flowerStrip→Left as points for turning on and off the hotspots. Those are the transitions that reposition the filmstrip. You don't want your hotspots active when the filmstrip is moving.

15. Repeat steps 10 through 14 for the remaining three flower photos. Name the instances of the hotspot symbol *hsDaisy*, *hsLilac*, and *hsTigerLily*.

    When you're done, you have hotspots that appear over the flowers as they're displayed. They're off when the flowers are off stage.

Create and Animate Your Callouts

At this point, you've created hot spots for each flower. (Now's a good time to make sure you've saved your project.) You can check the hotspots' timing and position by playing your animation Ctrl+Enter (⌘-Return). Use the Next Flower and Start Over buttons, and your hotspots should all remain over the flowers when the filmstrip is not moving. The next step is to create callouts for each flower and add the triggers and actions to make them work.

1. With the playhead back at the start of the timeline (0:00.000), select the Text tool (T), and then click the stage to create a text box.

   Don't worry too much about the size and position, you can always tweak those details later. Just put it in a place not occupied by the hsPoppy hotspot.

2. In the text box, type *Iceland Poppy* and press Esc to close the text editor.

   Your words appear on stage, but they need some formatting help.

3. With the text box selected, change the following settings in the Properties panel:

   • ID: tbPoppy

   • Display: On

   • font-family: Arial Black, Gadget, sans-serif

   • font-size: 30px

   • color: white (R=255, G=255, B=255, A=255)

   • text-align: center

   • textShadow black (R=0, G=0, B=0, A=255) with the horizontal and vertical offset 4px and the Blur Radius set to 6px

With the settings shown in Figure 6-19, your text is bigger and easier to see onscreen. The shadow settings help set the text off from the background image. Still you can give it a little more help by creating a background box.

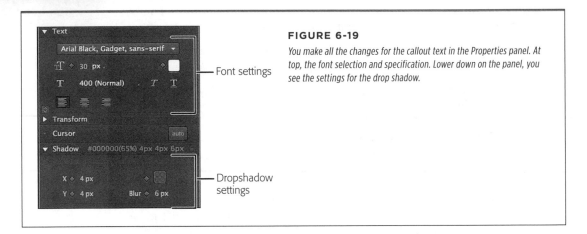

FIGURE 6-19

You make all the changes for the callout text in the Properties panel. At top, the font selection and specification. Lower down on the panel, you see the settings for the drop shadow.

4. With the Rectangle tool (M), draw a box around the text.

   Initially, your box hides the text, but you can fix that in the Elements panel. Your rectangle may be named something like Rectangle3 or Rectangle4. That's Animate's way of providing unique names for each element.

5. In the Elements panel, drag the Rectangle below the text box tbPoppy.

   If both the rectangle and the text box are white, it may be still a bit hard to see the text.

6. In Properties, change the rectangle's ID to bgPoppy, and change the Opacity to something between 40% and 50%.

   Now the callout looks pretty good. You can adjust the rectangle's edges or use Modify→Align commands to tighten things up.

7. Select both the tbPoppy and bgPoppy and right-click and choose "Group Element in DIV" from the shortcut menu. Name the group coPoppy (for callout Poppy).

   With the two elements grouped you can position, show and hide them as a single element.

8. With your newly created coPoppy group selected, set the Display property to Off at 0:00.

   You want the callout hidden when the animation begins. The hotspot hsPoppy will control whether or not the callout is visible.

9. Right-click the hsPoppy and choose Open Actions for "hsPoppy". Choose the mouseover trigger.

   The actions panel opens. When you choose the mouseover trigger a tab is created for the mouseover action.

10. On the right side of the actions panel, click Show Element.

    Generic Show Element code is added to the actions code.

    ```
    sym.$("Text1").show();
    ```

11. In the code, change "Text1" to "coPoppy".

    With the mouseover code reading:

    ```
    sym.$("coPoppy").show();
    ```

    The coPoppy callout will appear when the cursor is over the hotspot hsPoppy. Next step: Make it go away when the cursor moves off the hotspot.

12. In the upper-left corner of the actions panel, click the + button and choose the mouseout trigger.

    A new tab opens for mouseout actions.

13. On the right, click Hide Element. When the code appears, change "Text1" to "coPoppy".

    The mouseout code should read:

    ```
    sym.$("coPoppy").hide();
    ```

14. Hit Esc to close the actions panel. Press Ctrl+S (⌘-S) to save your work. Then press Ctrl+Enter (⌘-Return) to preview the project in a browser.

    When you preview the project, the callout that says Iceland Poppy should appear when the mouse is over the poppy. You can use the button controls at the bottom to control the filmstrip. At this point your hotspots are still visible. That's helpful for this stage of previewing, checking, and tweaking.

It shouldn't be hard to repeat the steps needed to create callouts for the remaining photos, as shown in Figure 6-20. In the cases where more than one flower visible, you can create several hotspots that show and hide a single callout. You don't need to turn on and off the callouts at particular points in the timeline, because they are controlled entirely by the triggers in the hotspots. Make sure all the callouts are turned off at 0:00. You don't want them showing up until someone mouses over a hotspot.

FIGURE 6-20

Here the rose hotspot is selected and the mouseover code is displayed. This code shows the callout that displays "A Pink Rose" on the screen. The mouseout code hides it.

Once you're done, check your callouts and actions. Make sure the hotspots are on and off at the right time. Check the spelling of your callouts. You may want to tweak the position or shape of different elements.

After you've created and tested all your hotspot triggers and actions and you're happy with everything, it's time to hide those hotspots. In the Library→Symbols panel, right-click hotspot. When hotspot opens for editing, select the rectangle and set the Opacity to 0. Because all the hotspot instances were made from a single hotspot symbol, you only have to make this change once. Exit the hotspot symbol by clicking Stage in the upper-left corner of the stage. Now, if you preview your animation, all the hotspots should be invisible.

Changing the Cursor to Provide User Feedback

As everyone learned the first time they visited a web page, a pointing-finger cursor indicates an item you can click, like a button or link. You can add cursor feedback as a finishing touch for the buttons and flower hotspots on your filmstrip animation. Fortunately, Animate has a tool that helps you do that in a snap. Make sure you're back at the main stage and timeline, then follow these two steps:

1. In the Elements panel, select the buttons StartOver and NextFlower.

2. Click the Properties→Cursor button and choose the pointing finger.

It's that easy to change the cursor property when it's over a button. Animate automatically creates both a mouseover and mouseout behavior. Because you selected two buttons, you're applying the behavior to both.

All the hotspots were made from a single symbol, so you can change the behavior of the one main symbol or you can select all the instances as you did with the buttons. Here's the way to change the main symbol:

1. In the Library→Symbol panel, right-click *hotspot* and choose Edit from the shortcut menu.

   The symbol opens for editing.

2. In Elements, select the rectangle.

   The rectangle's properties appear in the Properties panel.

3. Click the Cursor button and choose the question mark (?) cursor.

Now when the animation is running and the cursor is over a button, your audience sees the pointing finger. When the cursor is over a flower, they see a question mark, and the callout that answers the question, as shown in Figure 6-21.

FIGURE 6-21

The working model of the filmstrip with callouts is easy to use but provides plenty of user control and feedback. Here with the cursor over a flower hotspot, the cursor changes to a question mark and the callout identifies the flower. The buttons at the bottom give users control over the animation's playback.

Edge Animate with HTML5 and JavaScript

Working with Basic HTML and CSS

When you build a project, Animate automatically creates several different files. The Hypertext Markup Language file (.html) is the stuff web pages are made of. Web browsers read HTML files and display the results as web pages. The Cascading Style Sheet file (.css) supports HTML documents, providing formatting and positioning instructions. You don't have to be an HTML/CSS wizard to work with Animate. On the other hand, when you understand how HTML and CSS documents work, you're in a better position to customize your projects to meet your needs. Animate compositions live within the HTML/CSS environment, and your audience views your work in their web browsers. In some cases, the files that Animate produces will be all you'll need. In other instances, your Animate composition may be just a part of a larger page. For example, your project may be a banner ad. Knowledge of HTML and CSS helps you when it comes to sizing and positioning your project.

In this chapter, you'll learn how to read and interpret HTML and CSS documents. Along the way, you'll see how HTML's *IDs* and *classes* are used to identify elements on the web page. Toward the end of the chapter, you'll learn how to open and animate elements in existing web pages and how to position your Animate composition in another web page.

■ Reading HTML Documents

It's not hard to learn how to read HTML. If you've spent any quality time developing web pages, you likely have some skills. You can open an HTML document in any simple text editor like Notepad (Windows) or TextEdit (Mac). Nearly any web browser lets you view the source of the current web page. Just right-click (Control-click) on the page and choose View Source from the shortcut menu. The code behind complex web pages can be stunningly long and cryptic. However, once you know the basics, you can tackle a page chunk by chunk. With some practice, you can get a good idea of what's going on behind the scenes.

At its simplest, a complete "Hello World" web page might look like this:

```
<!DOCTYPE html>
<html>
<head>
    <title>Hello World</title>
</head>
<body style="margin:10px;">
    Hello World
</body>
</html>
```

Web pages are made up of different elements, sometimes referred to as nodes. Like all web pages, this document has a *head* element and a *body* element. Often the head holds special details that don't appear on the page. For example, the head is likely to hold style information that is applied to content in the body. Savvy web designers use special tags in the head portion of a page to provide a description of the page and a list of keywords. These details may be used by search engines to categorize the page. Sometimes, the head holds script tags that point to files of JavaScript code that performs some sort of automation or animation magic. Other times, the actual code may be present in the head portion of a page. CSS formatting instructions work in a similar way: There may be a reference to an external CSS file, or the formatting instruction may be placed in the page itself. The body holds the actual content that's displayed on the web page. This is where text, pictures, and your Animate compositions appear.

Playing Tag the HTML Way

If you want words to appear on a web page, all you need to do is place your text in the body portion of the document. For example, see the "Hello World" message on line 7? For this simplest of HTML documents, those words are the only thing that would appear in the document window. So what's with those brackets and all that other stuff? Those are tags. They don't show up on the web page, but they provide necessary information to web browsers. Tags are differentiated from content by their angle brackets (< >). Tags usually come in pairs, like the ones on line 4:

```
<title>Hello World</title>
```

These tags give the web page a title, and most browsers stick that title on the tab or title bar for the web page. The first tag lets the browser know that what follows is the title for this web page. The second tag is identical, except for its slash mark (/). That tag says to the browser, "OK, that's the end of the title." As you can see from a quick look at lines 3 and 5, it's common for one element to be completely inside another. In this case, the <title> element is a "child" of the <head> element, which in turn is a child of the <html> element.

Occasionally, you'll come across a single tag. For example, the tag for a line break in text is <br/>. Notice that in this case, the slash comes right before the last bracket.

> **TIP** A big part of being able to make sense of HTML code is knowing all the official tags and what they do. If you're looking for a cheat sheet, pick up *HTML & XHTML Pocket Reference* by Jennifer Niederst Robbins (O'Reilly). If you want a complete manual for learning the latest, greatest version of HTML, turn to *HTML5: The Missing Manual* by Matthew MacDonald (O'Reilly).

The first line of the code on the previous page is a single tag but an important one. It tells browsers what type of a document follows. That way the browser knows how to interpret all those tags. HTML is certainly the most popular DOCTYPE these days, but you might also come across xml or xhtml. Sometimes you'll see a version number displayed as in HTML 4.0 and other details. These generally aren't necessary for your Animate projects. Previous versions of HTML and XHTML used more complicated DOCTYPE details, but with HTML5, a simple "HTML" is all that you need.

The last thing to examine in the "Hello World" code is line 6. Here the <body> tag includes the attribute: style="margin:10px;". In this case, the attribute is named style and it sets the margin for the body of the web page. Attributes appear within the brackets of opening tags. The attribute name is followed by the assignment operator (=), which then assigns values to the attribute. Values appear inside quotes, which may be either double (") or single ('). In Animate, when you set the property for an element, often behind the scenes, Animate is setting the value for an attribute. The width and height of an image, the color and style of text—these are all attributes of specific elements.

> **TIP** Animate uses HTML tags, too. Select an element, and next to the name, you see the related tag. Often, you'll see the generic but versatile <div> tag. For a list of the common tags seen in Animate, turn to page 68.

Creating a Hyperlink with HTML

If there's one thing that's made HTML king of the World Wide Web, it's the hyperlink. Hyperlinks are the threads that form that web. Click a linked word, and suddenly you're in a different part of the universe (or at least, the Web). You create the links using the <a> anchor tags. Here's an example of a hyperlink:

```
<a href="http://www.stutzbearcat.net">click me</a>
```

Like most HTML tags, the anchor tag comes in pairs: *<a>in between stuff</a>*. In this case, the *href* attribute provides a web address. The *href* stands for hypertext reference; the equals sign assigns a value to the reference inside double quotes. The specific value here is a web address. The words in between the two <a> tags, "click me," are visible and clickable in the browser window. Depending on the tag's formatting, they may appear underlined or highlighted in some way to show that they're a link.

```
<font face="Cooper Black" size="3"> Home of the <em>legendary</em>
<strong>Stutz Bearcat</strong></font>
```

When a web browser like Chrome, Safari, Firefox, or Internet Explorer reads this text, it knows how to display the text in the browser window. For most browsers, the <em> tags indicate italics. Think emphasize. The <strong> tags specify bold text. The browser applies the formatting instructions and shows the text. It displays the proper typeface if it's available; otherwise it uses a substitute font. So HTML coding works fine from the audience's point of view. For designers, it can be a bit of a pain. One of the problems of HTML coding is that the message gets a bit lost in the formatting tags. Complicated HTML coding is hard for human eyes to read, and that makes it easy to foul up. When you want to make changes, it's a lot of work to go in there and tweak all those bits of embedded code. The solution? CSS to the rescue.

■ Reading CSS Files

CSS is the acronym for *Cascading Style Sheets*—an ingenious system for formatting HTML text. As the Web has matured, CSS has taken on more and more responsibilities. In HTML5, the role of CSS is even greater. If you want to read up on how CSS works, you can get an excellent introduction in David Sawyer McFarland's *CSS: The Missing Manual* (O'Reilly). A basic understanding of CSS will help you when you're working with Animate. Animate uses CSS behind the scenes to format and position elements. This book provides a quick overview of CSS and an example or two to get you started.

Formatting and style information can be stored in three different locations, as explained in the box on page 162. As the Web grew and pages became more sophisticated, new and better methods were developed to dress up those pages. These days, the fashionable technique is to use a separate Cascading Style Sheet (.css document) to format web pages. A line in the head of the HTML document links the style sheet definitions to the web page. It might look like this:

```
<link rel="stylesheet" href="barebones_edge.css" />
```

The link tag is a single tag; there's no corresponding end tag. The link tag is used to link more than just CSS files, so the *rel* (relationship) attribute is used to define the linked file as a style sheet. The *href* attribute points to the CSS file which, in this case, is named *barebones_edge.css*. There's no path in this case, because the CSS file is in the same folder as the HTML file. If the CSS document is in a different folder, a standard path description is needed with the filename. For example, if there's a special folder that holds all the CSS files, the complete path and name might be *css/barebones_edge.css.*

The underlying philosophy is that it's best to separate the formatting from the content. You create styles (type specs) for body text, major headlines, subheads, captions, and so forth. You store those definitions in a style sheet. Then, in the text, you tag different portions, indicating the styles they should use. In effect, you say: "This is a major headline, this is body text, and this is a caption." When the browser goes to display your web page, it comes to the text tagged as a headline, and then it looks up the type specs in the style sheet. It does the same thing for the body text and the captions. From a designer's point of view, this system is a tremendous timesaver. If you want to change the caption style for a website that has 400 captioned pictures, all you need to do is edit one definition in the style sheet. If all those type specs were embedded HTML code, you'd need to make 400 separate edits.

CSS style sheets are a little like those wooden Russian dolls where each one is nested inside another. Starting from the outside and working in, here's what you find in a CSS style sheet. A style sheet is a list of formatting specifications. Each formatting spec has a selector that identifies the HTML tag that it formats. That tag could be the paragraph tag <p>, the heading tag <h1>, or an anchor tag <a>. In CSS lingo, the formatting spec is called a *declaration block.* The declaration block is contained inside curly braces {}. Within those curly braces are specific declarations that define fonts, styles, colors, sizes, and all the other properties that can be defined in CSS. The declarations have two parts: a property and a value. So in CSS, if that property is *font-size*, then the value is a number representing the size. A CSS definition to format an <h1> heading tag might look like this:

```
h1 {
font-family: Arial;
font-size:18px;
font-weight: bold;
color: red;
}
```

The first line has the selector for *h1* headings, usually the biggest, boldest heading on a web page. The next four lines show pairs of properties and values. On the left side of the colon is the property, which is hyphenated if it's made up of more than one word. On the right side is the value assigned to that property.

Applying CSS Styles to Element IDs and Classes

You've seen how you can connect CSS styles to particular tags, like the heading1 tag <h1> or a paragraph tag <p>. Those formatting specs affect all of the headings and paragraphs that use the tag. But what if you only want to change the appearance of a specific heading or paragraph? That's the job for an ID or a class. You can give any element on the page an ID. That's exactly what Animate does behind the scenes when you name an element. Use IDs for elements that appear only once on the page. If you create a *LeftSidebar* ID, you can have only one *LeftSidebar* on the page. That's just how IDs work. If you need to apply a style to more than one element on the page, you can create a *class*. You can apply a single class name to several elements. For example, perhaps you're creating pull quote boxes (teasers that boldly display a line or two of text pulled from the main body of your document). So you specify a big, bold font and create text boxes that float on the right side of the page. Now you can create a *PullQuote* class and apply that to any chunk of text that you want to display those properties.

You assign a specific ID or class to an element through a tag attribute. For example, maybe you'd like to give a sales pitch its own ID. In the body of your HTML document, it might look like this:

```
<p id="pitch">What can I do to put you in a Stutz Bearcat today?</p>
```

Then in your CSS file, there'd be a definition for the *pitch* ID:

```
#pitch {
font-family: Arial;
font-size:18px;
font-weight: bold;
color: red;
}
```

CODERS' CLINIC

Three Places for Style Specs

There's more than one place to provide style and formatting details when you build a web page.

- **Inline styles.** As shown on page 160, formatting and style details can be interspersed with the HTML code and web page content. This method is considered old school and not used much today, except for an occasional bold or italic markup. It's also helpful for those cases where a particular element requires some exceptional formatting that isn't part of the template or previously defined styles.

- **Internal style sheet.** CSS styles can be listed in the head of the HTML document. In this case, the style specifications are separate from the content that they format. The listed style definitions are used only in the document in which they appear. This method is fine for standalone or unique pages.

- **External style sheet.** Styles can be stored in a separate document with a filename that ends in *.css*. This external style sheet contains only style definitions and no content. If it's helpful, the file may also include comments. A single style sheet can be applied to many HTML documents.

This is great when you have a big website with dozens of pages, many of which have a similar appearance. Also useful, a single document can have more than one style sheet applied to it.

When you build an Animate project, Animate creates CSS styles on the fly to format and position the elements. In Edge Preview 3 and earlier, actual style sheet files were created. In later versions, these details are hidden from view. HTML permits the use of multiple style sheets for a single page, so, if necessary, you can create another external CSS file to format other parts of your web page.

What happens when the same element has conflicting styles? Say a paragraph <p> element has an inline style applied to it, but there are also styles for <p> in an internal or external style sheet? CSS is designed so that the styles closest to the content take precedence. So an inline style will override the styles listed in the head of document , and that internal style sheet overrides an external style sheet saved as a separate file. This is a good method because it makes it easy to override a style occasionally. However, if your pages aren't behaving as expected, it's worth double-checking for CSS conflicts.

The pound sign (#) is what distinguishes an ID from any other tag. The process for defining a class is similar. If you want to apply a class named *pause* to a paragraph of text, it would look like this:

```
<p class="pause">Hang on a second. Let me check that price with my manager.
</p>
```

Then, in your CSS file, there'd be a definition for the *pause* class. And of course, that class might be applied to more than one paragraph. In the definition, it's the preceding period (.) that signals that a definition is for a class.

```
.pause {
font-family: Times;
font-size:12px;
font-weight: bold;
color: black;
}
```

The cascading aspect of CSS gives designers a double dose of formatting power. Suppose your web page has two main sections: the body and a sidebar. The body has a white background color, and the sidebar's background is a dark blue to set it off from the body. You're going to need a different font color for those two places. CSS has a solution. In effect, you can say, "When a paragraph is in the body, make the font color black. When a paragraph is in the sidebar, make the font color white." You create those instructions in your style sheet, like this:

```
body p {
font-family: Times;
font-size:12px;
font-weight: bold;
color: black;
}

#sidebar p {
font-family: Times;
font-size:12px;
font-weight: bold;
color: white;
}
```

In this way, that simple paragraph <p> tag takes on different characteristics depending on where it's located.

Reading the HTML Animate Creates

When you're in Animate and you choose File→Save, Animate creates several files, including an HTML file that describes a web page with your composition. You can open that HTML file and read the contents. You may be surprised to see that there's actually not a lot of code inside. For the most part, it's made up of links to other files that make your composition work. Here's the HTML from a bare-bones Animate project:

```
<!DOCTYPE html>
<html>
<head>
    <meta http-equiv="Content-Type" content="text/html; charset=utf-8">
    <title>Bare Bones</title>
<!--Adobe Edge Runtime-->
    <script type="text/javascript" charset="utf-8" src="07%20bare%20bones_
edgePreload.js"></script>
    <style>
        .edgeLoad-EDGE-27259565 { visibility:hidden; }
    </style>
<!--Adobe Edge Runtime End-->

</head>
<body style="margin:0;padding:0;">
    <div id="Stage" class="EDGE-27259565 edgeLoad-EDGE-27259565">
    </div>
</body>
</html>
```

The first line declares that it is an HTML5 document. Everything else is inside the two <html> tags. At the next level, the page has the two standard elements, <head> and <body>. The <head> includes a <title>. In this case, the text reads *Bare Bones.* The rest of the head fits in between two HTML comment tags: The first comment reads <!--Adobe Edge Runtime-->. The last reads <!--Adobe Edge Runtime End-->. Between these comments are statements that link a JavaScript (.js) file using the <script> tag. As you might guess from the word "Preload" in the name, this JavaScript code loads resources that Animate needs. Specifically, the preloader identifies other JavaScript files and libraries, some of which are in the *edge_includes* folder. Animate created all these files when you performed that Save command, and in many cases you don't have to mess with them. You won't need to change the links in this HTML document, unless you do something like move the files. And in most cases, you won't edit the external files. In fact, keep your hands off the four JavaScript files in the *edge_includes* folder. They contain the code that makes Animate compositions do their magic. They have names like:

- edge.0.1.6.min.js

- jquery.easing.1.3.js

- jquery-1.7.1.min.js

- json2_min.js

On the other hand, once you become proficient in JavaScript/jQuery, you may find yourself making changes to the JavaScript files that are in the same folder as your HTML document. If you save a project named *Bare_Bones*, you'll find these Java-Script files along with your .html web page and .edge project files:

- Bare_Bones_edge.js

- Bare_Bones_edgeActions.js

- Bare_Bones_edgePreload.js

You'll learn more about tweaking these guys in Chapters 8 and 9. In general, Animate is pretty good about placing warnings at the beginning of files you shouldn't edit and providing tips for making changes to the others.

NOTE The box on page 103 describes two types of comments shared by JavaScript and other programming languages like C. The <!-- and --> tags are used by HTML. These particular tags are useful with JavaScript. They provide a way to deliver JavaScript commands to browsers ready to handle JavaScript. If a browser isn't able to handle JavaScript, the commands are ignored—treated like comments.

◼ Opening an HTML Document in Animate

Want to apply some Animate magic to a web page that already has elements in place? You can do that by opening an existing document in Animate. For example, consider this web page, which isn't all that much more complex than the original "Hello World" example.

```
<!DOCTYPE html>
<html>
<head>
<title>Stutz Bearcat Sales</title>
</head>
<body>
<h1 id="headline">Stutz Bearcat Sales</h1>
<p><img src="images/StutzBearcat.png" alt-"The amazing Stutz Bearcat
automobile" name="bearcat" id="bearcat" /></p>
<p id="pitch">What can I do to put you in a Bearcat today?</p>
<p id="pause">Hang on a second. Let me check that price with my manager.</p>
</body>
</html>
```

This web page has three bits of text. One has a heading <h1> tag. The other two have paragraph <p> tags. There's also one image on the page with a source .png graphic identified. All the elements, both text and image, have IDs applied. You don't have to do this, but it does make it easier to identify the elements inside Animate. Animate doesn't provide a way to change IDs of elements once you've opened the HTML in Animate. In Animate, content that you create using Animate tools is called managed content. Content that is created outside of Animate is static content. In the Elements panel, move the cursor over an element's name; after a moment a tooltip appears. If it's static content, you see ("static") at the end of the element's name. In the Properties panel, you see a limited number of properties available for animation within Animate.

Open the page in a browser, and it looks like Figure 7-1.

FIGURE 7-1

Here's the simple web page that matches the code above. It consists of three blocks of text and the image of a snazzy auto. You can load this page in Animate and manipulate each of the elements.

If you want to experiment with opening an HTML document in Animate, get the Missing CD file *07-1_Load_HTML.html*.

1. In Animate, open *07-1_Load_HTML.html*.

   The Elements panel shows the elements existing in the HTML document (Figure 7-2), listing their IDs and tags.

2. Click the car on the stage.

   The Properties panel shows the image's properties such as Width, Height, and Opacity. The car's HTML ID (bearcat) appears at the top of the Properties, but it is grayed out. You're unable to rename a static element (that is, change its ID). You're also unable to change the element's tag. You can do those things only with elements that you've created inside Animate.

3. In the Elements panel, click "headline."

The Properties panel shows the same properties that were available for the image, as shown in Figure 7-3. However, the properties that you'd expect to see in a text box are missing. No Font, Size, or Color properties are available. In fact, you can't even change the text in the headline or the two paragraphs. If you need access to those properties in Animate, then you need to create text boxes inside Animate.

FIGURE 7-2

Give IDs to the elements in your HTML document when you create it in your favorite web-building tool. Then when you open that HTML in Animate, you see the IDs as element names. Here, headline, bearcat, pitch, and pause are all element IDs.

TIP   If you change your HTML file in a separate editor while it's open in Animate, you'll be prompted to reload the page in Animate. Most of the time, you'll want to do that. But beware, you'll lose any unsaved changes or animation you've applied to the project.

4. Animate the car.

You may want to start by making the car smaller; about 200 px wide works well. Then create a transition that moves the car across the stage. (See page 82 if you need to review the techniques to create a motion transition.)

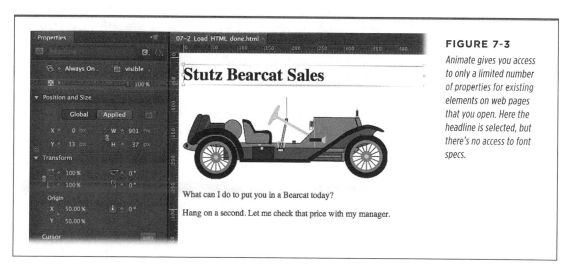

FIGURE 7-3

Animate gives you access to only a limited number of properties for existing elements on web pages that you open. Here the headline is selected, but there's no access to font specs.

5. Animate the headline and paragraphs.

Perhaps you want the headline to drop in from the top of the page. The two paragraphs are hidden at the beginning of the animation. Then the pitch appears first: "What can I do to put you in a Bearcat today?" Shortly, the pause paragraph appears saying: "Hang on a second. Let me check that price with my manager."

You can use many of the Animate animation tricks you've learned on elements in a pre-existing document. You just need to work with the properties that are exposed in Animate. If you want to provide interaction, you can use triggers and actions, as described in Chapter 5. For an example, check out *07-2_Load_HTML_done*.

You save your Animate-altered HTML file as you would any Animate project. When you do, Animate creates the usual suspects: JavaScript files. If you take a peek inside the HTML file after you've saved it in Animate, you'll see that it didn't change very much. Animate adds the usual links to external files mentioned in the box on page 181. The body of the document remains as it was originally.

TIP As of this writing, it wasn't possible to add a link to a few words inside a text box created with the Text tool without digging into JavaScript/jQuery code. You can add a link to the entire text box, but not specific words within. One workaround for this is to create text in an HTML file like the example above. Make your links before you open the HTML in Animate. The only drawback is that you will not be able to edit the text inside Animate. For the JavaScript/jQuery way to create a link within text, see the box on page 211.

■ Placing Your Composition in an HTML Document

You won't always be content to create entire web pages inside Animate. For example, suppose you want to create a banner ad in Animate. You'll want to place the ad on a web page that has other content. The banner ad is just one element on the web page. Horizontal banner ads usually appear at the top of the page. They may need to be centered or float to the left or the right. If you're in the mood to experiment, you can use *07-3_Banner_Ad* from the Missing CD.

Here's the process. First you create your banner ad in Animate in the normal manner. If you're making a horizontal banner like the one in Figure 7-4, the stage dimensions might be something like 468 × 60 pixels. When you save your project, Animate creates all the usual files. You'll want to copy all the files and folders in your Animate project to the folder on your website that holds HTML files.

In your favorite HTML editor, open the page where you want to place your Animate composition. In another window of your HTML editor, open the page that you created in Animate. What you're going to do next is really just a simple cut-and-paste operation. In the Animate file, find and copy the code that launches the preloader.

As explained on page 164, that code is in the head of the HTML file that Animate creates, and it is between two comment tags that look like this:

```
<!--Adobe Edge Runtime-->
```

and

```
<!--Adobe Edge Runtime End-->
```

For example, if your project was saved with the name Bare_Bones, the complete code that you need to copy looks like this:

```
<!--Adobe Edge Runtime-->

<script type="text/javascript" charset="utf-8" src="Bare_Bones_edgePreload.js"></script>

<!--Adobe Edge Runtime End-->
```

Copy the comments and everything that's in between them, and paste the lot into the head of your target web page.

FIGURE 7-4

Animate projects like this banner ad don't usually stand alone on a web page. You're likely to create Animate projects that end up sharing space on a web page with other elements.

NOTE Versions of Edge Animate before Preview 4 didn't use a preloader. In place of the preloader reference, you'd see several lines of code. Still, the procedure is the same: Copy the two comment tags and everything in between.

Next, in the body of the HTML file that Animate created, find the <div> tag with the *stage* ID. It looks something like this:

```
<div id="Stage" class="EDGE-225049589 edgeLoad-EDGE-225049589">
    </div>
```

Again, copy the tags and everything in between. This time, paste the code into the body of your web page. Close the Animate HTML file, and you can save or continue editing the web page. If you open your HTML page now, you'll find that the ad shows up where you placed it in the code. In most cases, you'll want to place it with more precision using CSS positioning tools. What you need to do is create a definition for the element with the *Stage* id. As explained on page 162, that code needs to be in the header for the page or in an external .css file that's linked to the page.

Here's an example:

```
#stage {

    margin: 4px;
    float: right;
    overflow: hidden;
    position: absolute;
    top: 200px;
}
```

CSS provides a number of properties that can be used to position elements on a web page. This definition gives the stage element a margin of 4 pixels. The float command positions the banner on the right side of the page. Overflow is set to "hidden" so elements outside of the stage don't appear. The position property is set to "absolute," which works well if other elements on the page are positioned in a similar manner. You can also use relative positioning if other page elements are "liquid." The last line in the definition moves the banner ad down 200 pixels from the top of the page.

NOTE For more details on CSS and positioning elements with CSS, see David Sawyer McFarland's *CSS: The Missing Manual* (O'Reilly).

■ Centering an Animate Composition

Frequently, you'll want to center your Animate composition on a page so it plays well with the existing elements, like the ones in Figure 7-5. You don't know the exact size of the window, so you can't simply use a *margin-left* value. Naturally, if the window width changes, you want your Animate composition to accommodate that change. This project is available on the Missing CD, *07-4_Centering_Composition_done*. Again, it's the code in the external CSS file (book.css) that does the magic. You can view and edit CSS files with any simple text editor. Here's the code that positions the Animate composition, which has the ID *Stage*.

```
#Stage {
    display: block;
    width: 468px;
    margin-left: auto;
    margin-right: auto;
}
```

The *Stage* ID is listed first. Then the properties all appear in between the curly braces. The property name is listed followed by a colon, followed by the property value. The display property is set to *block*, which means the element will be treated like a block (think of a block of text). Next, the width of the composition is provided. Don't forget to provide a unit of measure when giving dimensions. Finally, the important properties: *margin-left* and *margin-right*. When these properties are set to *auto*, the element is automatically centered and will adjust its position when the browser window changes dimensions.

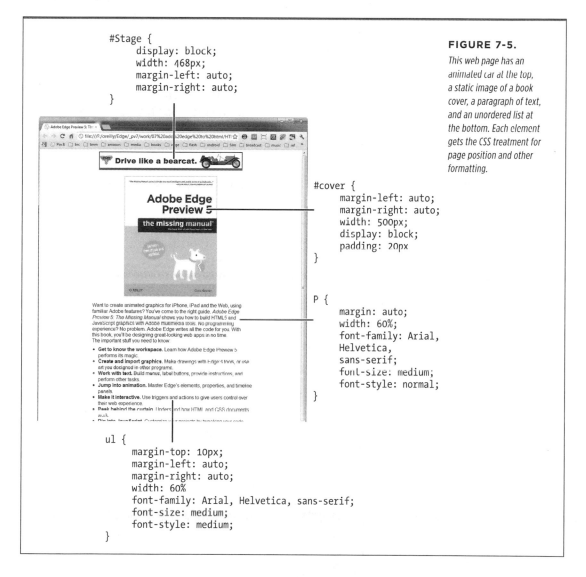

```
#Stage {
        display: block;
        width: 468px;
        margin-left: auto;
        margin-right: auto;
}
```

```
#cover {
        margin-left: auto;
        margin-right: auto;
        width: 500px;
        display: block;
        padding: 20px
}
```

```
P {
        margin: auto;
        width: 60%;
        font-family: Arial,
        Helvetica,
        sans-serif;
        font-size: medium;
        font-style: normal;
}
```

```
ul {
        margin-top: 10px;
        margin-left: auto;
        margin-right: auto;
        width: 60%
        font-family: Arial, Helvetica, sans-serif;
        font-size: medium;
        font-style: medium;
}
```

FIGURE 7-5.

This web page has an animated car at the top, a static image of a book cover, a paragraph of text, and an unordered list at the bottom. Each element gets the CSS treatment for page position and other formatting.

Placing Two Animate Compositions on the Same Page

Once you get used to all the features that Animate provides, you'll want to use it for all sorts of projects big and small. Sooner or later, you'll want to place two or more Animate compositions on a single web page. For example, suppose you have a page with an existing Animate composition that displays several book covers. When a web visitor clicks a book, with a little animation magic, it presents a large image of the book cover along with a sales pitch, as shown in Figure 7-6. To increase revenue, you decide to add a banner ad for the ever-popular Stutz Bearcat; you previously used this banner ad in a web page with a single composition (page 168). Putting two Animate compositions in one HTML document is best done outside of Animate in your HTML editor. So, roll up your HTML coder sleeves and get ready for some hand editing. To get started on this project, go to the Missing CD page (*www.missingmanuals.com/cds/animatemm*) and find the *07-5_Two_Compositions* file. It provides the original web page with the book's animation. You'll also want to get the *07-3_Banner_Ad* project, which is the second Animate composition that you'll add to the two compositions page.

Here are the chores you need to tackle when placing two Animate compositions on one page:

- In the head of your HTML document, add the preloader code for both compositions.

- In the body of your HTML document, add the <div> code that identifies the two compositions.

- Edit the <div> code so that each composition has a unique ID.

- Use your standard HTML or CSS tricks to position the compositions where you want them on the web page.

FIGURE 7-6

Here's a page with an Animate composition.

Left: Click on one of the books.

Right: With a little animated flourish, the page shows the cover and displays some details about the book. If you want to add another Animate composition such as a banner ad to the top of the page, you have to do some HTML hand-coding.

It's easiest if you start with a web page that already has one composition in place and working properly. That's exactly what you have in *07-5_Two_Compositions*. Open the HTML file in a browser, and you'll see it in action. The results should look like Figure 7-6. Here's the step-by-step process for adding the banner ad from page 168 to the top of this existing web page:

1. Examine the HTML and JavaScript files used to display the books page (*07-5_Two_Compositions*).

   The web page has the filename *07-5_Two_Compositions.html*. You see evidence of the existing Animate composition in *books.html*, *books_edge.js,* and other JavaScript files that make the project work. In addition, there's an *edge_includes* folder and an *images* folder. If you look in the *images* folder, you see a number of large and small JPGs for the book covers.

2. Add the files for the Stutz Bearcat banner ad (page 168) to the folder holding the books project.

   Copy all the files in the *07-3_Banner_Ad* folder to the folder with *07-5_Two_Compositions.html.* Copy all the images in the banner ad images folder to the book project *images* folder. Be careful; you don't want to delete or write over any of the existing images. You're going to need the images for both projects in this one folder. In this case, all the images have unique names. You don't need to copy the files in the *edge_includes* folder; they should be identical, as long as both projects were created with the same version of Animate.

3. Open *07-5_Two_Compositions.html* in your HTML editor. Then find the place in the <head> where the preloader for books is identified.

   It looks like this.

   ```
   <!--Adobe Edge Runtime-->

       <script type="text/javascript" charset="utf-8" src="books_edgePreload.
   js"></script>

       <style>

           .edgeLoad-EDGE-3521704 { visibility:hidden; }

       </style>

   <!--Adobe Edge Runtime End-->
   ```

4. Add a line in between the comments to identify the preloader for your second Animate composition.

   It's easiest to cut and paste lines of code; that way, you're less likely to make a mistake. In this case, you can open the file for the banner (*07-3_Banner_Ad.html*) to copy the line. Then, paste the result into *07-5_Two_Compositions.html*. When you're done it should look like this:

```
<!--Adobe Edge Runtime-->

<script type="text/javascript" src="http://ajax.googleapis.com/ajax/libs/
chrome-frame/1/CFInstall.min.js"></script>

    <script type="text/javascript" charset="utf-8" src="books_edgePreload.
js"></script>

    <style>

        .edgeLoad-EDGE-3521704 { visibility:hidden; }

    </style>

    <script type="text/javascript" charset="utf-8" src="07-3_Banner_Ad_edge-
Preload.js"></script>

    <style>

        .edgeLoad-EDGE-34947207 { visibility:hidden; }

    </style>

<!--Adobe Edge Runtime End-->
```

5. In the body portion of the banner ad HTML code, find and copy the line that provides an ID for the <div> tag and paste that into the books.html code.

You want your banner add to be at the top of the page, so you can paste it immediately underneath the <div class="content"> tag, above the rest of the HTML code. For example:

```
<div class="container">

  <div class="content">

    <div id="Stage" class="EDGE-34947207 edgeLoad-EDGE-34947207">

    </div>
```

There's still one issue that needs to be resolved. You may remember that an ID attribute like the one shown here must be unique. For example, there can be only one "Stage" ID on this page. The solution is to change the names of the two stage IDs to stageOne and stageTwo or something more meaningful to your project.

NOTE There's a number in the class attribute for the <div> that looks like: *class="Edge-225049589"*. This number changes with every project and is used by Animate for its own nefarious, identification purposes. So don't worry if your numbers are different from the ones in this book.

---

6. Give each composition a unique ID.

Change the ID to the banner ad:

```
<div id="Stage" class="EDGE-225049589"></div>
```

to

```
<div id="bannerStutz" class="EDGE-225049589"></div>
```

Then, change the ID for the book composition:

```
<div id="stage" class="EDGE-6141218">
```

```
</div>
```

to

```
<div id="galleryBooks" class="EDGE-6141218">
```

```
</div>
```

7. Open the *two_comps.css* file in a text or HTML editor. Add a definition for both #bannerStutz and #galleryBooks that centers the compositions in the browser. They should look like this:

```
#bannerStutz {

    margin: auto;

}

#galleryBooks {

    margin: auto;

}
```

The file *two_comps.css* is referenced as an external CSS style sheet in *07-5_Two_Comps.html*. It provides rules for the H1 headers and body text. You can apply CSS rules to position and format the <div> elements that hold your Animate compositions.

The pound sign (#) signals that bannerStutz is an ID. The margin property sets all margin values: top, bottom, left, and right. Setting that property to auto centers the composition.

You can see the finished project with both compositions in place on a web page that includes other non-Animate content in *07-6_Two_Compositions_done* (Figure 7-7).

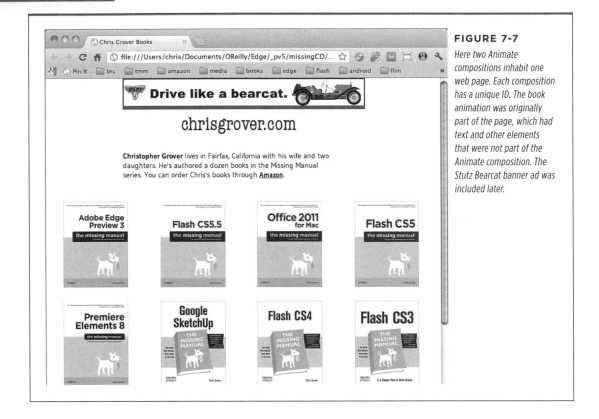

FIGURE 7-7

Here two Animate compositions inhabit one web page. Each composition has a unique ID. The book animation was originally part of the page, which had text and other elements that were not part of the Animate composition. The Stutz Bearcat banner ad was included later.

Controlling Your Animations with JavaScript and jQuery

I f you worked on some of the examples in Chapter 5, you've already dabbled in JavaScript and jQuery. When Animate creates triggers and actions, it produces JavaScript/jQuery code. Modern browsers all understand this code, and it works universally, unless someone has explicitly turned JavaScript off. Like the CSS code mentioned in Chapter 7, JavaScript can be interspersed within the HTML code for a web page, or a separate JavaScript (.js) file can be can be linked to the page.

This chapter isn't meant to be a complete study of JavaScript and jQuery, but it is meant to help you get started. You'll learn how to read the code that Animate produces, and you'll learn how you can tweak that code to customize your Animate compositions. Throughout, you'll find tips and techniques that help solve common issues when you're working in Animate. This chapter focuses mostly on JavaScript and jQuery theory. Chapter 9 explains how to put this theory into action.

■ A Very Brief History of JavaScript and jQuery

Once upon a time (in the 1990s), there was a company called Netscape, which de-livered one of the first widely used web browsers, Netscape Navigator. Soon, the company was in a death battle with another company called Microsoft, which put forth a competing browser called Internet Explorer. In an effort to keep a competitive edge over their nemesis, some Netscape wizards developed a scripting language that could be used to add automation and interactive features to web pages. The language had different names at different times, like Mocha and LiveScript, but the name that stuck was JavaScript. JavaScript was welcomed and widely used by the web-making masses. It proved to be so popular that Microsoft developed its own version, JScript...but that's another tale. At times, JavaScript suffered from all-too-familiar tech ailments: competing standards and implementation conflicts among browsers. (Translation: Microsoft's Internet Explorer behaves differently from every other browser.) As time went by, many of these issues were smoothed over. Support for JavaScript became more consistent among browsers. JavaScript libraries were developed, which made it easier for web designers to focus on building pages rather than dealing with browser inconsistencies. jQuery is one of the most popular libraries that serve this function. (Pardon the pun.) jQuery helped solve many other issues for JavaScript coders, truly living up to its motto: Write less, do more. With the advent of HTML5, many new and powerful tools were available for web building, and when combined, they were very powerful indeed. Web builders were happy, and the web page audience enjoyed visually entertaining and interactive experiences. Sadly, Netscape didn't survive, but JavaScript lives on.

JavaScript Versus ActionScript and Other Languages

If you're familiar with Flash and now you're adding Animate to your web-building toolbox, you're not alone. You'll find that JavaScript has a lot in common with ActionScript, Flash's programming language. Technically, they're both *scripting* languages, meaning that they're programming languages that run inside other environments—like web pages. On top of that, JavaScript and ActionScript both share the same programming language specification, ECMA-262.

> **NOTE** Since you're just dying to know, ECMA stands for European Computer Manufacturers Association, the standards group that established the spec.

Initially, programmers used both JavaScript and ActionScript in snippets to perform quick and easy chores. These snippets are similar to the triggers and actions in Animate. For example, in ActionScript, you'd write something like the following:

```
on (press) {
  startDrag(this);
}
```

Often, you'll find JavaScript interspersed throughout the HTML code that describes web pages. From a technical point of view, JavaScript and ActionScript are considered high-level languages, because they're closer to human language than the 1s and 0s of machine language.

■ Sleuthing Through the JavaScript Animate Creates

If you want to create a simple animation that runs from start to finish, you don't have to dig into JavaScript/jQuery code. However, if you want to add interactivity to your project or perform other magical feats, you'll want to add triggers and actions as explained in Chapter 5. If you want to modify those triggers and actions, you need to learn something about the way JavaScript and jQuery work. At first, programming and animation may feel like a curious match, since artists and programmers often seem to be such different people. But when you think about it, programming and drawing are both creative activities. Just like an artist, a programmer needs imagination and vision. And animation is a very programmatic visual art, complete with reusable chunks of action that branch off into separate scenes. On large creative teams, you'll find some people responsible for artwork and others responsible for code. However, there are plenty of small shops where the same person handles both duties.

One of the best ways to learn how JavaScript works is to read code. That's easy enough to do, and it's exactly where this chapter starts. You can begin by examining the code that Animate creates when you save a project. Then add an element or make a change, and examine the new code that Animate creates. Bit by bit, you can learn how certain chunks of code affect your project.

Follow these steps to see how this technique works:

1. Create a new Animate project and immediately save it with the name *Empty*.

    Animate creates HTML and JavaScript files.

2. Go to File→Preview In Browser.

    Your project opens in your web browser. Surprise—you see an empty page.

3. Right-click (Control-click) the web page in your browser and choose View Source (or View Page Source).

    Most browsers show the HTML code for a web page in a separate tab or window.

When you examine the source code for the empty web page, there's nothing much new that wasn't discussed in previous chapters. There's a <script> reference to the JavaScript preloader, *Empty_edgePreload.js*. The preloader is responsible for linking your project to all the resources it needs. Many of those are JavaScript libraries. For details, see the box on page 181. You won't be messing with the files in your *edge_includes* folder. Those are standard libraries, like jQuery. You want to examine the two JavaScript files that are specific to your project. Conveniently, they're in the same folder with the .html file for the page and the first part of the filename matches your project. So, as you see in the bottom of Figure 8-1, if your project name is "Empty," then the preloader filename is *Empty_edgePreloader.js*. If you inspect the preloader code at the bottom, you see an object called aLoader and its definition. Note the names of JavaScript files in the the definition, like *jquery-1.7.1.min.js*. These are files of JavaScript code that Edge Animate needs to do its magic. Another line that begins: loadResources(aLoader, doDelayLoad); is a function that makes use of the aLoader object. You can examine JavaScript files in some web browsers or in a text editor like Notepad (Windows) or TextEdit (Mac). Another option for viewing and editing HTML, CSS and JavaScript files is Adobe's Edge Code a sibling in the Edge family. You can get the application from the Adobe Creative Cloud (*http://creative.adobe.com*).

```
aLoader = [
    { load: "edge_includes/jquery-1.7.1.min.js"},
    { load: "edge_includes/jquery.easing.1.3.js"},
    { load: "edge_includes/edge.1.0.0.min.js"},
        {test: !hasJSON, yep:"edge_includes/json2_min.js"},
            { load: "Empty_edge.js"},
            { load: "Empty_edgeActions.js"}];

loadResources(aLoader, doDelayLoad);
```

TIP   Most browsers give you a way to view a web page's HTML source code. The command is usually View Source or View Page Source. If you're using Google Chrome for a browser, then after you choose View Page Source, you can click on the JavaScript filenames in the displayed code to view the JavaScript files in a new tab, as shown in Figure 8-2. This is a quick, handy way to study code, but you can't edit the files. Both Google Chrome and Mozilla Firefox have great developer tools that help you examine web pages and the files that make them work.

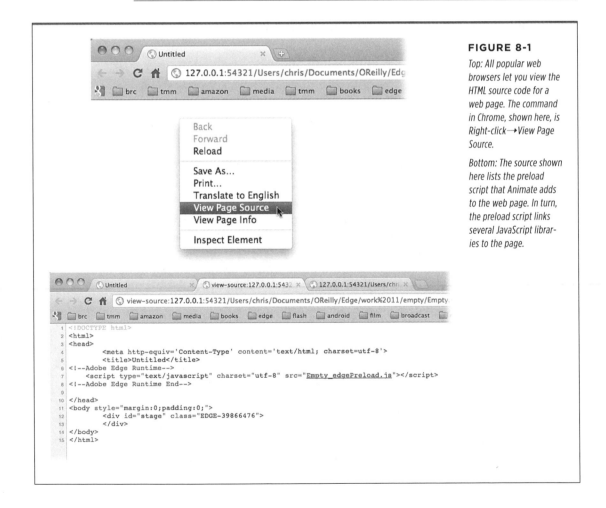

FIGURE 8-1

Top: All popular web browsers let you view the HTML source code for a web page. The command in Chrome, shown here, is Right-click→View Page Source.

Bottom: The source shown here lists the preload script that Animate adds to the web page. In turn, the preload script links several JavaScript libraries to the page.

Animate Project Files

As explained on page 1, when you save a project, Animate creates several files even if you don't do anything. What exactly are those files, and what do they do? Here's a quick rundown. Suppose you create and save a project named *Empty*. In the HTML file named *Empty.html*, you'll find a <script> tag that loads *Empty_edgePreLoad.js*. In turn, that preloader links to these files, though the version numbers may be different:

jquery-1.7.1.min.js. The official jQuery library. It includes all the routines that make it easy for you to write code that works with the whole spectrum of browsers that are out there. In addition, jQuery makes it easier to identify the elements on a web page. See the details on selectors, page 190.

jquery.easing.1.3.js. A plugin to the jQuery library that handles all those cool easing effects that you can use with transitions. This is a standard library, so if you're a JavaScript/jQuery wiz, you can use it outside Animate.

edge.1.0.0.min.js. The Edge Animate JavaScript library. When you create animations and other effects, the JavaScript code created refers to methods and functions in this library.

json2_min.js. A specialized JavaScript library that most often serves as a data interchange format.

If you want your web pages to load and display quickly in browsers, you want to minimize the amount of data that's loaded before the page appears. The JavaScript files with *min* in their names have been "minified," or made as small as possible. Upside: They load fast. Downside: They can't easily be read by humans. If you want to examine the readable jQuery source code, head over to *http://jquery.com*.

In general, you don't need to worry about the contents of these files. In fact, you're explicitly warned not to make any changes to them. They are safely tucked away in the *edge_includes* folder.

The other files that Animate creates are in the same folder as the HTML web page document. You can and should examine these files. As explained in this chapter, you can even tweak them a bit to make changes to your project. If you create the Empty project, you'll find:

Empty_edge.js. This is the file that defines the stage, timeline, and elements in your project. It defines the base state or starting point for each element. When you create a *transition*, the properties for your element transition *from* one state *to* another state over a period of time (*duration*).

Empty_edgeActions.js. When you add triggers and actions to your Animate composition, the details are stored in this file. If you want to tweak or customize those actions, you can do it in the Animate code panels, or you could make changes here.

Empty_edgePreload.js. The preloader file that's responsible for loading the resources and scripts Animate needs to perform its magic.

The first time you open the *Empty_edge.js* file, it may be a little confusing. There are lots of strange terms and characters, like { }, ( ), and $, sitting on indented lines. It starts off like this:

```
/** Adobe Edge: symbol definitions
*/
(function($, Edge, compId){
//images folder
var im-'images/';
var fonts = {};

var resources = [
];
```

```
var symbols = {
"stage": {
    version: "1.0.0",
    minimumCompatibleVersion: "0.1.7",
    build: "1.0.0.180",
    baseState: "Base State",
    initialState: "Base State",
    gpuAccelerate: false,
    resizeInstances: false,
    content: {
        dom: [
],
        symbolInstances: [

        ]
    },
    states: {
        "Base State": {
            "${_Stage}": [
                ["color", "background-color", 'rgba(255,255,255,1)'],
                ["style", "width", '550px'],
                ["style", "height", '400px'],
                ["style", "overflow", 'hidden']
            ]
        }
    },
        ...the .js file continues but is not shown here...
```

If you're new to this, try the drowning sailor technique: Grab hold of anything that looks recognizable. Comments are always good. (For a refresher on comments, see the box on page 103.) There's a block comment at the top that says, "Adobe Edge: symbol definitions." That's pretty clear. The code that follows must define the symbols in the project.

Around the tenth line in the preceding code, you see:

```
"stage": {
```

It seems likely that this is a reference to Animate's stage. Lines that follow appear to define the stage. There's a reference to "Base State" and later states, which sound suspiciously as though this code may set the starting values for specific properties for the stage. Sure enough, down around line 20, there are more Base State details, including height, width, and background-color. Animate master that you are, you remember that these are properties you can set in the stage's Properties panel. In fact, at this point, if you're daring, you can edit these properties from inside this JavaScript file. For example, if you change the line:

```
["style", "height", '400px'],
```

to:

```
["style", "height", '800px'],
```

and then save the *Empty_edge.js* file, then the next time you open *Empty.html* in a browser, the stage will be 800 pixels tall.

> **TIP** If you edit your Animate project's JavaScript file while it's still open in Animate, you tend to confuse Animate. You'll see a message noting that the file has been changed and you'll be asked if you want to reload the file. If you say Yes to reload the file, you load the file that was saved outside of Animate and you lose any change you made in Animate. If choose No, you won't see any changes in Animate. However, if you save the file, you'll overwrite any changes you made outside of Animate.

The next chunk of code appears to set values for the base state of the timeline. It looks like this:

```
timelines: {
    "Default Timeline": {
        fromState: "Base State",
        toState: "",
        duration: 0,
        autoPlay: true,
        timeline: [
        ]
    }
}
};
```

The duration property has a value of 0. That's about right for an Empty Animate project. Likewise, autoPlay is set to true, which seems about right.

As shown in Figure 8-2, the code near the bottom of the file, beginning with:

```
Edge.registerCompositionDefn(compId, symbols, fonts, resources);
```

...and through to the end, is used to set up the composition (Animate project). It checks to see that everything is loaded and that the browser window is ready. When it's ready, it runs the launchComposition method.

```
/**
 * Adobe Edge DOM Ready Event Handler
 */
$(window).ready(function() {
    Edge.launchComposition(compId);
});
})(jQuery, AdobeEdge, "EDGE-23150191");
```

The more code-sleuthing becomes a habit, the faster you'll learn JavaScript and its partner in crime jQuery. If you carefully duplicate and save projects, you can experiment with the code just to see what happens. If you mess up a duplicate file or project—no problem. Just delete it and try again.

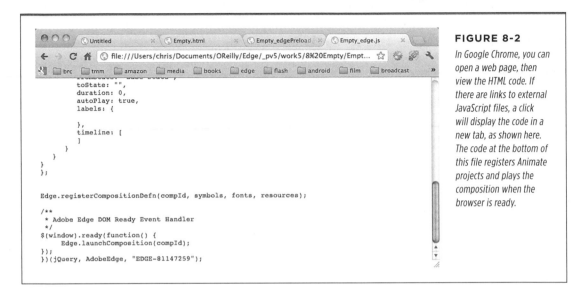

FIGURE 8-2

In Google Chrome, you can open a web page, then view the HTML code. If there are links to external JavaScript files, a click will display the code in a new tab, as shown here. The code at the bottom of this file registers Animate projects and plays the composition when the browser is ready.

Partial code visible in figure:

```
                toState: "",
                duration: 0,
                autoPlay: true,
                labels: {

                },
                timeline: [
                ]
            }
        }
    }
};

Edge.registerCompositionDefn(compId, symbols, fonts, resources);

/**
 * Adobe Edge DOM Ready Event Handler
 */
$(window).ready(function() {
    Edge.launchComposition(compId);
});
})(jQuery, AdobeEdge, "EDGE-81147259");
```

Adding a New Element to the Stage

The next step in the sleuthing expedition is to add a new element to the stage and see how that changes the code in *Empty_edge.js*. It's best to start simply, so you don't get lost in a sea of code, so just add a square that's 100 × 100 px and name it Square.

> **TIP** Hold the Shift key down when you drag out a rectangle to create a square. Keep your eye on the Properties panel, and it's not hard to create a 100 px square.

Open the *Empty_edge.js* file in a code editor or plain text editor and you see the new code that defines your square. Under these lines that were already in the project when it was empty:

```
content: {
        dom: [
```

you see:

```
        {
                id:'Square',
                type:'rect',
                rect:['146px','78px','104px','104px','auto','auto'],
                fill:["rgba(192,192,192,1)"],
                stroke:[0,"rgba(0,0,0,1)","none"]
        }],
```

The first few lines are pretty clear. There's an element with the ID of Square. That's the name you gave to the rectangle. The next line confirms that the element is the "rect" type. The other lines describe the rectangle properties you'd find in the Properties panel (Figure 8-3). The next three lines describe the appearance of the rectangle. For example:

```
rect:['146px','78px','104px','104px','auto','auto'],
```

The first two numbers set the position of the rectangle (X=147, Y=89). The next two numbers describe the width and height. A couple of the rectangle's properties are set to "auto." Following that, the fill and stroke properties are set in *rgba* terms: red, green, blue, and Alpha.

```
fill:['rgba(192,192,192,1)'],
```

In this case, the fill is gray, because of the even red, green, and blue values. With Alpha set to 1, the square is 100 percent opaque. Want to change your square to be red? Edit that line to read:

```
fill:['rgba(255,0,0,1)'],
```

Want to make the square semi-transparent? Change that last number (a) to a decimal, like this:

```
fill:['rgba(255,0,0,.5)'],
```

Now, there may not be a great value in being able to edit values like these on a new Animate project; you can easily make those changes in Animate when you begin a project. But there is a value in experimenting to see how changes like these affect elements in your project. The things you learn at this stage can be applied to other chunks of code you create using triggers and actions. From time to time, you may get JavaScript code from members of your project team or other sources. The more fluent you are in JavaScript/jQuery, the better you'll be at solving problems and building masterpieces.

■ JavaScript and jQuery Basics

JavaScript shares many programming concepts with other popular languages. If you have any programming experience, from C to Java to ActionScript, you certainly have a head start with JavaScript. This section covers some of the JavaScript and jQuery basics that are helpful to know when you're working with Animate. It's certainly not a complete reference or a tutorial on the subjects. If you're looking for a complete study of JavaScript and jQuery, that'll take an entire book. The name of that book happens to be *JavaScript and jQuery: The Missing Manual* by David Sawyer McFarland (O'Reilly). You can find online information about JavaScript at *www.w3schools.com/js* or *https://developer.mozilla.org/en/JavaScript.*

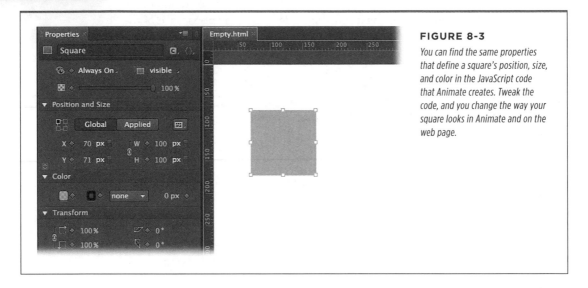

FIGURE 8-3

You can find the same properties that define a square's position, size, and color in the JavaScript code that Animate creates. Tweak the code, and you change the way your square looks in Animate and on the web page.

When it comes to types of data, JavaScript provides the usual suspects:

- **Numbers** can be whole numbers like *756* or decimals like *7.56*. Numbers are expressed without any particular punctuation. For example, you might have a statement like:

```
var myNumber = 12 + 5;
```

The 12 and 5 are added together, and the result is stored in the variable myNumber.

- **Strings** are groups of characters, like your name or the words "Moby-Dick." Strings must appear inside quotes, either single or double. Statements with valid strings might look like this:

```
var author = "Herman Melville";
var firstSentence = 'Call me Ishmael.';
```

You can combine two strings using the + operator. For example:

```
var author = "Herman " + "Melville";
```

Stores a single string "Herman Melville" in the *author* variable.

- **Booleans,** as usual, have two values: *true* or *false*. They're often used to determine if a certain condition exists. Here's an *if* conditional statement that checks to see if the sun has come up:

```
sunRise = true;
if (sunRise == true) {
  newDay();
};
```

The first line assigns the value "true" to the variable sunRise. If it's true that the sun has come up, then the *newDay()* function is performed. The details of *newDay()* are defined elsewhere. It's important to remember that the operator to compare equal values is ==, not a single =.

- **Arrays** provide a convenient way to group several items together. For example, an array of colors might look like this:

```
var colors = ['red','blue','green','alpha'];
```

In that case, you could retrieve values from the array with a statement like this:

```
myFavorite = colors[1];
```

The numbering for arrays always begin with 0, so in this example *colors[1]* references *blue*.

A single array can hold different types of data. So for example, an array for an employee could have strings that store first and last names, and numbers that store age and number of years employed. There are a number of ways to add items, remove items, and change items in an array. Details are available online at *www.w3schools.com/js* or *https://developer.mozilla.org/en/JavaScript*.

- **Functions** consist of one or more statements that can be executed. You may be surprised to see functions listed among the *data types*, but in JavaScript, functions are considered a data type. As a result, functions have some interesting capabilities. For example, they can be stored in variables or arrays. A function might be declared like this:

```
function fullName(first, last) {
return first + ' ' + last;
}
```

The word "function" explains that the code that follows is a function. The name of the function is *fullName*, and it takes two arguments: *first* and *last*. These arguments need to be provided when the function is called. One or more statements for the function appear in between curly braces { }. This function joins three strings to create one string. The arguments *first* and *last* are strings, presumably the first and last names. In between, a *string literal* is used to insert a space character. Code to call the function might look like this:

```
name = fullName(firstName, lastName);
```

In this case, the variables *firstName* and *lastName* are presumed to be strings that have already been defined to represent someone's name. So if previously the variable firstName was given the value *Umberto* and lastName was given the value *Eco*, then this statement would assign the string "Umberto Eco" to the variable *name*.

Here are some other features you should keep in mind when you work in JavaScript:

- **JavaScript is loosely typed.** Unlike many other languages, variables do not have a specific data type when they are created. This means a variable could be assigned a number value and then later a string value.

- **JavaScript is case sensitive.** Capitalization matters in JavaScript. That means "javascript," "JavaScript," and "javaScript" could be used to name three separate variables.

- **Variable names must be specific characters.** Variables must begin with a letter, $, or _. They cannot begin with a number. The rest of the characters in a variable must be letters, numbers, $, or _. Variables can't contain any other characters or punctuation.

- **JavaScript has reserved words.** Like most programming languages, JavaScript has a number of words that have special meanings. These are usually called *reserved words* or *keywords*. You don't want to confuse the process by using these words for variables or in other places. The following are examples of reserved words:

  - *var*—used to create variables.

  - *if*—used to begin if...else conditional statements.

  - *while*—used to begin while conditional statements.

  - *new*—creates a new instance of an object.

  - *function*—used to define a function.

  You can find the complete list of JavaScript reserved words at *https://developer .mozilla.org/en/JavaScript/Reference/Reserved_Words.*

- **JavaScript uses semicolons (;) to end statements.** To properly interpret JavaScript code, browsers need to know where one statement ends and the next begins. JavaScript uses semicolons to separate statements. If there's only one statement on a line, many browsers will let you get away with not putting a semicolon at the end, but it's considered a best practice to always put a semicolon at the end of a statement.

- **JavaScript ignores whitespace.** In general, JavaScript ignores spaces, tabs, and new lines. That leaves you free to add whitespace to your code to make it more readable. Naturally, if you put whitespace in the middle of something like a number, that would change *736* into two numbers, *7 36*.

Operators in JavaScript

Programs and scripts perform their magic through a sequence of operations where variables are assigned values, calculations are performed, and comparisons are made. These operations require operators like + for addition and / for division. The operators used in JavaScript are similar to those used in other programs and scripting languages.

The assignment operator is =. You use this to assign a value to a variable, as in:

```
age = 23;
name = "James Joyce";
```

Basic math operations use these standard operators:

OPERATION	OPERATOR	EXAMPLE
Add numbers	+	45 + 21
Subtract numbers	-	45 - 21
Multiply numbers	*	45 * 21
Divide numbers	/	21 / 7

You can use these operators with literals—that is, actual numbers—or you can use them with variables that have number values assigned to them. Sometimes you'll end up with a string that is a numeral, as in:

```
age = "23";
```

The variable "age" has been assigned a string. You can tell by the quote marks. That string happens to be numerals. What if you want to perform a math operation with *age*? JavaScript gives you an easy way to convert that string to its numerical value.

Just put a + sign in front, like so:

```
doubleAge = +age * 2;
```

Then you can calculate to your heart's content.

A special set of operators is used to compare values. The trickiest one is the equal-to operator. It's easy to forget you want two = signs, as in ==.

Here are the comparison operators. The result of each example is true:

OPERATION	OPERATOR	EXAMPLE
Are two values equal?	==	(4+1)==5
Are two values unequal?	!=	(4+1)!=3
Is the left value greater than right value?	>	24 > 12
Is the left value greater than or equal to the right value?	>=	24 >= 12 24 >= 12 + 12
Is the left value less than the right value?	<	12 < 24
Is the left value less than or equal to the right value?	<=	12 <= 24 12 <= 6 + 6

Conditional Statements in JavaScript

Comparison operators are often used in conditional statements. For example, as a programmer for the Department of Motor Vehicles you might say, "If this applicant's age is less than 16, then deny driver's license." Written in JavaScript, the statement might look like this:

```
If (applicantAge < 16) {
    denyLicense();
    alert('License is denied, due to youthful recklessness!');
}
```

Understanding the Document Object Model (DOM)

JavaScript gives you a way to modify and rewrite HTML documents. JavaScript does this by accessing elements in the document and then making changes. CSS formatting works in a similar way when it applies formatting to individual elements in a web page. In effect, it amounts to rewriting the HTML that defines the page. The document object model, affectionately known as the DOM, is the skeleton of any web page, as visualized in Figure 8-4. It's a conceptual definition of a web page that describes the elements.

Before you can make changes to an element in an HTML document, you need to identify or *select* that element. There are three common ways to identify the elements in a web page: by tag, by ID, or by class.

- **Tags** are HTML's basic method for identifying things like headings <h1> or paragraphs <p>. Tags always use angle brackets: < >.

- **IDs** are used to identify one unique item on a page. An ID can be assigned to an element using an attribute within a tag. For example, a picture could be given an ID of mainPhoto within the <img> tag:

  ```
  <img id="mainPhoto" src="images/bearcat.jpg">
  ```

- **Classes** are used to identify similar elements on a page. To identify a photo as part of the "gallery" class, you'd write:

  ```
  <img class="gallery" src="images/bearcat.jpg">
  ```

JavaScript has methods for getting an element by ID and for getting an element by tag. It also provides ways to move around the DOM to select different elements. This technique is called traversing, and if you're not used to using it, it's likely to cause headaches. However, there's good news and more good news: jQuery provides ways to select elements that are much easier to use. And, for the most part, Animate uses jQuery methods to select elements.

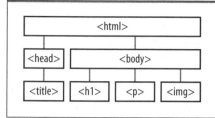

FIGURE 8-4

A web page is the sum total of its elements. There's a certain hierarchy, as some elements reside inside others. Here, for example, all the elements are inside html, and the paragraph or <p> tag is inside <body>. There are many elements defined by the DOM. They aren't all shown here.

■ Natural Selection the jQuery Way

In Animate, when you name an element, something is going on behind the scenes. Animate is giving that element an ID. So if you name a photo *mainPhoto* in Animate, it's just as if you'd written *id="mainPhoto"* in the <img> tag. Remember how CSS references IDs by placing a # (pound sign) in front of the name? (For a reminder, see page 161.) jQuery uses the same system. If you want to reference your *mainPhoto* using jQuery, you'd write:

```
$('#mainPhoto')
```

Remember how CSS references classes by placing a period in front of the name? jQuery uses that system to identify classes, too. If you want to select all the elements in the gallery class, it looks like this:

```
$('.gallery')
```

Finally, if you want to select all the elements with <img> tags, you don't need any special character at the front. That would look like this:

```
$(img)
```

■ "this" and "sym" Are Special Words

In JavaScript, the word "this" has a special meaning. A great deal of your effort in writing and editing JavaScript and jQuery code involves identifying exactly the right element so that you can do something to it. You may want to move it to a new position. You may want to change its color. You may want to replace all the text that it displays. The reserved word "this" is often used to identify an element that has been clicked or the object from which a function (method) is called. However, "this" is more flexible in JavaScript than it is in other languages, so its use may surprise you. In Animate, "this" usually refers to the symbol. When you first fire up Animate, that symbol is the main stage and its timeline. The *lookupSelector()* function may be used to identify specific element—in other words, children of that symbol. For example, this statement will identify an element named "text1" and then hide it:

```
$(this.lookupSelector("text1")).hide();
```

Early versions of Animate used this code in the Actions panel, and it still works. However, later versions of Animate use a slightly different syntax:

```
sym.$("Text1").hide();
```

In this case, "sym" stands for "symbol." If you're working on the main stage, sym refers to the stage and its timeline. If you've created new symbols and opened one up for editing, the word sym refers to that symbol's stage and timeline. The dollar sign is the jQuery selector that looks up the element by name (ID). The *.hide()* function remains the same. You can add this statement using the Actions panel and then edit it for your own purposes. Change text1 to the name of the element you want to identify. Then, if needed, change the function *hide()* to one that you want to use. One great advantage of this "build-it-yourself snippet" is that you'll cut down on typos in your code.

Helpful JavaScript Tricks

Here's the payoff for learning the JavaScript/jQuery basics covered in Chapter 8. You can apply those skills to your Animate projects. One of the easiest ways to start is to use Animate's triggers and action snippets to write code, and then apply your own modifications to customize that code. That's exactly how this chapter begins. Then it presents yet another version of the photo gallery, using a nifty image source swapping technique. Along the way you learn how to change an element's dimensions, position, and background colors the JavaScript/jQuery way. This chapter explains how you can simplify your code by assigning symbols and elements to variables. Symbols have their own independent timelines. If you want to start, stop, and control those timelines, you'll be interested in the example that shows how to do that from within and without the symbol. Last, but not least, you'll learn how to create Animate compositions that make decisions for themselves through the use of conditional statements.

More Showing and Hiding Tricks

Chapter 5 showed several examples using the Show and Hide actions. Now it's time to revisit that subject and see how you can bend those simple tricks to your own iron will. Consider a simple Animate composition like the one in Figure 9-1. You can find *09-1_HideAndSeek* with the exercises for this chapter on the Missing CD at *www.missingmanuals.com/cds/animatemm*.

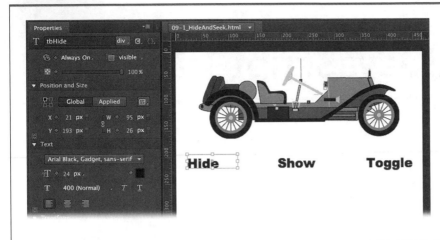

FIGURE 9-1

This Animate composition has an image of a car and three text boxes with the words "Hide," "Show," and "Toggle." Guess what happens next.

The idea is to make the text boxes with the words Show, Hide, and Toggle behave like buttons. Click on the word and the car picture disappears or reappears. For example, as covered in Chapter 5, this is the quick way to make Hide work:

1. In Animate, right-click (Control-click) the word "Hide" and choose Open Actions for "tbHide" from the shortcut menu.

2. Choose *click* from the triggers menu.

3. In the Actions panel, click the Hide Element button on the left.

> **NOTE** In this example, the letters tb are added to the front of each element that is a text box. As your projects grow, you may want to use similar techniques to further distinguish the many elements inside. Two or three letter prefixes or suffixes work well.

That inserts the generic hide code, Figure 9-2, which looks like this:

```
sym.$("Text1").hide();
```

You need to change "Text1" to *car* so that a click on the word hides the image of the car. When you're done, it reads like this:

```
sym.$("car").hide();
```

You go through a similar process when you create a trigger for the text box with the word "Show." Just make sure you use the Show Element action.

> **NOTE** Check back on page 99 if you need to brush up on showing and hiding elements using triggers and actions.

So what about that word "Toggle"? It can be awfully handy to have a single button or command to turn an element on the web page on and off. You could write something with one of those conditional statements like, "If the car is visible, hide the car; else show the car." But there's an even easier way. jQuery has a companion to the show and hide functions called *toggle*. All you need to do is follow the steps above to apply a *click* trigger and a *hide* action to the car element. Then you can edit the statement. You want to change the *hide* action to a *toggle* action. When you're done, the code for Toggle looks like this:

```
sym.$("car").toggle();
```

Save your work and give it a test. If the car is visible, clicking either Hide or Toggle makes it disappear. Likewise, if the car is hidden, clicking Show or Toggle makes it reappear.

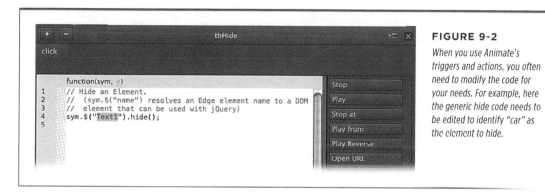

FIGURE 9-2

When you use Animate's triggers and actions, you often need to modify the code for your needs. For example, here the generic hide code needs to be edited to identify "car" as the element to hide.

Delaying Action for Show, Hide, and Toggle

If you read through Chapter 8, you may recognize that *show()*, *hide()*, and *toggle()* are functions. Somewhere deep in the JavaScript code that's linked to your Animate composition are the routines that make these functions perform. When your browser comes across a function name like *hide()*, it looks up those routines and applies them to the car element. You don't have to know the nitty-gritty coding details that make a function work; it's enough to understand what they do and how to use them. It's like the difference between driving a car and being an auto mechanic.

Here's one more hide, show, and toggle trick. You can add *arguments* (sometimes called parameters) to the *hide()*, *show()*, and *toggle()* functions that change the way they behave. Open the click actions for the text box "hide." Change the code by placing the number *4000* inside the parentheses after "hide." The statement should look like this:

```
sym.$("car").hide(4000);
```

Do the same for the *show()* function of the text box with the word "Show." Now test the composition. When you click on "Hide" and "Show," the box gradually shrinks from view or grows into view from the upper-left corner. You may have seen this technique used to show and hide menus on a navigation bar. Without any argument, "Toggle" still works instantaneously.

You may recall that JavaScript likes to divide time into milliseconds—that is, thousandths of a second. That's exactly what's happening in your *hide()* and *show()* functions. It takes 4 seconds for the shrinking and growing to take place. If you'd rather use words to specify the timing, try "slow," "normal," and "fast." Don't forget to include the quote marks.

Fading In and Out

As the infomercial salesperson likes to say: But wait! There's more! The shrinking and growing from the previous example works well for some chores, like menus. For photos and other images, a nice dissolve animation works well. Sure, you can create this effect on the timeline and use "Play from" triggers, but why bother if you can do the same thing by swapping functions?

If you want to keep using the same composition, you can change the words in the text boxes to read "Fade Out" and "Fade In" or you can add new text boxes to do the job. You can continue to use *click* as the trigger. The action uses new functions:

- *fadeOut()*: The element dissolves (becomes less opaque) until it disappears.

- *fadeIn()*: The element increases in opacity until it is fully visible.

- *fadeToggle()*: Shows or hides the element by changing its opacity.

Keep in mind, as always, JavaScript and jQuery are case sensitive, so be sure to *fadeOut()* rather than FadeOut or fadeout. As with the *hide()* and *show()* functions, you can use arguments to control the speed. These fading actions accept both numbers (in milliseconds) and the words "slow," "normal," and "fast."

Slip Sliding Up and Down

Order now and you'll get sliding action, too! You guessed it: You can swap these functions in place of *show()* and *hide()*.

- *slideUp()*: Slides an element up until it disappears.

- *slideDown()*: Slides an element down until it is fully visible.

- *slideToggle()*: Shows or hides the element using the sliding action.

As with the *hide()* and *show()* functions, you can use arguments to control the speed. These sliding actions accept both numbers (in milliseconds) and the words "slow," "normal," and "fast."

If you completed all the steps, you'll have a hide-and-seek sampler that you can view in your browser, as shown in Figure 9-3. If you haven't followed along, you can find *09-2_HideAndSeek_done* on the Missing CD at *www.missingmanuals.com/cds/animatemm*.

FIGURE 9-3

The text boxes in this example all work like buttons. Click on a word to see how the function affects the image of the car. Examine the code, and you'll see the different delay settings that control the timing of the animated effect.

The Fickle Finger of Click

Why don't I see that pointing finger when my cursor moves over a clickable item?

We're all well-trained. We expect to see that pointing finger when we move our cursor over a button or a hyperlink. Yet when you create clickable elements in Animate, that's not always the case. Page 152 explains how to set the cursor property for an element. See Figure 9-4. Then, that cursor appears automatically when you mouse over the element.

There is a JavaScript/jQuery fix to this problem, too. It involves only one piece of code. First right-click (Control-click) an element in your project, and then choose the *mouseover* or trigger. In the actions planel, add a line of code that looks like this:

```
sym.$('tbHide')).css('cursor','pointer');
```

In this example, *tbHide* is the ID for the text box that holds the word "Hide." It is the element with the *mouseover* trigger. With this action in place, the cursor changes to a pointing finger when it's over the text box. In the earliest preview versions of Edge Animate, there was no cursor property for elements, so this was the standard way to add that familiar pointing finger. There are several other cursor variations that you can use. They match the options shown in Figure 9-4. In the example on page 202, simply replace the word pointer with one of these: crosshair, e-resize, help, move, n-resize, ne-resize, nw-resize, progress, s-resize, se-resize, sw-resize, text, w-resize, and wait. (The resize cursor options display an arrow. The letters in front indicate the direction of the arrow. For example, for nw-resize, think "northwest-resize.")

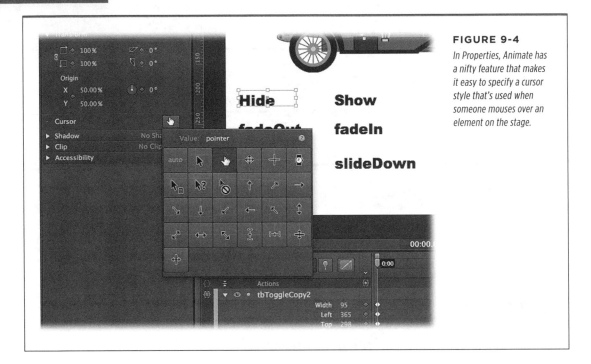

FIGURE 9-4

In Properties, Animate has a nifty feature that makes it easy to specify a cursor style that's used when someone mouses over an element on the stage.

More Visual Effects with *animate()*

As explained in Chapter 7, formatting chores for web pages can be handled by CSS (Cascading Style Sheets). JavaScript and jQuery statements can rewrite the CSS rules and, in the process, change the way elements appear on a web page. The *animate()* function does just that. For example, using *animate()*, you can change the opacity of the car image, or you can change the appearance of the text in a text box.

The *animate()* function works a little differently from the previous ones, because it can use several arguments at once. For example, you can change the opacity of an image and crop the image at the same time. To do that with the car image, you'd write the function like this:

```
sym.$("car").animate(
{
   opacity: .25,
   width: 200px
}
);
```

There are a few new things to note in this example. The *animate()* function holds arguments inside parentheses like any self-respecting function. The opening paren-thesis is at the end of line 1, and the closing parenthesis is at the beginning of line 6.

Inside those, there are curly braces that hold multiple arguments. In this case, the arguments specify the opacity and width of the image. These arguments match up with standard CSS specs, and they're separated by commas. The function is considered a single command, so there's only one semicolon at the end of the command.

In this case, the width spec scales the image by changing its width. Since the car graphic is over 380 pixels wide, the code scrunches the car, making it shorter.

You can use triggers to run more than one action, so you can change the car image and change the specs for a block of text all at once. This time, let's suppose you want to use a rectangle as a button.

1. At the bottom of the *09-1_HideAndSeek* example, draw a rectangle. Name it *btnBar*.

2. Right-click (Control-click) btnBar and choose Open Actions for "btnBar" from the shortcut menu.

3. Choose the *click* trigger.

4. In the btnBar Actions panel, write these lines of code:

```
sym.$("car").animate(
{
    opacity: .25,
    width: 200
}, 2000
);
sym.$("tbHide").animate(
{
    fontSize: '12',
    fontFamily: 'Times'
}, 2000
);
```

The font changes work for tbHide because it has a <p> tag associated with it. Paragraphs have font properties. If it had a <div> the changes wouldn't work, because in HTML divs don't have any font properties. If you're familiar with CSS, you may remember that you specify font size using a hyphenated identifier: *font-size*. Typefaces are also specified with a hyphenated identifier: *font-family*. In JavaScript, these identifiers don't use a hyphen, which might be confused with a subtraction operator. Instead they use what's known as camel text, where the first word begins with a lowercase letter and subsequent words start with an uppercase letter, as in *fontSize* and *fontFamily*.

You can specify the delay for *animate()* effects as you do with *show()* and *hide()* functions. In this example, the delay is set to 2000 for both the car image and the *tbHide* text box. The 2000 appears right before the closing parenthesis, and it is also separated by a comma. For a working copy of the Hide and Seek exercise, see *09-2_HideAndSeek_done* from the Missing CD.

What, No Slide Left and Slide Right?

You may have noticed the absence of "slideLeft" and "slideRight" methods in the tips that began on page 193. That's because they don't exist. The slideUp and slideDown methods are built into JavaScript, but if you want to slide left or right, you have to roll your own. Fortunately, it's not that hard, now that you know the power of the *animate()* method. All you have to do is find out the position of the left edge of an element, and then change the position of that edge.

In the filmstrip project back on page 92, several photos of flowers were combined into one long JPG image. That example was accomplished using the timeline: By moving the left edge of the filmstrip, you make different photos slide into view. (You can check out the finished project from the Missing CD: *04-6_Film_Strip_done.*) You can create the same effect using triggers, actions, JavaScript. The first thing you need to do is find the left edge of the filmstrip, which you can do with a JavaScript statement like this:

```
sym.$("flowerStrip").position().left;
```

The *sym.$("flowerStrip")* portion of the statement identifies the flowerStrip element. Then the *.position()*.left method gets the left edge or the X position for the element. So, what can you do when you know the value of the left edge of an element? As explained on page 208, you can display that value using an *alert()* method, which is helpful when you're debugging a project. An even more powerful use for the value is to store it to a variable. The last example in this chapter (page 221) does that using the value in a *switch()* conditional statement.

You can use the *.animate()* method to move the element to a new position on the stage. That statement looks like this:

```
sym.$("flowerStrip").animate({left: "-=500px"}, "slow");
```

That code changes the position of the left edge of flowerStrip, slowly moving it 500 pixels to the left, as shown in Figure 9-5. Just what you want to make your filmstrip work. There's a little JavaScript sleight of hand going on here that might not be apparent at first glance. It has to do with the -= operator, which is a kind of shorthand. It assigns a value and performs the subtraction at the same time. In this case, it's saying "Get the value of the left edge of flowerstrip. Subtract 500px and then make that the new value for the left edge." There's a similar operator that performs addition and assignment (+=).

TIP You can use the *animate()* method with the right, top, and bottom edges, too. In the case of the filmstrip, the left edge is the most logical choice for positioning.

If you want to experiment, use *09-3_Slide_Left* from the Missing CD. If you'd rather cut to the chase, you can see a finished example: *09-4_Slide_Left_done.* You'll notice that there's something lacking in the finished example: One click moves the filmstrip one image and that's the end of the show. It takes a few more JavaScript tools to develop a smoothly functioning filmstrip, as you'll see later in this chapter (so keep your files handy). You'll need to know how to store a value to a variable where it can be manipulated (page 207). You'll also need a conditional statement that knows how to make a decision, like "If the left edge of flowerStrip is at -500px, change the value of the left edge to -1000px." To perform this kind of JavaScript wizardry, check out the *switch()* conditional statement on page 221.

FIGURE 9-5

The animate() method is used with a click trigger to slide the filmstrip 500 pixels to the left. This statement displays a different flower photo on the stage.

Swapping Images in Animate

One of the keystones of web design is the image swap. You see it used all over the place, and JavaScript is usually the engine that's working behind the scenes. In the earlier examples, you saw how JavaScript could rewrite CSS specifications for formatting and positioning. In the case of an image swap, JavaScript is rewriting the *src* (source attribute) for an image tag. Want to make a button change its appearance when the cursor is over it? Use the *mouseover* trigger. You'll need a *mouseout* trigger to change it to its normal state when the cursor moves away. Want a button to change when it's clicked? You can use *mousedown* and *mouseup* to change its appearance. In each case, you want to swap the source of the button image. The perfect place to practice your image swapping chops is a photo gallery.

Photo Gallery Revisited

One common technique for displaying a group of photos is to have one large main photo and smaller thumbnail images, as shown in Figure 9-6. Your audience can click or mouse over a thumbnail to display that pic as the main photo. This type of gallery works well for up to about a dozen photos. If you try to use too many photos, the thumbnail images are too small to be useful. The project *09-5_Rollover_Gallery* is ready to go. If you want to see the end result, check out *09-6_Rollover_Gallery_done*.

FIGURE 9-6

Here's a common layout for a rollover photo gallery. Point to one of the images at the bottom, and it is displayed as the main photo at the top. This technique uses simple image swapping code and works on computers, tablets, and phones.

Examine the gallery files and you'll find that some of the work has been done for you. The main photo and thumbnails are in place on the stage. In the Elements panel, you have four thumbnail images, each beginning with *sm_* (think "small"). The main photo is named "bike." Select it, and you'll notice the filename listed in Properties. All the images, big and small, are in the *images* subfolder of your project. In fact, there are three other images that don't appear on the stage: farmhouse, squirrel, and flowers. The project will use these photos, but they don't need to be imported as long as they're in the *images* subfolder. They'll be referenced as sources for the main photo. Follow these steps to finish up the rollover gallery:

1. Select the large bike photo. Then, in Properties, change the div tag to *img*.

   Animate automatically applies the <div> tag to everything you import. In this case, you want to use the src attribute of an <img> tag. This step is important, because later you want to use CSS properties that are unique to an img element.

2. With bike still selected, in Properties, change the image name to *mainPhoto*.

   In the Elements panel, you see mainPhoto when the image is selected. The bike won't remain a bike for long, so it's best to give it a more generic name that will make sense in your code.

3. Right-click (Control-click) the farmhouse thumbnail and choose Open Actions for sm_farmhouse, and then choose *mouseover* from the triggers.

   You're making life easy for gallery visitors. They won't even have to click to swap photos; all they have to do is move the cursor over a thumbnail.

4. On the left side of the Actions panel, click the Hide Element button.

   You don't really want to hide anything, but this is an easy, typo-free way to write much of the code you need. In the next step, you'll make alterations.

5. Change "text1" to "*mainPhoto*". Then change the *hide()* function to *attr()*.

   With these changes, your code should look like:

   ```
   sym.$("mainPhoto").attr();
   ```

6. Inside the parentheses for the *attr()* function, type: *'src','images/farmhouse.jpg'*.

   Now the line of code looks like this:

   ```
   sym.$("mainPhoto").attr('src','images/farmhouse.jpg');
   ```

   Make sure you use quote marks around the src and photo attributes. They can be single or double quotes as long as the pairs are matched up correctly.

   The src attribute identifies the source for an image. The *images/farmhouse.jpg* text provides the path and name of the photo. You use similar code for each of the thumbnails.

7. On a new line in the Actions panel's mouseover tab, type this line:

   ```
   sym.$("sm_farmhouse").css('cursor','pointer');
   ```

   As explained in the box on page 197, this line will change the cursor to that familiar pointing finger when it is over the farmhouse thumbnail. The box also explains how to use the cursor button in Properties to create this effect.

8. Click the X button in the upper-right corner of the Actions panel. Go to File→Save and then press Ctrl+Enter (⌘-Return).

   The Actions panel closes, and you preview your project in your browser.

9. Move your mouse over the farmhouse thumbnail.

   The cursor changes to the pointing finger and the main photo changes to show the farmhouse. If your project behaves differently, go back and double-check your code. Pay particular attention to the parentheses and those single quote marks. Make sure the photo path references the *images* folder, not the *image* folder. Make sure that you changed the mainPhoto's tag to *img*, as described in step 1.

10. Open the Actions panel for *sm_farmhouse*. Select and copy (Ctrl+C or ⌘-C) the code in the panel.

    You need to add similar code to the other three thumbnails. You might as well save time by copying, pasting, and editing the code.

11. Open one of the other thumbnails. Choose the *mouseover* trigger, and then paste (Ctrl+V or ⌘-V) in the code.

    When you paste it in, the code looks like this:

    ```
    sym.$("mainPhoto").attr('src','images/farmhouse.jpg');
    sym.$("sm_farmhouse").css('cursor','pointer');
    ```

    The text that needs to be edited to match the thumbnail is shown in bold.

12. Repeat the copy-and-paste process for the rest of the thumbnails.

When you're done, you have a working photo gallery. The thumbnails are big enough that they should work for an iPhone as well as a computer. If you want to dress the project up a little more, you can create rollover highlights or a drop shadow to mark the currently selected pictures.

■ OTHER USES FOR ROLLOVERS

All you need to do is roam the Web a bit, and you'll see all sorts of rollover examples, like changing the cursor to a pointing finger. They give your audience useful feedback. If you tackled the previous exercise, then you can see how you'd create a simple rollover button. Create two images for your button, one for its normal state and one for the mouseover state. As with the gallery example, give your images helpful names when you create them. With buttons, you may want to add something to the end of the name that identifies the state. For example, if you're creating website navigation buttons, you could have image filenames like *home.jpg, home_ovr.jpg, contact.jpg,* and *contact_ovr.jpg*. Import the normal state button to your project, and make sure the mouseover state button is in your images file, and you're ready to swap.

■ Identifying and Changing Elements and Symbols

When you're working with triggers and actions, half the battle is identifying the element that you want to change. The other half of the battle is changing its properties. When learning new coding techniques, it's best to start simple and build your skills. Consider a composition with two elements: a rectangle and a text box. In this case, the text acts as a button changing the width of the rectangle. Here's the lay of the land, as shown in Figure 9-7:

- The rectangle's ID is Square.

- The text box's ID is tbChangeSquare.

- There's nothing else on the stage.

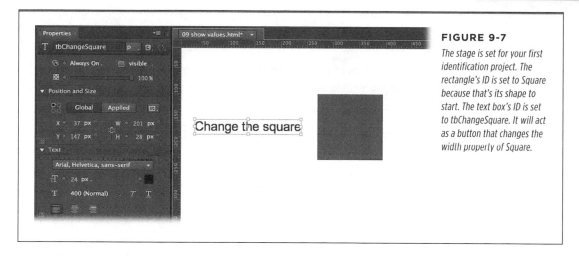

FIGURE 9-7

The stage is set for your first identification project. The rectangle's ID is set to Square because that's its shape to start. The text box's ID is set to tbChangeSquare. It will act as a button that changes the width property of Square.

You want to put your code in the "click" trigger for the text box tbChangeSquare. (For a refresher on using a click trigger, see page 194.) Your code is like building blocks that you use to identify an element and its properties. You almost always start at the outermost level—that's the main stage symbol. As explained back on page 191, you use the word "sym" to identify a symbol. The main stage and its timeline are the mother of all symbols for a project.

```
sym.
```

Animate, like JavaScript, uses dot (.) notation to separate elements that are inside of other elements. Here the stage (sym) is one element and Square is another. You also use dots to separate the properties and methods that belong to elements. Now that the stage is identified, it's time to zero in on the rectangle with the ID "Square."

```
sym.$("Square").
```

Think back on page 193, during the discussion of *show()* and *hide()* functions, where the car element is identified using the jQuery selector. That's what's going on here. The dollar sign ($) along with the ID is used to zero in on a specific element. You're going to use CSS to change the format of this element, so the next step is to add another building block:

```
sym.$("Square").css()
```

A number of properties can be changed using CSS and, as explained on page 160, the process involves pairs: a property name and a value. These pairs go inside the parentheses, with each listed inside quotes. The name/value pairs are separated by a comma. Suppose you want to change the width of Square to 400 pixels: The final bit of code looks like this:

```
sym.$("Square").css("width","400px");
```

The units for width and height values are given in pixels (px). Lastly, you need to end the statement with a semicolon.

Right-click (Control-click) the text box tbChangeSquare and choose the click trigger. Paste or type your line of code and then test your project. It should look like Figure 9-8.

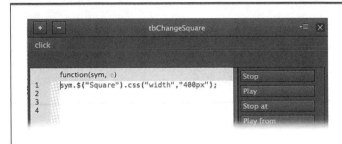

FIGURE 9-8

Here's the code that gets attached to the "click" trigger of the text box ID'd as tbChangeSquare. When the text gets clicked, Square will be square no more.

Assigning Variables

It's common to use variables to identify different symbols, elements, or values. In fact, that's what many of Animate's action buttons do. Look for ones with names like Get Symbol or Get Element. You get to choose the variable name, and then you assign a value to the variable. Suppose you want to shorten the way you identify Square. A line of code like this does the trick:

```
var theSquare=sym.$("Square");
```

Now you can use the variable theSquare to reference the element with the ID of Square. No more need to mention the stage (sym) or use the jQuery selector with dollar signs, parentheses, quotes, and brackets. It gives you an easier way to make changes to that element. So, you can change the width, height, and fill color with commands like:

```
var theSquare = sym.$("Square");
theSquare.css("width","400px");
theSquare.css("height","400px");
theSquare.css("backgroundColor","blue");
```

But there's an even better way to change multiple properties of a single element. You don't have to repeatedly identify Square. You can identify it once and change multiple properties at once as long as the changes appear within curly braces. It works like this:

```
var theSquare = sym.$("Square");
theSquare.css({
    "width" : "400px",
    "height" : "400px",
    "backgroundColor": "blue"
});
```

Put curly brackets inside of the parentheses, and then you can list several properties within those brackets. As usual, you need to put both the property name and the value in quotes. In this case, separate property names and values with a colon, then separate each property/value pair using commas.

Using Actions to Assign Variables

The Actions panel gives you snippets of code that can be used to assign symbols and elements to variables. For example, when you click on Get Element, Animate provides this snippet:

```
var element = sym.$("Text1");
```

As always, you can change the code for your own purposes, replacing "element" with any variable name you want. In this case, sym identifies the stage level element. Then replace Text1 with the ID of the child element you want to identify.

Click the Get Symbol button to add this snippet:

```
var mySymbolObject = sym.getSymbol("Symbol1");
```

In this case, the *getSymbol()* function replaces the jQuery selector, but really the drill is the same. Change the variable name (mySymbolObject) to something meaningful for your project. Then swap "Symbol1" with the ID of a symbol that's on stage or listed in your Element panel. Remember, there may be many instances on stage of a single symbol in the Library. When you're animating, you'll want to identify specific instances on the stage. *The getSymbol()* method identifies a specific instance of a symbol by its ID, which you'll find in the Properties panel when it's selected. You can also see the instance names in the Elements panel whether the instance is visible on stage or not. Once you've identified a specific instance of a symbol, you have access to its timeline and any child elements within the symbol.

TIP For more details on working with the getSymbol method, go Help→Edge Animate JavaScript API (application programming interface). This opens Adobe's technical notes on the using JavaScript with edge in your web browser. Search for "getSymbol" and you'll find a section called Working with Symbols.

CODER'S CLINIC

Move On Up to the Code Window

When you're just beginning to learn JavaScript and jQuery, the action panels directly associated with elements are helpful. Their whole system prompting you with triggers and offering action buttons makes it easy to keep your place and learn the new language. As your projects get more complex and your coding skills improve, you may be willing to give up some of that hand-holding for the ability to work more quickly. If that's the case, it's time to move on up to the Code window, where you can quickly access all the code in your project. You'll spend less time opening and closing windows for individual elements and more time writing and learning code.

Go to Window→Code or press Ctrl+E (⌘-E) to open the window. On the left side you see the elements in your project, beginning with the Stage. If an element has a trigger and code attached, you'll find it there. Click the element name to examine the code. Want to add code for an element that's not listed? Click the + button next to Stage, then choose Elements. Choose from the list of elements and then choose the trigger. That adds the element and trigger to the column on the left. You're ready to add your code. If you'd like to use some snippet buttons like the ones in the action panel, click the bracket button in upper-right corner. Your snippet friends will join the fun.

The Code window has one other nifty trick up its sleeve. It checks the syntax of your statements while you work. If it sees an obvious mistake, an error message appears at the bottom of the window. See Figure 9-9. As is often the case with syntax checkers, the messages can be puzzling. Perhaps the most helpful thing they do is point you to a specific line in the code where Animate found something unexpected. The error is in that line or sometimes the line preceding it.

The choice between the Code window and the Actions panels isn't an either/or decision. You can use both. For example, you may want to start off your project using Action panels to add code snippets to some elements. Then, as your project grows, you may want to use the Code window to copy and paste some of that code to other elements. For an advanced code editor that you can use outside of Animate, consider Adobe's Edge Code. You can use it on HTML, CSS, and JavaScript documents. Just announced when this book was going to press, it's still in its development/preview phase. That means new features are being developed. You can get Edge Code through your Adobe Creative Cloud account (*http://creative.adobe.com*).

Checking Values with Text Boxes and Alert Dialogs

When you begin assigning values to element properties and variables, you may want to check them. One quick and dirty way to do that is to create a temporary text box and then place the property or variable in question in the box. For example, perhaps you'd like to check the width of the variable theSquare.

1. Add a new text box to your project and change its ID to tbValue.

   Initially, you need to have some placeholder text in the box. Something like "Values" will work.

2. Open the click trigger that changes the size of theSquare.

   In the previous exercise, tbChangeSquare had the click trigger.

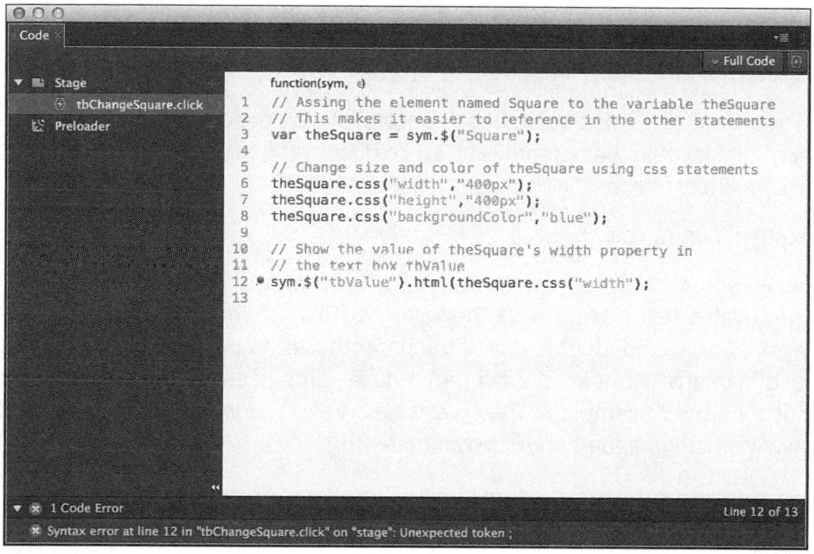

FIGURE 9-9

The Code window is a great tool when your code and projects get more complex. With all the code for all the elements in one place, you can quickly and easily automate your composition. The Code window even checks for errors, as shown in the warning at the bottom. It caught an error in Line 12 of the displayed code. Someone forgot a closing parenthesis.

3. Add this line below the other code:

```
sym.$("tbValue").html(theSquare.css("width"));
```

Here's the breakdown of that new line: sym identifies the main stage and timeline. $("tbValue") identifies the text box. html is a property of textboxes and it expects text—a string of characters.

Now, with a few explanatory comments, the code for the click trigger looks like this:

```
// Assign the Square element to the variable theSquare

var theSquare = sym.$("Square");

// Change the width, height and backgroundColor properties of theSquare
theSquare.css({
    "width"           : "400px",
    "height"          : "400px",
    "backgroundColor" : "blue"

})

// Show the "width" value of theSquare in the text box tbValue
sym.$("tbValue").html(theSquare.css("width"));
```

There are some new things going on in that last line of code. The *.html()* method is used to add html code to a web page. (See the box on page 211 for more details on adding hyperlink tags to your text boxes.) Put a string of text inside of those parentheses and it appears on the page. In this case, it appears within the tbValue text box. You could put a string literal in the text box like this:

```
sym.$("tbValue").html('My manual is missing');
```

If you want to see the value of a property, all you need to do is put the property name within the parentheses. So, to display the theSquare's width you put *theSquare.css("width")* inside of the parentheses.

4. Test your composition.

   When you click "Change the square," all the width changes take place and the tbValue text box displays the value "400px." If your composition doesn't work as expected, double-check the parentheses. In particular, make sure the last line ends with two closing parentheses and a semicolon. You can check out a finished example in *09-7_Variables_Values_done* from the Missing CD (*www.missingmanuals.com/cds/animatemm*).

TIP If you think your value-checking text box will be getting a lot of use, you probably want to assign it to a variable, too. For example:

```
var valueBox=sym.$("tbValue");
```

Then you can check values in this manner:

```
valueBox.html(theSquare.css("width"));
```

Using variables often simplifies the identification of elements. It not only speeds things up when you're coding, it means you're less likely to create a script-stopping typo.

■ USING *ALERT()* DIALOG BOXES TO CHECK VALUES

If you don't want to clutter up the stage with temporary text boxes, you can use the alert() dialog box in a similar fashion. It works in a browser like a pop-up window. One of the downsides of this method is that you need to close the alert() window before you can continue previewing your animation. The code for an alert box looks like this:

```
alert("text appears here");
```

TIP If you place an *alert()* function in your code and the dialog box never appears, that's a sign that there's an error somewhere. Often, the error occurs before the *alert()* and so the script stops and the alert() function never runs.

The text within the quotes is displayed literally. However, you can use it just like the html property of the text box to display values of properties or variables. For example, you can do this:

```
alert(theSquare.css("backgroundColor"));
```

The result is that the background color of theSquare is displayed in the alert dialog box. You used the shorthand "blue" to describe the background color. JavaScript prefers to refer to the color's RGB values, so you see: rgb(0, 0, 255).

TIP If you're ready to move up to more powerful debugging tools for your JavaScript/jQuery projects, consider Firebug (*http://getfirebug.com*), an extension for the Firefox browser. Firebug, itself, has many extensions for different scripting languages and libraries. If you use Google's Chrome browser, check out the built-in Developer Tools. You can find them by clicking the wrench icon in the upper-right corner, then choosing Tools→Developer Tools.

CODER'S CLINIC

Adding HTML Anchor Tags to Text Boxes

Back on page 159, you saw that it's easy to apply an HTML anchor tag <a> (sometimes called a hyperlink) to an entire text box, but not so easy to apply a link to specific words within a text box. If you've delved into the HTML for a web page, you've undoubtedly seen anchor tags like:

```
Why not buy a <a href=
"http://missingmanuals.com">Missing
Manual</a>?
```

In this example, the words "Missing Manual" appear on the web page as a hyperlink that opens the page identified by the URL within the quotes.

If you enter a line like that in a text box, you end up with everything. The tags, which should be hidden, are visible and there's no hyperlink. The solution lies in the *.html()* method that works with text boxes. The exercise on page 209 shows how to use the *.html()* method to display text or the value of a variable. The main purpose of the *.html()* method is to add HTML code to a web page. Just place the code you want inside of the parentheses and inside of quotation marks. So that line shown earlier might look like this if it were placed inside of an Animate action:

```
sym.$("tbText").html("Why not buy a <a
href='http://missingmanuals.com'>Missing
Manual</a>?");
```

You can use all your favorite tags, like <h1>, <p>, <br/>, and of course, <a>. Squeeze as much as you want inside of those parentheses and your box will display it all.

The big question is, what do you want to use to trigger the *html()* method? You can use any trigger you want, but in most cases you won't use a "click" trigger to change big chunks of text on a page. More often, you'll want to use the stage's compositionReady trigger.

Identifying Elements Within Symbols

When you start putting elements inside of symbols, you add another layer of complexity to identifying parts of your composition. Just remember to start on the outside and work your way in. Think of onion layers or those wooden Russian dolls nested inside each other. Suppose you have a symbol instance on the stage and an element inside of that symbol. The order to identify that interior element is: *stage* then *symbol instance* then *element*.

For experimentation, draw a square, a circle, and a text box with "Words" shown, as shown in Figure 9-10. Give them these IDs:

- Square ID = Square

- Circle ID = Circle

- Text Box ID = Words

Select all three elements and press Ctrl+Y (⌘-Y), the Modify→Convert to Symbol command. In the Library, name your symbol *BoxSymbol*. Drag two instances of BoxSymbol on to the stage. They'll need better unique names than the ones Animate provides. Give them IDs of *BoxInstanceOne* and *BoxInstanceTwo*.

If you're going to change the elements within an instance of a symbol on the stage, your first step should be to identify the instance. For ease of use later, you might want to assign that instance to a variable, like this:

```
var boxTwo = sym.getSymbol("BoxInstanceTwo");
```

If you click the Get Symbol button, as explained on page 207, you need to replace Symbol1 with the ID of the symbol instance. You may also want to change the variable name mySymbolObject to something more helpful. The next step is to identify the element within the symbol. Suppose you want to change the text in the Words text box in boxTwo. You can zero in on the text box like this:

```
boxTwo.$("Words")
```

Next on the to do list is identifying the property for your text: html.

```
boxTwo.$("Words").html();
```

Your text can be a string literal (as explained on page 210) or it can be a variable that has a string assigned to it. A string literal might look like this:

```
boxTwo.$("Words").html("To be or not to be");
```

If you're going to use a variable, it needs to be defined in advance. Like this:

```
var Hamlet = "To be or not to be";
boxTwo.$("Words").html(Hamlet);
```

If you want to change the height property of the element with the ID of Square, the code would look like this:

```
var boxTwo = sym.getSymbol("BoxInstanceTwo");
boxTwo.$("Square").css("height", "400px");
```

If you want to trim down the code even more, you can create a variable that identifies Square within the symbol:

```
var boxTwo= sym.getSymbol("BoxInstanceTwo");
var theSquare = boxTwo.$("Square");
theSquare.css("height","400px");
```

The first line is identical to the previous code. The second line creates a new variable called "theSquare" and assigns the element inside of boxTwo with the ID "Square" to the variable. The last line uses "theSquare" to identify the element within the symbol and assigns a value to the height property of the element. Even if there are several instances of the symbol on the stage, only the Square inside of boxTwo will change. For some more details about working with nested symbols, see the box on the next page.

You can explore some of these symbol and element techniques in the completed example called *09-8_Get_Symbol_done*. See Figure 9-10. It shows how to change specific elements inside of two instances of the same symbol.

UP TO SPEED

Getting Symbols and the Elements Inside

When you're starting out, it's easy to get confused working with nested symbols. The first and most important thing you need to know is where you're working in the hierarchy of nested symbols. If you have a symbol open for editing, you can identify an element in that symbol with a fairly direct statement like:

```
sym.$("myElementID");
```

That's the same way you'd identify an element if you're on the main stage and timeline and identifying an element that isn't inside a symbol. The difference here is that "sym" is referring to the symbol that you have open for editing. You're working on the symbol's stage and timeline, which is independent of the main stage and timeline.

When you're working on the main stage and you have a symbol that's closed—you're working from the outside. You need to get the symbol and then identify the element within the symbol. That's how it is done in the examples starting on page 205. In those examples, variables are used to identify the symbol and the element inside. It's also possible to identify elements more directly without variables. Suppose you have an instance of a symbol on the main stage with the ID *nestedStuff*. You are writing actions from the main stage for a button or text box. To identify the symbol you can use:

```
sym.getSymbol("nestedStuff")
```

To identify the element "Square" inside of nestedStuff, tack on this code:

```
sym.getSymbol("nestedStuff").$("Square");
```

Finally to access a property of Square use a statement like this:

```
sym.getSymbol("nestedStuff").$("Square").
css("height","400px");
```

This example performs the same chores as those on page 206, with the exception that no variables are created or used. You can examine this project in the file *09-9_Nested_Symbol_done*.

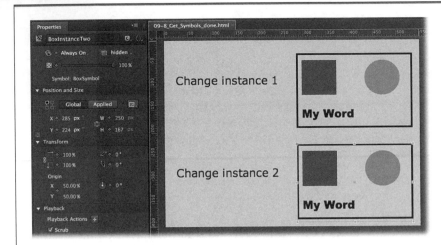

FIGURE 9-10

This composition has two instances of a single symbol. The text boxes have click triggers that change the colors of the square and circle and the text in the text boxes. Because these are unique instances, each symbol can change independently.

Playing a Symbol's Timeline

One of the great features of Animate symbols is that they have their own timeline, just like the main stage. You can start and stop that timeline using triggers, actions, or your own custom code. Here's a project called *09-10_Control_Symbol_Timeline*. As shown in Figure 9-11, it has a symbol that acts as a simple counter. Outside of the symbol are two text boxes: tbStop and tbPlay. The text serves as buttons to stop and start the timeline in the counter. If you've followed along since page 204, the technique for identifying the symbol with the ID myCounter should look familiar. The methods *stop()* and *play()* are part of all symbols. That includes the main stage and its timeline, and the timeline of any symbol that you create. Here's the code in the click action for tbStop:

```
var mySymbolObject = sym.getSymbol("myCounter");
mySymbolObject.stop();
```

You can create that first line using the Get Symbol button in the actions panel. Just replace Symbol1 with myCounter, the ID for the symbol in your project. The code for tbPlay shouldn't come as a surprise:

```
var mySymbolObject = sym.getSymbol("myCounter");
mySymbolObject.play();
```

In this case, the object with the trigger (the text box) is not part of the symbol, so it is necessary to identify the stage (sym) and the symbol you want to control (my-Counter). A variable (mySymbolObject) is created to easily identify the symbol. Then, the *stop()* and *play()* methods are used to control the timeline. If the object with the trigger were part of the symbol, or if everything were on the stage, you can use sym to identify the current symbol. Then the code to stop and play the timeline would be:

```
sym.stop();
sym.play();
```

Check the actions for the red and green blocks in the symbol, and you find exactly that code. You can also use some of the tricks you learned on page 111 to jump to a particular point on the timeline. For example, you can make the timeline Play from a particular point in time:

```
var mySymbolObject = sym.getSymbol("myCounter");
mySymbolObject.play(4000);
```

The basic unit of time is the millisecond, so 4000 is the point four seconds into the timeline. As an alternative, you can use a timeline label as described on page 112:

```
var mySymbolObject = sym.getSymbol("myCounter");
mySymbolObject.play("myLabel");
```

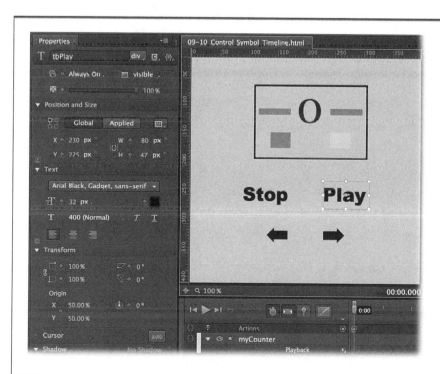

FIGURE 9-11

Animate provides several methods for playing and stopping the timeline. These methods work for symbols as well as the main timeline. To see the code for the examples described in this section, get 09 10_Control_Symbol_Timeline from the Missing CD at http://missingmanuals.com/cds/animatemm.

Getting the Current Playhead Position

Sometimes you'll want to know the current position of the playhead in a symbol or in your main timeline. Animate provides a function that does just that: *getPosition()*. It returns the number in Animate's favorite unit of time, the millisecond, where 1000 equals a second. Suppose you have a variable for a symbol named theCounterSymbol. A statement that assigns the current playhead position to a variable looks like this:

```
var playPosition = theCounterSymbol.getPosition();
```

What can you do when you know the playhead position? For one thing, with a little arithmetic you could make the playhead jump ahead a couple of seconds.

```
var playPosition = theCounterSymbol.getPosition();
playPosition = playPosition + 2000;
theCounterSymbol.play(playPosition);
```

Line two adds 2000 (two seconds) to playPosition and then assigns the result to playPosition, giving it a new value that's two seconds farther down the timeline. Want to go backwards? Just use subtraction. The third line uses playPosition with its new value to reposition the timeline playhead.

■ Using Conditional Statements

There's one problem with the previous exercise that positions the playhead on the timeline. If the current position is too far along the timeline, the updated value for the variable playPosition may be greater than the duration of the symbol. That means you want to check the value and then perform different actions based on the result. That's the perfect job for the *if* conditional statement described on page 190. The basic form is this:

```
if (this statement is true) {
    do these actions;
    }
    else {
    do these other actions;
    }
```

The parentheses and curly brackets are all vitally important. Forget one, and your carefully constructed conditional won't work. The else portion of the statement is optional, but you need it for the current dilemma. Here's a statement that checks to see playPosition is under the ten-second mark. If it is, the playhead is moved to playPosition. If not (the else portion of the statement), the playhead is moved to 0, the start of the timeline.

```
if (playPosition < 10000) {
    theCounterSymbol.play(playPosition);
    }
    else {
    theCounterSymbol.play(0);
    }
```

Attach this code to the click trigger of a forward pointing arrow, and you have a way to jump ahead in your animation. With a little tweaking, you can create a back arrow and code that moves in the other direction. If you'd like to examine this code and some of the other symbol controls, take a look at *09-10_Control_Symbol_Timeline*.

Slideshow Control with the *if()* Conditional

The great thing about using conditional statements like *if()* is that your programs and compositions get smart. They literally can make their own decisions. With a little careful coding, you can create compositions that are adaptable to different situations. For example, wouldn't it be great to create a slideshow composition that can quickly be adapted to handle a varied number of photos? Using variables (explained on page 206) to keep the count and an *if()* statement to make decisions, you can do just that. The end result looks like Figure 9-12. The completed project on the Missing CD is named *09-11_Photo_Show_If*. Here are some of the goals for this composition:

* Create a slideshow viewer that can handle up to 99 photos.

* Make adding new photos quick and easy.

* Display the total number of photos and the current position along with the photo.

* Use simple controls that work as well on mobile devices as they do on computers.

FIGURE 9-12

This versatile variation on the slideshow has hidden buttons that cover the left and right side of the photo. Click or tap on one side or the other to show the next photo or the previous one. For user feedback a semi-transparent button, like the one shown on the right side, appears briefly on mousedown then disappears on mouseup. The extra big buttons make this slideshow useful for mobile devices.

To handle multiple photo projects, this composition uses a common naming system: *photo-01.jpg, photo-02.jpg*, and so forth, up to *photo-99.jpg*. If you want to change photos, adding more or fewer, you can simply put new photos with the same naming convention in the *images* folder for your Animate project. After you add photos, you need to tell your composition the total number of photos in your project. That number is stored in two places—the "click" actions for the *goNext* and the *goPrev* buttons. To get at those actions panels, follow these steps:

1. Open *09-11_Photo_Show_If.edge*.

   One symbol is on the stage named thePhotos. If you explore the Library's Assets panel, you see the photos starting with *photo-01.jpg* and the graphics for the goNext and goPrev buttons (arrowNext and arrowPrev). In the Symbols panel there are three symbols: thePhotos, goNext, and goPrev.

2. In the Elements panel, right-click thePhotos and choose Edit Symbol "thePhotos" from the shortcut menu.

   In the innards of the symbol thePhotos, you see tbCount (a text box), mainImage (the photo visible on stage with an *img* tag), and the two symbols that work as buttons: goNext and goPrev.

3. In the Elements panel, click the Open Actions button next to goNext.

As shown in Figure 9-13, here's the code for the "click" trigger of the *goNext* button.

```
var numOfPhotos = 22;
var pic = sym.$("mainImage");
var textCount = sym.$("tbCount");

var imageSource = pic.attr('src');
var imageCount = +(imageSource.slice(13,15));
imageCount = imageCount+1;
if (imageCount>numOfPhotos) {imageCount = 1}
var newCount = imageCount + ' of '+numOfPhotos;
if (imageCount<10) {imageCount = '0'+imageCount}
imageSource = 'images/photo-'+imageCount + '.jpg';
pic.attr('src',imageSource);
textCount.html(newCount);
```

On the first line a variable called numOfPhotos is declared. For the Car Show project, the value is set to 22, since there are 22 car photos.

If you change the number of photos for a new project, you need to change *numOfPhotos* from 22 to a new value. The code for the *goPrev* button is similar and you'll find the numOfPhotos variable in the same place. When you add or remove photos, you can update the composition by changing those two numbers.

FIGURE 9-13

The hardworking code in this project is inside of the numOfPhotos symbol. Open it, then open the "click" actions for the goNext and the goPrev buttons. Tucked in there you'll find the variables that keep the count and the if() statements that control the view.

While you have the goNext button's click action displayed, take a look at the three variables created at the top:

```
var numOfPhotos = 22;
var pic = sym.$("mainImage");
var textCount = sym.$("tbCount");
```

After numOfPhotos, the *pic* variable is created to provide a short way to identify the mainImage. Next is a variable called *textCount* that is used to identify the text box (tbCount) that displays a message like "12 of 22".

So, how does Photo Show keep track of the currently displayed photo? It steals that bit of information from the JPEG filename. Remember each photo is named something like *photo-03.jpg* or *photo-05.jpg*. The first task is to get the entire photo name:

```
var imageSource = pic.attr('src');
```

The new pic variable is used to identify the mainImage. Then, its src attribute is stored in another new variable *imageSource*. That stores an entire path and filename like *images/photo-03.jpg* in imageSource as a string. The next line of code slices the number out of the filename.

```
var imageCount = +(imageSource.slice(13,15));
```

The value is stored in yet another variable, *imageCount*, but don't yawn. This one's important because it's used all over the place in the rest of the code. For example, since this code is in the "click" action of the goNext button, the first thing it does is add one to imageCount.

```
imageCount = imageCount+1;
```

That new number will be used to advance to the next photo. But first there are a couple of conditions to check. For example, what if that new number is greater than the total number of photos in the project. In that case, Photo Show needs to display the first photo, looping back to the beginning. Here's the *if()* statement to handle that condition:

```
if (imageCount>numOfPhotos) {imageCount = 1}
```

When the new photo is displayed, you want to update the text box (tbCount) that keeps count. That's done with a string of text that is stored in a variable called newCount.

```
var newCount = imageCount + ' of '+numOfPhotos;
```

The variable is created and the string is assembled from three pieces. The first is the photo number: imageCount. In the middle is a *string literal*—the text that appears in the middle: " of ". Lastly, the total number of photos is added to the string, in the case of the Car Show that number is 22. The result is that tbCount displays text like 3 of 22, providing handy, unobtrusive feedback to the viewer.

The next *if()* statement handles a sticky issue. When JavaScript sees a number like 03, it automatically lops off the leading zero. That's great for showing the count in a text box like tbCount, but it's a problem when you are trying to identify photos with names like *photo-02.jpg* and *photo-04.jpg*.

```
if (imageCount<10) {imageCount = '0'+imageCount}
imageSource = 'images/photo-'+imageCount + '.jpg';
```

So, the first line determines if imageCount<10. If that's the case, it manually adds a 0 to the front of the string imageCount. Immediately, the next line builds the filename for the image that is to be displayed. The name includes the path to the images folder. So, a complete name might be: *images/photo-03.jpg*.

> **TIP** One caution about the names of the photo files. JavaScript and many web servers are extremely picky about the case of filenames. Make sure all filenames are lower case. It's highly possible that a photo with a name like *photo-03.JPG* will not be displayed.

The last two lines of code update the visuals displayed on stage. Finally!

```
pic.attr('src',imageSource);
textCount.html(newCount);
```

The first line performs the old image swap using that carefully constructed filename. The second line updates the count that is shown in the tbCount text box. That's how the goNext button works. The goPrev button has similar code except that it subtracts from imageCount to identify the previous image and it uses conditionals to provide smooth backward navigation.

> **TIP** When this project is displayed in a browser, the Photo Show is centered. The code to do that is placed in the compositionReady trigger of the stage. That single line of code reads: *$("#Stage").css("margin", "auto");*.

Using switch() to Handle Multiple Conditions

The *if..else* conditional statement works fine when you only have a couple of possible conditions. It gets a little unwieldy when there are several. On page 92, there is an example of a filmstrip with five photos of flowers. The photos are arranged horizontally edge to edge, and individual photos are displayed on the stage by sliding the filmstrip left or right. Suppose you want to write a click action that checks the position of the filmstrip and then moves it to show the next photo. If the filmstrip is on the last image, it rewinds to the first photo. With five possible conditions, that's a little more than can be handled gracefully by *if..else*. The solution is to use JavaScript's *switch()* conditional, which lets you handle as many cases (conditions) as you want. The basic format looks like this:

```
switch(value) {
    case value1:
        do this;
        do that;
        do the other;
    break;
```

```
    case value2:
        do a different this;
        do a different that;
        do a different other;
    break;

    case value3:
        do this 3;
        do that 3;
        do the other 3;
    break;

    case value4:
        do this 4;
        do that 4;
        do the other 4;
    break;

    case value5:
        do this 5;
        do that 5;
        do the other 5;
    break;
}
```

When you call the *switch()* conditional, you pass a value to it. That value is used to determine which *case* statements are performed. When the code reaches the *break*; statement, it skips the rest of the code. To use this with the filmstrip example, you get the value for the left edge of the filmstrip. You store that value to a variable with a helpful name like *posLeft*. Then, pass that variable to a *switch()* statement:

```
switch(posLeft)
```

Inside of curly braces, you assemble your cases. For the filmstrip, there are five possible posLeft values that display the flower photos: 0, -500,-1000,-1500,-2000:

```
switch(posLeft) {
    case 0:
        do this;
        do that;
        do the other;
    break;
    case -500:
        do a different this;
        do a different that;
        do a different other;
    break;
...continued with the rest of the five possible cases
}
```

To see a working example of the filmstrip project using the *switch()* statement, check out the *09-12_Film_Strip_Switch* project (Figure 9-14). You'll find plenty of comments in the code that explain its inner workings.

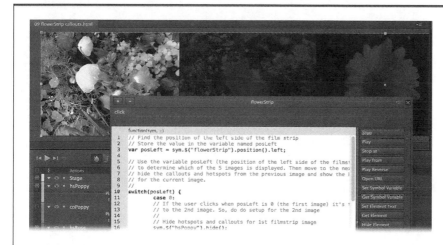

FIGURE 9-14

The Missing CD project 09-12_Film_Strip_Switch shows how to use the switch() *conditional statement to reposition the filmstrip based on its current position. The* switch() *conditional is also used to show and hide hotspots that trigger callouts for the various flower images.*

Publishing Your Composition

CHAPTER 10:
Publishing Responsive Web Pages

Publishing Responsive Web Pages

Designing compositions so they look great in Adobe Edge Animate is just half the battle. Those compositions usually go out into the world as web pages and are viewed in web browsers of all shapes and sizes—giving you limited control over how your audience sees them. This chapter provides tips for publishing compositions that look good whether they're viewed on smartphones, desktops, or high-def TVs. You'll learn to add background images to the stage and other elements. Then, you'll learn how to make the stage and its background image fill the browser window. You'll also learn how to create graphics that cleverly resize and reposition themselves for browser windows of different sizes. Along the way, you'll get tips about creating a preloader for your composition and designing a composition poster (placeholder) if someone views your page in a browser that's not up to HTML5 standards.

■ Adding Background Images to Compositions and Elements

When you build a composition, the stage can be transparent or any color that you choose from the color picker, as explained way back on page 8. For an even livelier option, you can use an image or photograph for the background. For example, if you create an animation about the epic battles between a rapidly running bird and a not too bright coyote, you might want to use an image of Monument Valley as the background. In other cases, you may prefer to use a simple textured image.

Here are the steps for adding a background photo to the stage. You can use one of your own photos or you can use one of the images in *10-1_Background_Image* from the Missing CD (*www.missingmanuals.com/cds/animatemm*).

1. Create a new Animate composition.

   Leave the size settings for the stage at 550px × 400px or a similar relatively small size.

2. Use the File→Import command to import the photo you want to use for a background image.

   The photo appears in the Assets panel in the Library. If you don't have a photo handy, you can grab one from *10-1_Background_Image*.

3. Drag the photo onto the stage.

   The image may be larger than the stage at this point.

4. Position and resize the photo so it completely covers the stage.

   The top, right corner of the image should be positioned at X=0, Y=0. When you're done resizing, the size of the image (W and H properties) and the stage should be the same.

TIP   If you change the width to height proportion of some images they can look awkward. However, if your photo is on the abstract side, like the rock wall photo in *10-1_Background_Image*, it may not matter if the proportions don't match perfectly.

---

5. Press Ctrl+Enter (⌘-Return) to preview your project.

   Your browser opens and displays your composition, scrunched up in the upper-left corner of the window (Figure 10-2, left). As expected, your photo is displayed in the area allocated to the composition's stage.

6. Drag the edge of the browser to resize the window.

   No surprises here. If you make the browser window bigger than the stage and the image, you see whitespace around the edges. Make it smaller than the image and hide parts of the image.

This kind of setup works well when the composition is only a small part of a web page. For example, if you're creating a banner ad, you probably need to have fixed dimensions. In other cases, you may want to make a bigger statement.

Making the Stage Fill the Browser Window

If you're creating an Animate composition that isn't going to be part of an existing web page, you may want to use as much of the browser window as you can. The web designer's standard dilemma is that you never know how much space your audience and their devices are likely to provide. Fortunately, Animate has a few solutions for this problem. First of all, you want to make the stage fill 100% of the available space in the browser window. Then, you want to make the image fill 100% of the stage.

Here are the steps to accomplish both of those tasks.

1. In the Elements panel, select Stage.

   The Stage properties appear in the Properties panel.

2. In Properties, click the button labeled "px" next to W (width).

   The "px" label changes to % (percentage). Now, instead of using an absolute value, the width of the stage is set to a percentage of the available browser window. There are only two units of measure available, so this button works as a toggle, switching between pixels and percentage. Initially, Animate sets the width to 100%. If you'd prefer a different percentage, you can make that change in the value.

3. In Properties, click the button labeled "px" next to H (height).

   You can choose different units of measure for the width and height of an element. In this case, setting both to 100% makes the stage fill the available space.

4. Select the background image on the stage.

   In the previous steps, this image was manually resized to fill the stage. That process gave the image an absolute size in pixels.

5. In the Position and Size properties, click the Layout Preset button.

   As shown in Figure 10-1, the Layout Preset panel opens displaying presets that work for different design situations.

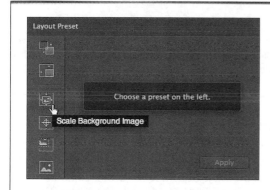

FIGURE 10-1

Layout Presets are a timesaver because they make several position and size property changes with a single click. You can make the same changes manually, by adjusting several properties. The advantage of the preset is that it bundles all those settings into a single command.

6. Choose the Scale Background Image preset and then click Apply.

   When you click a preset, the panel explains the purpose of the preset and provides details about the property settings. When you click Apply, those settings are applied to your project.

7. Press Ctrl+Enter (⌘-Return) to preview your project.

Now when your browser displays your project, the stage is set to fill the available space in the browser window. In turn, the image is set to fill the available space provided by the stage. You can see the result on the right in Figure 10-2. Resize the browser and your image accommodates the new dimensions. What's more, because the image was fairly high resolution to begin with, it looks pretty good even when it's expanded to fill a display with a resolution of more than 2500 x 1400 pixels.

FIGURE 10-2

Left: You see the image as it appeared with an absolute size provided in pixels.

Right: Here's the image as it appears after setting the stage W and H properties to 100% and then applying the Scale Background preset.

Congratulations—you've created a responsive design that automatically adjusts for browser windows of different sizes. For example, if you used the rock wall photo, that image will fill a browser window whether it appears on a computer screen or a handheld device. If someone resizes the browser or turns the tablet from a landscape to a portrait position, the background adjusts in response.

> **TIP** There's one gotcha to be aware of regarding image size. Apple's operating system for phones, pods and tablets has limitations. It doesn't gracefully handle images over 1024×1024px. One workaround is to slice large images into smaller parts and then piece them together in Edge. For ease of handling, you can put the parts into a symbol.

Setting Minimum and Maximum Widths for Elements

Being able to fill up the browser window with the stage and an image helps to make your compositions look better in a variety of circumstances. Still, there are limits to how small you can scrunch an image before it becomes distorted. Likewise, there are limits to how wide you can stretch a composition before the individual elements are spaced so far apart that they begin to look disconnected and odd. Animate provides two settings to help with these problems. Select the Stage in Elements and you see the Min W and Max W settings (for Minimum Width and Maximum Width). The width is usually the most significant dimension for a couple of reasons. Web pages are often designed to automatically accommodate content by extending the height (length) of the page. Width, on the other hand, is often adjusted by users for readability. On big screen monitors, users adjust the width of their web browsers to avoid overly long lines of text. Phone and tablet users switch between portrait and landscape orientation for similar reasons.

Using the Min W and Max W properties you can set limits to that stretching and scrunching. To experiment with these controls, try this:

1. Create a new Animate project and set the stage background to a color other than white.

   Giving the stage a background color makes it easier to identify the stage area in a browser window.

2. In Properties, change W and H to 100%.

   As explained in the previous example (page 228), setting the stage W and H properties to 100% makes the stage fill the browser window.

3. Change the value of Min W to 550px.

   This setting overrides the setting in step 2, setting a minimum width for stage scrunching. If a visitor provides less than 550px in their browser window, the width of the stage will become clipped.

4. Click the Max H button and then change the Max H value to 700px.

   This setting overrides how far the stage can be stretched. So, using a combination of a Min W and Max W values, you can create a range for the stage width.

5. Make sure that Rulers (Ctrl+R for Windows, ⌘-R on Macs) are visible.

   Once you change the stage width to a percentage, a pin appears in the ruler. You can use this pin to simulate different stage widths.

6. On the horizontal ruler, drag the stage resize pin to the left and right.

   When you drag the pin to the left, the workspace simulates the appearance of your composition in a narrower browser window. See the top of Figure 10-3. Dragging the pin to the right shows what your composition will look like in a wider browser window.

You set Min W and Max W values for the elements on your web pages, too. For example, you set minimum and maximum values for a photograph or other image. Even the rectangles, rounded rectangles, and ellipses created in Edge can be constrained. If you don't see the Min W and Max W widgets in the Properties panel, click the button in the lower-left corner of the Position and Size subpanel to expand it.

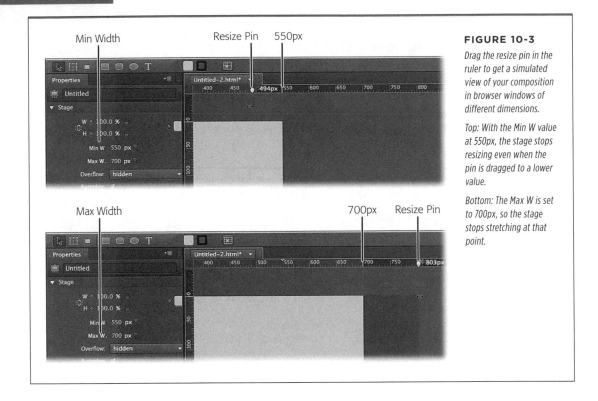

FIGURE 10-3

Drag the resize pin in the ruler to get a simulated view of your composition in browser windows of different dimensions.

Top: With the Min W value at 550px, the stage stops resizing even when the pin is dragged to a lower value.

Bottom: The Max W is set to 700px, so the stage stops stretching at that point.

■ Creating Responsive Designs

The art of creating responsive designs is to carefully apply properties to each element so it behaves the way you want under different circumstances. Primarily, those circumstances relate to the amount of real estate available to the composition. An earlier example showed how to scale an image to fill the stage. The next step is to add more elements and choose the right property settings for them. Here are questions you should ask about each element:

■ SIZE QUESTIONS
- What size should this element be?
- When the stage dimensions change, should the size of this element change? If so, how should it resize itself?
- Should this element have minimum and maximum width settings?

■ **POSITION QUESTIONS**

- Where should this element be on the stage?

- When the stage dimensions change, should the position of this element change? If so, how should it move?

- Which corner of the stage should be used as a reference point? Upper-left? Lower-right?

Chances are, you'll use different settings for different elements. You may want the main image for your composition to change in size and have a position relative to the upper-left corner of the available space. On the other hand, you may have a sidebar that consists of a text box and a rectangle for background color. For that element, you may want to position it relative to the upper-right corner. You want the text to be readable, so you may want to use an absolute size or perhaps set a minimum width for the text box. These decisions are often made through testing—also known as trial and error. As usual with web pages and browsers, you never have complete control as a designer. The best you can do is develop settings that are acceptable in most circumstances.

The best way to learn responsive design techniques is to play with different layouts and different settings. In fact, when you're learning how the many size and position widgets work, it's best to experiment with just a couple of basic elements on the stage. Later, you can apply the things you learn to your more complex compositions.

Making Graphics that Scale Size

When the stage shrinks and grows, often you'll want to change the size of elements too. If you've followed along in this chapter, the methods for making elements scale shouldn't come as much of a surprise. You can change the W (width) and H (height) units from px (an absolute setting) to % (a variable setting). Note you don't have to change both to the same unit. For example, you may want an element to scale with the width of the browser window, but you'd like the height to remain an absolute value in pixels. Perhaps you'd like to create a text box that is always 60% of the width of the browser window. Here's what you need to do:

1. Make sure the stage is set to Scale its size by changing its W property to a percentage (%) as explained on page 229.

2. Select the text box you want to scale. Then, change the units for W to a percentage (%).

3. Change the value for W to 60%.

You can position your text box wherever you want on the page and its width will be 60% the width of the stage. You can set the height (H) to an absolute value in pixels or you can change it to a percentage, too. Keep in mind that when you scale the size of a text box, you're changing the size of the container, but not the font-size of the text. That remains controlled by the Text settings (page 49). Depending on the position and your display settings, some of the text box may be hidden. With text boxes, it's likely that you'll want to set up some parameters for the minimum and maximum acceptable width. Those details were covered back on page 230.

TIP   When you're scaling the size of elements on the stage, you can get a quick preview of the changes by adjusting the "resize pin" on the ruler. For details, see steps 5 and 6 on page 231.

Making Graphics that Scale Position

When the stage and background of the composition changes dimensions, you may want to change the relative position of elements on the stage. Often, you'll want to use different settings for photos, graphics, and text boxes. As usual, the best way to learn how the various tools work is to add one or two elements to the stage and tweak the settings. With that in mind, try these experiments with the example begun earlier in this chapter (page 229):

1. Draw a 200px square and position it in the center of the stage. Then, press Ctrl+Enter (⌘-Return) to preview your composition.

    The view. If you view this composition on a larger monitor or screen, the background image fills the browser window, but instead of being centered, the square is positioned near the upper-left corner. If you change the size of the browser window, the background changes size and shape, and the square remains the same distance from the upper-left corner.

    The position settings. When the X and Y position setting units are *px* (pixels), they represent an absolute value. In this case, the square is an absolute distance from the upper-right corner of the browser window.

2. With the square selected, in Properties→Position and Size→"Relative to," click the upper-right corner as shown in Figure 10-4. Change the X and Y properties to 200px. Then, press Ctrl+Enter (⌘-Return) to preview your composition.

    The view. In your browser, the 200px square is position 200px from the top of the window and 200px from the right edge of the window. If you resize the browser window, the square repositions itself so that it remains 200px from the top and right edges.

    The position settings. In this step, the reference point has changed from the upper-left corner to the upper-right corner using the "Relative to" tool. New absolute values of 200px determine the distance from the upper-right corner.

FIGURE 10-4

Choose a corner in the "Relative to" tool to determine which corner of the browser window is used as a reference point. Here, the upper-right corner is selected.

3. In Properties and Size, click the Applied button. Then, click the X and Y unit buttons (px) and change them to %. Then, change both the X and Y values to *50%*. Then, press Ctrl+Enter (⌘-Return) to preview your composition.

The view. In Animate, the top-right corner of the square is placed in the middle of the stage both horizontally and vertically. In the browser window, it is also centered. If you change the size of the browser window, the square is repositioned in the window, so that its upper-right corner is at the center of the browser window.

The position settings. The Global and Applied buttons change the scope of the Position and Size settings. When Global is selected, the settings are relative to the stage. When Applied is selected, the settings are relative to the DIV or Symbol that contains the element. When you change from pixels to a percentage, or vice versa, you should change the unit before entering a value. Using a percentage instead of pixels gives the square a relative position. In this case, X=50% and Y=50%, the upper-right corner of the square is centered in the browser window.

You can scale the position of photos, imported graphics, and elements drawn in Animate using these techniques. As with the size properties, you can mix and match absolute units (pixels) with relative units (percentage). For example, you can create a right sidebar that's 10% from the top of the stage and 50px from the right edge of the stage.

TIP When you're scaling the position of elements on the stage, you can get a quick preview of the changes by adjusting the "resize pin" on the ruler. For details, see steps 5 and 6 on page 231.

◼ Creating a Preloader for Your Composition

No one likes to wait, but it's particularly annoying when you don't know what's going on. When you're waiting for a web page to load, these kinds of questions run through your mind: Is this website broken? Is my connection down? Is this web site worth the wait? I wonder if anyone's left me a Facebook message? It's relatively easy to hang on to your audience by providing a preloader graphic that lets them know something is going on behind the scenes and pretty soon they'll see the results. Preloader graphics are usually animated GIF images: circles or bars that display some kind of motion. They're lightweight (small in file size) so they can load quickly, before the other bigger elements.

1. With the stage selected, in Properties→Preloader, click the Edit button.

The workspace changes to show the Preloader in place of the stage. Also, the Preloader is the only element shown in the Elements panel. The Properties panel shows a single button: Insert Preloader Clip-Art. Below that is a panel that tells you the size of the Preloader in kilobytes. This is helpful because you want your preloader to be lightweight (small file size).

2. Click Insert Preloader Clip-Art.

As shown in Figure 10-5, a dialog box opens displaying several pre-designed preloader graphics. These are animated GIF images.

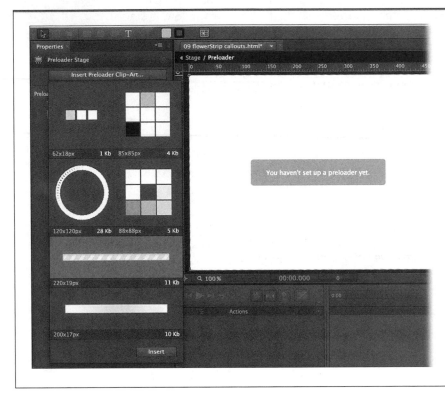

FIGURE 10-5

Edge comes with a few quite serviceable preloader graphics. These animated GIFs provide some movement and activity to let your audience know things are happening behind the scenes and it's worth the wait. If you don't like Adobe's preloaders, you can create and use your own.

3. Choose one of the preloader graphics and then click Insert.

The dialog box closes and your preloader graphic is on the stage. You can reposition and resize it if you wish. In Properties, under Preloader Size, you see the total size of your preloader, which includes the graphic and the JavaScript code required to display the preloader.

4. In the main workspace, click Stage.

The preloader closes and you're back at the main stage for your composition. Later, if you need to go back and make changes to the preloader, select the Stage in the Elements panel and then go Properties→Preloader→Edit.

If you want to display a message while your composition is loading, you can add text to the preloader. You can also add a background image, but keep in mind you want your preloader to be as lean as possible (as in, as small a file size as possible, to allow for quick download).

There's one more setting you can make in regard to the preloader in the Properties panel. In the Preloader subpanel, there's a button where you can choose between

Immediate and Polite. Even though your mother told you it always pays to be polite, the Immediate option is initially chosen here. That means the preloader will load the needed JavaScript libraries as soon as possible. If you choose the Polite option, Animate waits until the page's load event fires before it starts loading those resources. In most cases, the Immediate option works well. If you're working with a very large composition or have other special circumstances, it may be worth testing both options after your project has been uploaded to a web server.

Accommodating Older Web Browsers

Sadly, not everyone roaming the web has up to date equipment or browsers. That means some visitor's to your Animate web page may not be equipped to see it in all its glory. Your first reaction may be: "Tough! Why don't you get with it?" After that passes, you may want to set up a way to let those poor Neanderthals know what's going on. You do that by creating a Down-level Stage. Translation: Build a relatively static web page that visitors see when their browsers can't handle highly Animated pages. Here are the things you need to do to set up an effective Down-level Stage:

- Create a "poster" image.

- Add the poster to the Down-level Stage.

- Add explanatory text to the Down-level Stage.

- Redirect ill-equipped visitors to a new location.

All the action takes place in the Properties panel when you have the stage selected. You can follow these steps with any of your Animate compositions. In most cases, you want to set up your Down-level Stage when your composition is nearly complete. Why? Because, the first thing you want to do is snap a screenshot with interesting graphics that illustrate the purpose of your composition. Here are the steps:

1. With the Stage selected in the Elements panel, position the playhead to display the image you want to capture.

   This image needs to convey as much information as possible about the composition.

2. In the Properties panel, click the camera icon in the Poster subpanel.

   The Capture a Poster Image dialog box appears with buttons that provide two options: Capture and Refresh. There's a brief explanation for each. In short, choose Capture the first time you create a Poster image and choose Refresh if you want to update a Poster that you've already captured.

3. Click Capture.

   The image is saved as Poster.png in the Library→Images folder. The dialog box title changes to Poster Image Captured and two new buttons appear: Publish Settings and Edit Down-level Stage. See Figure 10-6.

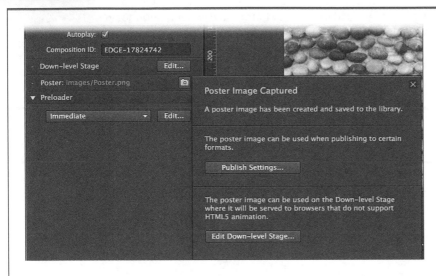

FIGURE 10-6

After you've captured a poster for the Down-level Stage, you see this dialog box where you can open the Publish settings or edit your Down-level Stage.

4. Click Edit Down-level Stage.

   The workspace changes to show the Down-level Stage, which is empty the first time you see it. In the Elements panel, you see that the Down-level Stage is the only item available and it is selected. The Properties panel shows a single option, which lets you insert the captured Poster.png into the Down-level Stage.

5. In Properties, click Insert.

   Poster.png becomes the background for Down-level Stage. With Poster.png selected, you see additional options in Properties: Position and Size, and Link. As expected, you can change the size of the image. You also have the option to change from pixels to percentages for a more responsive design.

6. In the Tools panel, click the text tool (T) and add a message to the Down-level Stage.

   Provide whatever message is necessary for a visitor who is unable to view your composition. You can tell them what they're missing. Suggest that they upgrade to a new browser. Suggest they visit another web page.

7. In Properties→Link URL, type in a complete web address for an alternative web page.

   The link you provide should be related to the message in step 6. If you're giving a browser recommendation, you may link to the page where they can download a new browser. If you're providing a low-tech alternative to your composition, you want to link to that alternative page.

■ Publishing Your Composition as a Web Page

The last task that you perform inside of the Adobe Edge Animate workspace is to publish your composition. During the creation process, you end up with lots of different files in your project folder, some of which aren't needed on the web server and page that hosts your composition. When you use Animate's "publish" feature, only the necessary files are copied to the publish folders. Other files, such as JavaScript resources, are "minified" in the process. That means that they're reduced in file size so that your web pages and compositions load as quickly as possible. Before you publish your composition, you'll want to double-check your Publish Settings.

1. Go File→Publish Settings.

   The Publish Settings dialog box opens as shown in Figure 10-7. It displays three publish target options: Web, Animate Deployment Package, and iBooks/OS X.

NOTE This book covers publishing to the Web, the most common destination for Animate projects. For details on publishing deployment packages and iBook publishing, visit the Adobe Forums (*http://forums.adobe.com*).

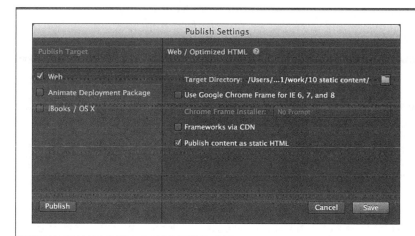

FIGURE 10-7

Before you publish the files needed to place your composition on a website, visit the Publishing Settings shown here (File→Publish Settings). The most critical step is to choose the folder where your published files are stored.

2. Choose Web.

   The dialog box displays the publish settings for web pages, including a target directory.

3. Click the folder and choose a folder on your computer where you want to publish your Animate files.

For example, you may choose to publish your Animate composition in a folder that is already part of an existing website. If you don't choose a folder, Animate creates a "publish" folder within your project folder. This works fine in many cases, because you later upload these files to a web server.

4. Choose Optional Publish Settings.

No other settings are needed to publish a working composition; however, there are three optional settings you can choose to turn on:

- **Use Google Chrome Frame for IE6, 7, and 8.** Internet Explorer is notorious for not following the standards used by other browsers. This is especially true of the versions before Internet Explorer 9. This setting may help your composition work with these older browsers.

- **Frameworks via CDN.** The term CDN stands for content delivery network. Use this option to get the necessary JavaScript libraries via the Internet, rather than publishing them with your composition.

- **Publish content as static HTML.** Usually, Animate creates elements using code in the JavaScript files. When you choose this option, Animate creates some of those same elements in the HTML file. If you examine the web page, you will see DIV tags that describe elements from your composition. This feature improves accessibility and makes your project more compatible with screen readers.

5. Click Publish.

When you click Publish, Animate writes the necessary files for your composition to the designated folder.

TIP If you don't click the Publish button in the settings dialog box, you can always publish your composition later using File→Publish.

Your animate composition may be a standalone web page or you may want to place it inside of an existing web page. That process is explained on page 168. After you've published your composition to a folder on your computer, you probably still need to move it to your web server. You can do this using a web design program, such as Dreamweaver or using a FTP (file transfer protocol) tool.

Appendixes

Installation and Help

While there are many programs out there that have double-digit version numbers, Adobe Edge Animate is a youngster at version 1.0. After about a year of "preview" versions (seven of them), it's now ready for its debut. Animate has matured into the kind of design/web page building program that you'd expect from Adobe. There's a lot of power under the hood. The widgets and tools are well thought out and let you tinker with just about everything on the page. Still, you may need help getting started and support when you're working with Animate. Because it hasn't been on the scene that long, it might not be obvious where to turn for Adobe Edge Animate support. But you've come to the right place because that's the purpose of this appendix. After all, even Lewis and Clark had guides to help them in their explorations.

NOTE This section was based on Adobe Edge Animate version 1.0. Your mileage may vary if you're using a different version.

■ Edge Animate System Requirements

Adobe Edge Animate runs in Windows 7 and Mac OS 10.6. That means Windows XP and Mac OS 10.5 and below are not supported. For those of you who are interested in such details, Animate is a 32-bit application but will run on 64-bit machines, too. Adobe has not listed any other requirements, but Animate doesn't seem to require a lot of processing power or disk space. If your system can comfortably run a web browser and another application, like a photo editing program, at the same time, you won't have trouble with Animate. Typically, the application folder, Windows or Mac, requires less than 150 megabytes of space. That's less than half of what's required for Dreamweaver or Photoshop.

■ Installing Edge Animate

Installing Animate is fairly easy. The first step is download the file for your computer from Adobe's website. There's a version for Windows and a version for Mac. You need an Adobe Creative Cloud account to log in, and get access to the files. If you don't already have an account, don't worry. It's free. All you have to do is provide the usual information: name, email, and so forth.

> **NOTE** If you have an Adobe Cloud subscription, you'll find Animate listed with the other applications. Installation is as simple as selecting Edge Animate in the Adobe Application Manager tool.

You can find the download links at: *http://labs.adobe.com/technologies/edge/.* The Windows version is a ZIP file. The Mac version is a DMG file.

Installing Edge Animate for Windows

1. Double-click the ZIP file. Extract the contents of the ZIP file to the desktop.

2. Open the folder containing the extracted files, and double-click *Set-up.exe.*

   The Welcome screen appears.

3. Click Accept to start the installation.

   The Install Options screen opens.

4. Click Install to install Animate or Back to return to the Welcome screen.

   The Installation Progress screen appears; when installation is complete, the Thank You screen is presented.

5. Click Done to close the installer or the Adobe Animate button to launch Animate.

Installing Edge Animate for Mac

1. Double-click the DMG file.

2. Open the Adobe Edge Animate folder and double-click the Install application.

   The Welcome screen opens.

3. Click Accept to start the installation.

   The Install Options screen appears.

4. Click Install to install Animate or Back to return to the Welcome screen.

5. The Installation Progress screen appears; when installation is complete, the Thank You screen is presented.

6. Click Done to close the installer or the Adobe Edge Animate button to launch Animate.

Uninstalling Edge Animate

If you've taken an Adobe Edge Animate test drive with one of the preview versions, it's important that you completely uninstall it before you move up to the latest and greatest version.

Uninstalling Edge Animate for Windows

1. Select Start→Control Panel and, in the Programs section, click "Uninstall a Program."

2. In the list of programs, double-click Adobe Edge Animate.

   The Uninstall Options screen appears.

3. Click Uninstall and wait while Windows deletes Animate.

   To back out now and keep Animate around for a while, click Cancel.

Uninstalling Edge Animate for Mac

1. In the Applications→Adobe Edge Animate Preview folder, double-click the Edge Animate Uninstaller application.

2. Click Uninstall and wait while your Mac deletes Animate.

   To back out now and keep Animate around for a while, click Cancel.

TIP Sometimes Adobe applications leave remnants on your hard drive even when they've been uninstalled. That can be a particular problem with "preview" applications. The remnants interfere when you install a new version of the same application. If you have these kinds of problems, you can use Adobe's "cleaner" tool to remove those remnants. Follow Adobe's instructions carefully when using the cleaner utility. You can find the tool and the instructions at *www.adobe.com/support/contact/cscleanertool.html*.

Getting Help

As a relative newcomer, Animate may not have the kind of extensive help documentation that you're used to with other applications. What's available you'll find under the the Help menu. It includes online documentation and links to Adobe's video tutorials. There's also "getting started" help in the Lessons window (Window→Lessons).

If you have a specific question, you may want to turn to the Animate community forum that's hosted on Adobe's website: *http://forums.adobe.com/community/labs/edge/*. You need to use your Adobe ID to log in, but you already have that if you downloaded Animate. What you'll find in the forum is an active community of Animate fans. Other Animate explorers, like you, post some of their projects and share info about how they work. Post a question, and soon you'll have an answer—if not a full-blown debate.

Books for HTML, CSS, JavaScript, and jQuery

A few of the books in the Missing Manual series cover HTML, JavaScript, and jQuery: *HTML5: The Missing Manual* by Matthew MacDonald (O'Reilly); *CSS: The Missing Manual* by David Sawyer McFarland (O'Reilly); *JavaScript and jQuery: The Missing Manual* by David Sawyer McFarland (O'Reilly); and *Creating Websites: The Missing Manual* by Matthew MacDonald (O'Reilly).

Head First jQuery by Ryan Benedetti and Ronan Cranley (O'Reilly) also serves up a great introduction to jQuery coding. If you're looking for the Bible on JavaScript, turn to *JavaScript: The Definitive Guide* by David Flanagan. Just be prepared for some serious technical detail.

Online Help

There are a number of non-Adobe resources for help with Animate, JavaScript, and jQuery. Do a Google search for "Adobe Edge Animate," and you're likely to find websites where people post examples and maintain blogs that discuss Animate. Darrell Heath, this book's technical reviewer, has just such a site at: *www.heathrowe.com*.

For help with JavaScript, you can turn to *www.w3schools.com/js* or *https://developer .mozilla.org/en/JavaScript*.

The official jQuery website provides tutorials, forums, and lots of ways to learn. Here's a link to its tutorials: *http://docs.jquery.com/Tutorials*.

Chris Grover, the author of this book, has a website at *www.edgemanual.com*. The site displays working examples of some of the projects in this book. It also provides hints, tips, and how-to projects not covered in the book.

Menu by Menu

A dobe Edge Animate: The Missing Manual is full of details, explanations, and examples. This appendix provides quick thumbnail descriptions of every command in every menu.

NOTE   Adobe is frequently updating the Edge Animate program, so it's possible some of these menu commands may not match your version. You can always find the most recent version of Animate at *http://edge.adobe. com.*

▉ File

The File menu commands work on your Animate projects as a whole. Use the File menu for major events like starting a new project, opening a file you created previously, and adjusting Animate's publishing settings.

New

Windows: Ctrl+N

Mac: ⌘-N

The new command creates a new, empty HTML document, complete with a new Animate stage and timeline. Animate uses the stage settings from your previous project, but you can always make changes to stage properties such as dimensions and background color. Just adjust the settings in the Properties panel.

Open

Windows: Ctrl+O

Mac: ⌘-O

Opens the standard dialog box where you can navigate through your folders and select Animate Files. Use the Open command to quickly find and then open files in Animate.

Open Recent

Leads to a submenu that shows a list of the last 10 Animate project (.edge) files that you opened and saved. Click a file name to open the Animate project.

Close

Windows: Ctrl+W

Mac: ⌘-W

Closes the active Animate project. If you made changes to the project, Animate asks if you want to save it before closing.

Close All

Windows: Ctrl+Alt+W

Mac: Option-⌘-W

Closes all open Animate Projects. If you made changes to the projects, Animate asks if you want to save them before closing.

Save

Windows: Ctrl+S

Mac: ⌘-S

Saves the changes you've made to your Animate document. If you haven't made any changes since opening the document, the Save command is dimmed.

Save As

Windows: Ctrl+Shift+S

Mac: Shift-⌘-S

Use Save As to save the active Animate project with a new name. Keep in mind, you probably want to keep your newly named project and all the resulting files in a new or separate folder.

Revert

Discards any changes you made to your document and reverts to the last saved version.

Publish Settings

Opens the dialog box where you can choose options for publishing your project (see Figure B-1). Different options are available for publishing to the Web, InDesign, or iBooks.

Publish

Windows: Ctrl+Alt+S

Mac: Option-⌘-S

After you've adjusted the Publish Settings (above), use this command to publish your project. Animate produces HTML and JavaScript (.js) files that are needed for your animation to run properly. If these files are moved or missing, your animation won't work as expected.

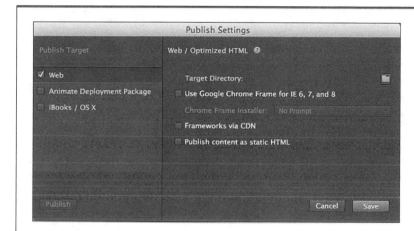

FIGURE B-1

In the Publish Settings dialog box, Animate gives you several options for publishing your project to the Web, to InDesign (Adobe's page layout application), or to iBooks (Apple's book publishing tool).

Preview in Browser

Windows: Ctrl+Enter

Mac: ⌘-Return

Publish Preview runs your Animate animation in your web browser. If you have more than one web browser on your computer, Animate uses the one that's set as the default.

Import

Windows: Ctrl+I

Mac: ⌘-I

Opens a standard folder/file dialog box where you can select graphics to add to your project. Animate can import PNG, GIF, JPG, and SVG files. You can select and import multiple files at once. After images are imported, they appear in the Library panel's Assets→Images folder.

■ Edit

Use this menu to cut, copy, paste, and change items you've selected on the stage. In addition to the usual suspects, the Edit menu also lets you transform elements, set keyboard shortcuts, and use special characters in text that may not show up on your keyboard.

Undo

Windows: Ctrl+Z

Mac: ⌘-Z

This command undoes that last command you applied. So if you accidentally deleted a drawing from your stage, the Undo command brings it back like magic. Remember the Undo command for those moments when you smack your forehead and say, "Oh, no! Why'd I do that?" You can backtrack through your last few steps by hitting the Undo command repeatedly.

Redo

Windows: Ctrl+Shift+Z

Mac: Shift-⌘-Z

Redo is for those moments when you have second thoughts a second time. If you've used Undo and decide you liked things better before you issued the command, use the Redo command to put things back the way they were.

Cut

Windows: Ctrl+X

Mac: ⌘-X

Removes the selected element from the stage and places a copy on your computer's Clipboard. Once it's on the Clipboard, you can paste it to a new location or a new document.

Copy

Windows: Ctrl+C

Mac: ⌘-C

Makes a copy of any selected elements and places a copy on the Clipboard. The original elements remain on the stage. Once you've copied an element or group of elements to the Clipboard, you can paste them to a new location or a new document.

Paste

Windows: Ctrl+V

Mac: ⌘-V

Any elements that are on the Clipboard due to cutting or copying (above) are pasted onto the stage. At that point, the elements are like any other. You can move them or change them through the Properties panel.

Paste Special

The Paste Special command handle special circumstances usually having to do with the timelines keyframes and transitions after they've been cut or copied.

Paste Transitions To Locations

Pastes keyframes and transitions to the timeline at the current playhead position.

Paste Transitions From Location

Pastes keyframes and transitions from one element or symbol to another.

Paste Inverted

Reverses the order of keyframes and transitions while pasting them back into the timeline. This command is good for back and forth motion like a bouncing ball.

Paste Actions

Use this command to paste actions from one element to another. This command works well when several elements have identical actions or you can use it to copy action that you will later modify.

Paste All

Paste transitions and actions to the target.

Duplicate

Windows: Ctrl+D

Mac: ⌘-D

A copy and paste command all rolled into one. Copies any selected objects, and then immediately pastes a duplicate on the stage.

Select All

Windows: Ctrl+A

Mac: ⌘-A

Selects all the elements on the stage and in the work area offstage. If you select an element in the timeline before using Select All, the command selects all elements, keyframes, and transitions in the timeline. If you want to deselect individual elements, use Shift-click.

Transform

If you have an element selected, this command switches to Transform mode where you can scale, rotate, and skew elements.

Delete

Windows: Del

Mac: Delete

Removes any selected element from the stage or timeline. Animate doesn't store deleted elements, keyframes, or transitions on the Clipboard, so you can't use the Paste command to put them back.

Keyboard Shortcuts

Windows: Alt+K

Mac: Option-K

Keyboard shortcuts are the key combinations used to run a command, like Alt+K and Option-K above. Animate lets you change or create keyboard shortcuts for any menu command. This command brings up the dialog box shown in Figure B-2, where you can make changes.

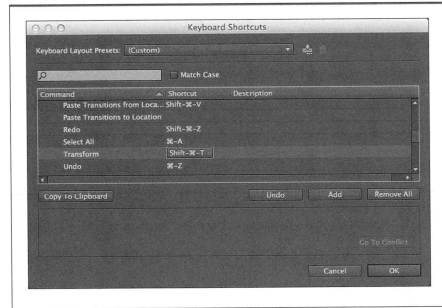

FIGURE B-2

Use the Keyboard Shortcuts dialog box to make Animate work they way you want. You can reprogram any command to use new shortcut keys.

Special Characters (Mac only)

Mac: Option-⌘-T

Displays the Mac's standard dialog box for showing and inserting special characters that don't appear on the keyboard.

■ View

Use this menu to alter the onscreen display, with features such as zoom, guides, and rulers. This menu also gives you access to the Animate Preloader and Down-level Stages.

Zoom In

Windows: Ctrl+=

Mac: ⌘-=

Changes the view of the stage by zooming in around any selected object. It may help to think of this key as Ctrl++ or ⌘-+, as that is the shifted version of this key. The minus (-) key lives next door in the number row at the top of your keyboard.

Zoom Out

Windows: Ctrl+-

Mac: ⌘--

Changes the view of the stage by zooming out.

Actual Size

Windows: Ctrl+1

Mac: ⌘-1

Resets the view to the actual size after you have zoomed in or out.

Rulers

Windows: Ctrl+R

Mac: ⌘-R

Shows or hides rulers along the top and left side of the stage. At the time this was written, Animate's rulers were a bit underpowered compared to other Adobe products. For example, the Selection tool's position is not indicated on rulers and it is not possible to pull guidelines from the rulers. These popular features will most likely appear in later versions.

Guides

Windows: Ctrl+;

Mac: ⌘-;

Shows or hides the guides you create by clicking a ruler (horizontal or vertical) and dragging on to the stage. This command works like a toggle; click to show or hide guides on the stage. A checkmark appears next to the command when it is turned on.

Snap to Guides

Windows: Ctrl+Shift+;

Mac: Shift-⌘-;

Toggles snapping on and off for guides. With snap to guides on, elements you move on the stage will automatically snap to guides when they are positioned near them.

Lock Guides

Windows: Alt+Shift+;

Mac: Option-Shift-;

Locks guides in place so they won't be inadvertently moved when you're positioning other elements. This command works like a toggle; click to show or hide guides on the stage. A checkmark appears next to the command when it is turned on.

Smart Guides

Windows: Ctrl+;

Mac: ⌘-;

Smart Guides pop up when you position elements on the stage next to other elements and, frankly, they're pretty smart and helpful. Use this command to toggle them on or off as needed.

Preloader Stage

Used to view the stage that is displayed while Animate is loading the main composition.

Down-level Stage

Used to view the stage that is displayed when the audience has a browser that is incompatible with an Animate composition.

 # Modify

The commands in the Modify menu help you to arrange elements on the stage. This menu also includes commands for creating and editing symbols.

Arrange

The Arrange submenu's commands act on the elements in your animation's layers.

Bring to Front

> Windows: Ctrl+Shift+]
>
> Mac: Shift-⌘-]
>
> Brings the selected element to the top level on the stage so that the element appears to be in front of all other elements.

Bring Forward

> Windows: Ctrl+]
>
> Mac: ⌘-]
>
> Brings selected elements forward one step in front of other elements on the stage.

Send Backward

> Windows: Ctrl+[
>
> Mac: ⌘-[
>
> Moves the selected elements back one step, placing it behind other elements on the stage.

Send to Back

> Windows: Ctrl+Shift+[
>
> Mac: Shift-⌘-[
>
> Sends the selected elements to the bottom level on the stage so that they appear to be behind the other elements on the stage.

Align

The Align submenu's commands help you position your animation's elements neatly in relation to the edges of the stage or to one another:

Left

> Aligns selected elements along the left edge.

Horizontal Center

> Aligns the center of the selected elements to the same horizontal position.

Right
> Aligns selected elements along the right edge.

Top
> Aligns selected elements along the top edge.

Vertical Center
> Aligns the center of the selected elements to the same vertical position.

Bottom
> Aligns selected elements along the bottom edge.

Distribute

Use the Distribute menu to arrange three or more elements with even, in-between spacing. These commands don't have keyboard shortcuts.

Left
> Spaces the left edge of selected elements an even distance apart.

Horizontal Center
> Spaces the center of elements an even distance apart in the horizontal direction.

Right
> Spaces the right edge of selected elements an even distance apart.

Top
> Spaces the top edge of elements an even distance apart.

Vertical Center
> Spaces the center of elements an even distance apart in the vertical direction.

Bottom
> Spaces the bottom of elements an even distance apart.

Convert to Symbol

Windows: Ctrl+Y

Mac: ⌘-Y

Use this command to turn selected elements into a Symbol. Symbols give you a way to group elements own independent timeline. When you use this command, a dialog box appears where you can name the symbol and set its initial timeline action to play automatically.

Edit Symbol

Opens a selected symbol for editing, giving you access to the grouped elements and the symbol's timeline.

◾ Timeline

The longest and most complicated of Animate's menus, the Timeline menu lets you Play, Stop, and control your animation while working in Animate. In addition, there are commands for adding keyframes, transitions, labels, and triggers.

Play/Stop

Windows: Space

Mac: Space

Starts and stops animation playback. This command works only while you're working inside of Animate. There are other methods for starting and stopping the timeline when it is being viewed by your audience. See page 214.

Return

Windows: Enter

Mac: Return

Moves the playhead back to its previous position before playback.

Go to Start

Windows: Home

Mac: Home

Moves the playhead to the beginning of the timeline.

Go to End

Windows: End

Mac: End

Moves the playhead to the end of the timeline.

Go to Previous Keyframe

Windows:

Mac: ⌘-Left Arrow

Moves the playhead to the previous keyframe of the selected element.

Go to Next Keyframe

Windows:

Mac: ⌘-Right Arrow

Moves the playhead to the next keyframe of the selected element.

Auto-Keyframe Mode

Windows: K

Mac: K

Toggles Auto-Keyframe mode on and off. When Animate is in Auto-Keyframe mode, keyframes are automatically created when element's properties are changed on the stage.

Auto-Transition Mode

Windows: X

Mac: X

Toggles Auto-Transition mode on and off. For example, a streetlight changing from red to green is an instant transition. A car driving from one point to another is not an instant transition—it's a gradual transition.

Add Keyframe

Keyframes are used in the timeline to mark the point in time where an element's property changes. That property might be width, height, position on the stage, color, or any of the properties that appear in the Properties panel. Keyframes mark the ends of a transition, where a property changes from one value to another. The Add Keyframe submenu changes to display the available properties for the selected element.

Insert Label

Windows: Ctrl+L

Mac: ⌘-L

Use labels to mark points in the timeline that you want to refer to later. Labels are particularly helpful when you use JavaScript to automate timeline actions.

Insert Trigger

Windows: Ctrl+T

Mac: ⌘-T

Inserts a trigger in the timeline at the point of the playhead. Timeline triggers initiate actions that are written in JavaScript/jQuery code.

Create Transitions

Windows: Ctrl+Shift+T

Mac: Shift-⌘-T

Use this command to create a transition between two property keyframes with different values.

Remove Transitions

Windows: Ctrl+Del

Mac: Shift-Delete

Removes the selected transition, but leaves the property keyframes in place.

Invert Transition

Reverses the keyframes in a transition. For example, if the original transition is an apple falling from a tree, the reversed transition would show the apple rise from the ground and reattach itself to the tree branch.

Insert Time

Automatically inserts time into the timeline. A dialog box appears where you can set the amount of time you want to add. Adding time makes your animation run longer. Inserting time in the middle of a transition makes it take place more slowly.

Toggle Pin

Windows: P

Mac: P

The Playhead's pin is used to mark two positions on the timeline at once. For example, you use the pin and playhead to mark the beginning and end of a transition you're about to create. For details, see page 10.

Flip Playhead and Pin

Windows: Shift+P

Mac: Shift-P

The pin can be placed before or after the playhead. This command swaps their positions.

Snapping

Windows: Alt+;

Mac: Option-;

Snapping makes it easier to align keyframes, the playhead, and the edges of transitions. When you position an object close to another object, it automatically snaps into place.

Snap To

Use the options in the Snap To submenu to apply snapping to Quarter Seconds (in the Timeline), the Playhead and Transition Edges.

Show Grid

Shows and hides a grid that marks off time on the Timeline.

Grid

Leads to a submenu where you can choose the interval for grid that overlays the timeline. Choices range from 1 grid line per second to 30 lines per second.

Zoom In

Windows: =

Mac: =

Zooms in to the Timeline, making it easier to see smaller segments of time. This command only affects the Timeline and is not to be confused with the Stage view commands.

Zoom Out

Windows: -

Mac: -

Zooms out from the Timeline, making it easier to see a longer period of time in your animation. Like the other commands on this menu, it only affects your view of the Timeline, not the stage.

Zoom to Fit

Windows: \

Mac: \

Zooms to display all the time in your animation.

Expand/Collapse Selected

Windows: Ctrl+.

Mac: ⌘-.

In the Timeline, elements properties are grouped in collapsible, outline fashion under each element. This command shows and hides the properties for selected elements.

Expand/Collapse All

Windows: Ctrl+Shift+.

Mac: Shift-⌘-.

Shows or hides all the element properties in the Timeline.

◼ Window

Like all of Adobe's design tools, Animate is made up of many panels, all of which are listed in the Windows menu. This is where you show and hide the panels you need for your work.

Workspace

With so many panels to deal with, designers can spend an awful lot of time managing their position and visibility. Fortunately, Adobe gives you tools to save different workspace configurations.

Default

Use this command to choose the Default workspace, the original arrangement of panels provided in Adobe Edge Animate.

New Workspace

Move your panels to a new arrangement and then choose this command to save your new workspace. At that point, the newly saved workspace is listed in the Workspace menu, where you can choose it at any time.

Delete Workspace

Choose this command to remove unneeded workspaces that you've saved.

Reset

As you work, you're likely to show and hide panels and move them around. Choose this command to return to the saved configuration of the selected workspace.

Timeline

Show and hide the Timeline with this command. The Timeline is where set the timing for transitions in your animation.

Elements

Show and hide the Elements panel with this command. The Elements panel lists all the elements in your animation. You can use the Elements panel to show and hide elements on the stage. You can also use the Elements panel to open the Actions panel for each element.

Library

Show and hide the Library panel with this command. The Library panel lists all the assets in your project whether or not they're placed on the stage. For example, images imported into your project appear in the library before they're placed on the stage. The Library also holds any symbols you've created, giving you a way to create new instances of symbols and to edit existing symbols.

Tools

Use this command to show and hide the Toolbar that runs along the top of the Animate workspace. The Toolbar holds the Selection, Transform, Rectangle, Rounded Rectangle, and Text tools. Color swatches give you a quick way to change the background color and border color for selected elements. On the right end of the toolbar, a drop-down menu provides a way to select workspaces.

Properties

Show and hide the Properties panel with this command. The Properties panel gives you access to the properties of a selected element. If more than one element is selected, you can change the properties the elements have in common.

Code

Show and hide the Code panel with this command. Unlike the Actions panel for an individual element, the Code panel puts all the JavaScript code you've created for your project in one place.

Lessons

Use this command to show and hide the lessons that Adobe provides for Animate.

■ Help

Adobe Edge Animate is a brand new, version 1.0 product, so its Help documents are minimal. That means the Help that you'd expect to find is either missing or provided in terms that only geeks, engineers, and programmers would appreciate.

Animate Help

When this was written, Animate Help opens your web browser and delivers you to a page that combines product promotion with lessons, videos, links to other resources, and Adobe forums.

Edge Animate JavaScript API

The Edge Animate JavaScript API provides short and sometimes cryptic descriptions for using JavaScript with your Animate projects.

Edge Animate Community Forums

This command leads to Adobe's public forum where other interested Animate users discuss Animate and answer each other's questions. If you're stuck on a problem, this is a good place turn to turn. Post a question and you're like to get several responses in short order.

Change Language

Use this command to set the language used in menus and dialog boxes.

Adobe Product Improvement Program About Animate (Windows only)

Lists the version number for your installation of Animate. You'll also see copyrights and the names of the clever folks who developed this nifty program. For Macs, the About Animate command is listed under the Animate window.

Index

Symbols

\<a> (anchor tags), 161, 211
+ (add numbers) operator, 189
\<address> tags, 68
\<> (angle brackets) tags, 158
\<article> tags, 69
* (asterisk), at file name at top of Animate window, 7
\<blockquote> tags, 69
\<body> tags, 159
**\
 line break tags,** 159
\<code> tags, 69
{} (curly braces)
   in conditional statements, 217, 222
   in CSS declaration block, 161
   in JavaScript functions, 187
/ (divide numbers) operator, 189
\<div> tags, 68, 20
. (dot)
   used in JavaScript, 205
   used to identify classes, 191
" (double quotes) tags, 159
= (equal sign) tags, 159
== (equals) operator, 189
> (greater than) operator, 189
>= (greater than or equal to) operator, 189
\<h1> (heading) tag, CSS applied to, 161
\<h1> through \<h6> tags, 69
--> (HTML comment tag), 165

\<! (HTML comment tag), 165
< (less than) operator, 189
<= (less than or equal to) operator, 189
- (minus button), deleting triggers and actions, 107
* (multiply numbers) operator, 189
() (parentheses), in conditional statements, 217
+ (plus button), adding triggers to element, 107
\<p> (paragraph) tags, 69, 161, 163
\<pre> (preformatted) text tags, 69
\<script> links, 179
; (semicolons), in JavaScript, 188–189
' (single quotes), tags, 159
// (slashes), in comments, 103
*/ (star slash), in block comments, 103
- (subtract numbers) operator, 189
!= (unequal) operator, 189

A

About Animate command, in Help menu, 262
actions and triggers
   about, 97–98, 110
   adding triggers to point in time, 76, 113–114
   adding trigger to loop animation, 111–112
   changing properties, 204–211
   click triggers, 98, 103

C

Have it your way.

©2011 O'Reilly Media, Inc. O'Reilly logo is a registered trademark of O'Reilly Media, Inc. 00000

Get even more for your money.

Join the O'Reilly Community, and register the O'Reilly books you own. It's free, and you'll get:

- $4.99 ebook upgrade offer
- 40% upgrade offer on O'Reilly print books
- Membership discounts on books and events
- Free lifetime updates to ebooks and videos
- Multiple ebook formats, DRM FREE
- Participation in the O'Reilly community
- Newsletters
- Account management
- 100% Satisfaction Guarantee

Signing up is easy:

1. **Go to: oreilly.com/go/register**
2. **Create an O'Reilly login.**
3. **Provide your address.**
4. **Register your books.**

Note: English-language books only

To order books online:
oreilly.com/store

For questions about products or an order:
orders@oreilly.com

To sign up to get topic-specific email announcements and/or news about upcoming books, conferences, special offers, and new technologies:
elists@oreilly.com

For technical questions about book content:
booktech@oreilly.com

To submit new book proposals to our editors:
proposals@oreilly.com

O'Reilly books are available in multiple DRM-free ebook formats. For more information:
oreilly.com/ebooks

O'REILLY®

Spreading the knowledge of innovators   oreilly.com

©2010 O'Reilly Media, Inc. O'Reilly logo is a registered trademark of O'Reilly Media, Inc. 00000